Spirituality Without God

CELEBRATING THE TRANSCENDENT IN HUMANITY

Möller de la Rouvière

Llumina Press

© 2005 Möller de la Rouvière

All rights reserved. No part of this publication may be reproduced or transmitted in any form or by any means electronic or mechanical, including photocopy, recording, or any information storage and retrieval system, without permission in writing from the copyright owner.

Requests for permission to make copies of any part of this work should be addressed directly to the author at mollerdlr@telkomsa.net

ISBN:1-59526-141-9
Printed in the United States of America by Llumina Press

Library of Congress Control Number: 2004115909

CONTENTS

Acknowledgments   i
Introduction   v

PART ONE: THE VIEW

Chapter 1…..Vision and Practice	1
Chapter 2 … Spiritual Humanism: The Quest for Human-Centric Spirituality	16
Chapter 3…..The Thought/Attention-Knot	27
Chapter 4…..Components of the Separate Self-Sense	49
Chapter 5…..Intellectualism and Reality-Consideration	67
Chapter 6…..On Sense Perception	77
Chapter 7…..The Destiny of 'I'-Consciousness	87
Chapter 8…..Attachment and Detachment	94
Chapter 9…..Self-Enquiry, Psychology and Right Attitude	102
Chapter 10….The Question of Will	118
Chapter 11….Three Fundamental States	126
Chapter 12….Spirituality, Science and Art	135

PART TWO: THE PRACTICE

Introduction   141

Chapter 13…..The Practice Of Passive Awareness   145
- General Introduction
- The Practice of Passive Awareness
- 'Minding?' and the Thought/Attention-Knot
- Insight
- Attention and Awareness
- Samatha

Chapter 14…. The Practice Of Direct Awareness   177
- Understanding Direct Awareness
- Practicing Direct Awareness
- Full Bodily Awareness

Chapter 15.....Working With Contemplation   194
Chapter 16.....Contemplation and Reality Consideration   208
Chapter 17.... Working With Psychological and   219
             Emotional Reactivities
   - General Introduction
   - Self-Transcendence and Emotions
   - Looking at the Problem
   - The Broader Context of Emotional Disturbance
   - Primal Contraction
   - The Ego-process and Emotional Reactivity
   - Discovering the Right Instruments
   - Beginning the Process
   - Direct Awareness and Emotional Reactivities
Chapter 18.... Integration –   239
             Toward the Wholeness of Being

About the Author   247

Dedicated to the human spirit of enquiry.

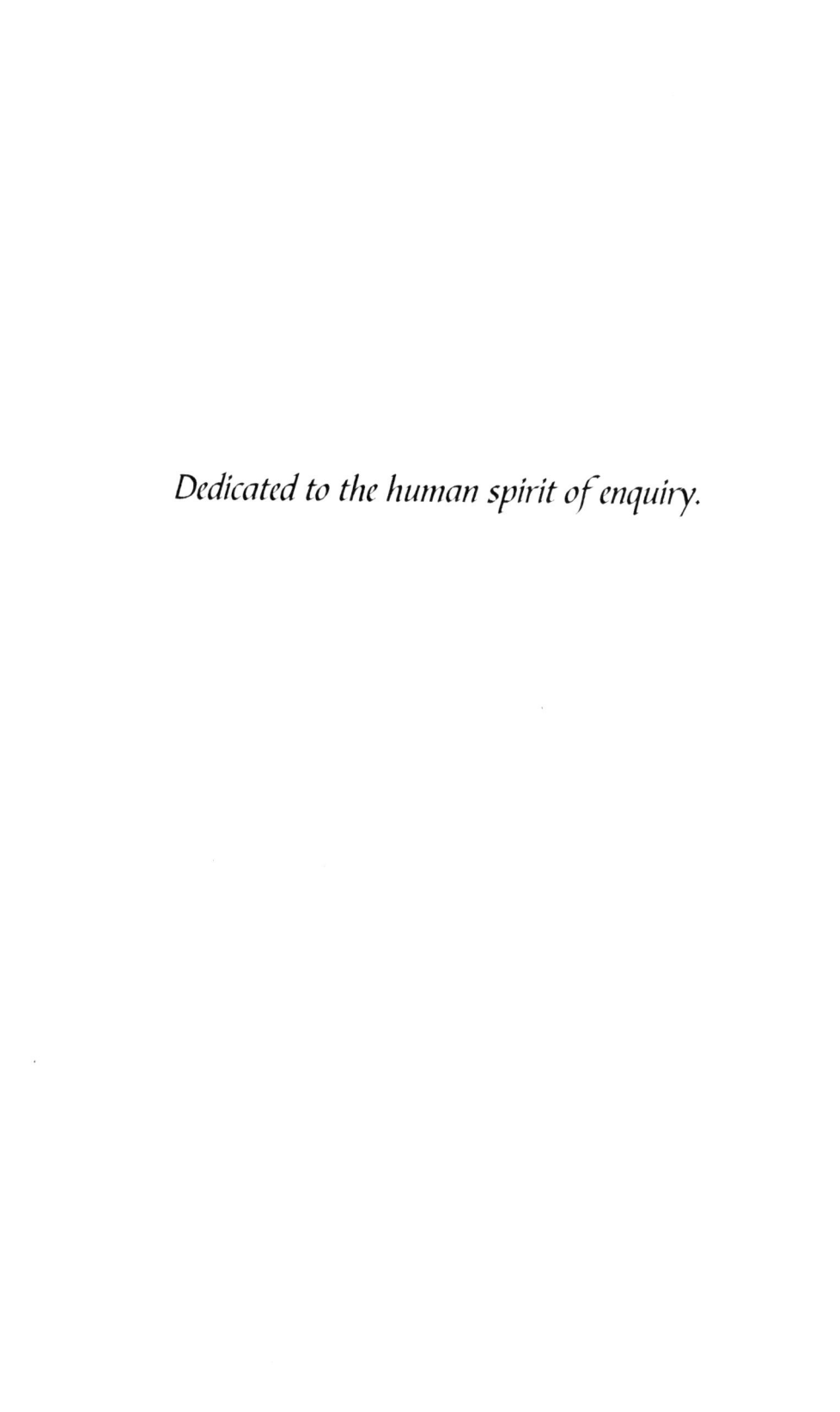

*' There is only one god,
and that is man made perfect.'*

-J. Krishnamurti

Acknowledgments

Without the penetrating insights of those great students of life whose teachings I have had the privilege of stumbling upon, and the good fortune of being able to make use of, this book would not have been possible. I feel deeply indebted to them and immensely enriched having been brought into the broader communicating sphere of their work.

At the age of twenty-five, when my own enquiry into spirituality was just beginning to dawn from the slumber of my pre-inspected early life, I was introduced to the teachings of J. Krishnamurti. Although I felt myself immediately drawn to the insights of Krishnamurti, it took many years before I was able to grasp the full extent of his work. Today, while firmly established in the insight of my own understanding and the living reality of the material I wish to share in this book, it often occurs to me how closely related my own rather iconoclastic approach is to his.

In fact, the insights which life has brought to my own enquiry could perhaps be seen as a natural evolution and expansion of many of the themes around self-enquiry and self-observation he introduced to the world. My indebtedness to J. Krishnamurti is deep and profound.

It was at Brockwood Park, England, where I had the good fortune of meeting Dr. David Bohm, a close associate of J. Krishnamurti and one of the most penetrating thinkers of the twentieth century. His understanding of the human situation was quite remarkable and, although far too subtle for me to grasp at the time, many of the ideas he shared with us during private conversations remained somewhere in my mind and recollected themselves in the form of deep insights as the years passed.

A truly modest man of extraordinary ability and clarity, he alerted me to the crucial difference between 'that which is created and sustained by thought and that which is not'. Over the years this statement served as the inspiration for deep insights into my own functioning, many of which could be considered fundamental to the issues discussed in this book.

The teachings of Zen and Hinayana Buddhism also served to broaden my outlook and to present me with many penetrating shifts in consciousness, confirming much of what had been revealed to me from my involvement with the work of J. Krishnamurti. What particularly attracted me to Zen was the Soto Zen notion of 'silent illumination', or 'serene reflection'. Here I sensed resonance with the process as it was gradually unfolding in me. The challenges these teachings presented to my enquiring mind greatly assisted me in the intuitive grasp of concepts such as 'non-doing', no-effort, no-mind etc.

Special mention should be made of a book by Nayanaponika Thera, *The Heart of Buddhist Meditation*. In his book this renowned Buddhist monk explains much about the transformative potential of the Hinayana path of Mindfulness and Insight. Many of the meditation practices he explores find resonance with that of J. Krishnamurti's intimations of 'passive observation'. This encouraged me to explore afresh the path of inner silence and insight. The approach to contemplative enquiry suggested by these teachings afforded me with a sound and openhearted point of departure from where I could continue with my own inner explorations.

At some point I felt myself drawn to the teachings of Da Free John (Adi Da). After years of struggling on my own, I found in aspects of Adi Da's earliest teaching a reflection of many of the enquiries which occupied my search at the time. He has a wonderful way with words, and managed to describe some of my own experiences to myself with considerable lucidity.

Although I now find myself critical of the way Adi Da allows his followers to develop a dependence on him as guru and Giver (Da) of Light, I nevertheless feel it appropriate to mention his work with regard to some crucial aspects of my own enquiry.

As my development began to take on a more humanistic tone, and I found myself moving further away from the traditional approaches to mysticism and spirituality, I regard myself fortunate to have come across the Dzogchen teachings as explained by Namkai Norbu. Dzogchen has a truly remarkable non-dual message. Though I never studied directly under Norbu, I was nevertheless deeply moved by the way Dzogchen addresses the issues of non-doing and effortlessness.

It was in Dzogchen, more than in any other teaching I had come across, where I sensed a truly non-dualistic message. This came at a time when the sense of wholeness was beginning to shine through in my own case, and I could evaluate my own non-dual experiences in the light of this teaching.

Then, in the later years of my enquiry, I stumbled across the non-teachings of U.G. Krishnamurti. Although one cannot but agree with U.G. that he has truly no teaching to offer, he nevertheless makes a very clear point relative to the domination of thought over our total field of experience. This resonated powerfully with my own experiences in this regard and confirmed an aspect of my enquiry which has become one of the pivotal insights I explore in this book.

Finally, there remains only life to be grateful to. This book is not a synthesis of the teachings I have come across. It is also not merely the result of years of mental and intellectual enquiry, although naturally such enquiry forms part of it. *Spirituality Without God* stands as a description of actual experience made possible by life itself.

It is my hope that others may find value in what has been revealed to me, which, to the best of my ability, I endeavor to share in this book.

Möller de la Rouvière
Barrydale, South Africa.
2005

Introduction

Spirituality Without God could be seen as a fresh and original approach to spiritual life, founded in a truly humanistic perspective. Being an expression of our deepest need, as well as the fulfillment of our greatest potential, spiritual life is a profoundly *human* affair which has to be given its rightful place in the context of human life. For this to happen, the development and refinement of the human spirit has to be set free from the religious and mystical traditions with their dependence on God and all other forms of the Great Beyond. Spiritual awakening is a process whereby the human spirit is allowed to reveal itself as a many-faceted well of wisdom, compassion and wholeness. For this we do not need God. We need only to allow for the recognition and unfolding of the truly humane within us.

One of the most important insights which this book explores and communicates is that we need not place our trust in any specific tradition, philosophy, religion or teacher for the complete fulfillment of our spiritual journey. It is not necessary to complicate our enquiry with all the traditional forms of spiritual, metaphysical (other worldly) or religious ideas presented to us as revelatory truths. Rather, if we approach our situation with a true spirit of enquiry we will soon discover that we are naturally endowed with an Intelligence and purity of heart - the expression of which will satisfy our deepest quest for human well-being. It does this not only in a coherent and practical way, but most characteristically as an awakened sense of compassion and charity, which naturally extends itself towards other human beings and life in general.

For this *humanizing* process to unfold and to become our living reality, our starting point would be the recognition that there is absolutely nothing suspect about our born condition. As humans we lack nothing for the complete fulfillment of our deeply felt need for inner and outer order, happiness, emotional equanimity and a fully integrated, spiritual life. We are born into a wholeness of life that will naturally express itself through unconditional Intelligence and pure emotion, if only we could allow for its unfolding.

If we could become sensitive to this primary truth, we will discover that our deepest potential has only been *obscured* by a vast and complex network of thought-projections and emotional reactivities which have prevented our natural state from revealing itself in our everyday living. These created the *appearance* of fragmentation and duality whereas we already inhere in an undivided, natural condition of wholeness.

Spirituality Without God brings clarity and insight to this entire field of presumed fragmentation. Through self-enquiry we discover how we fragment our world into nationalities, religious factions, competing economic models, racial discrimination, sexual dominance, philosophical ideologies, egocentrism, nuclear family units and so on. Through these structures of opposing energies we participate consciously and unconsciously in inner and outer division and fragmentation of our lives. And as we immerse ourselves in these as individuals, we need only to observe our own personal functioning with clarity and insight to discover how we create and perpetuate our own suffering and discontent. In the process we will also discover what needs to be done to free ourselves from these self-imposed limitations.

Such self-observation does not require us to become more complicated or philosophical. The path of self-enquiry and self-transcendence suggests quite the contrary: we learn how to observe ourselves with Intelligence and clarity. Once we become sensitive to our own inner functioning, we naturally begin to appreciate the extent of the damage we do to ourselves and our world through uninspected living. Here we also become aware of the unfolding of our deeper Intelligence which heals and re-orders our lives in resonance with the natural order of things – an order that is non-fragmented and whole.

Through this path of self-observation, meditation and contemplation we will also uncover many hidden aspects of ourselves. In *Spirituality Without God* we are offered clear guidelines on how to restore our sanity through insightful participation in every aspect of our being. During this investigation it will become clear that to arrive at a complete understanding of ourselves, we need never look outside the already-existing truth of our living reality. This makes our journey truly humanistic where we never feel the need, or urgency, to look for any assistance or guidance from some presumed God, Essence or Ground beyond human life.

Yet, to find our human measure, we will need the courage to look afresh at every aspect of our interaction with our world as a whole. Approaching both ourselves and objective reality in this openhearted way, we will discover that nothing we may encounter during this investigation will have the power to deter us from our quest for true integral living. In fact, our enquiry will reveal that the closer we keep to the truth of our present experience, the more liberating our path will be. Truth literally sets us free. But our first gesture towards the freeing of our being from illusion and misapprehension is to observe ourselves intimately in our everyday functioning. We need to get to know ourselves *as we are*. This is why so much emphasis is placed on self-discovery and self-knowledge throughout this enquiry.

Through self-enquiry we discover the right instruments with which to work most effectively in each situation. It would be of little use to attempt deep investigations into our own being before we have established the appropriate means to facilitate such work. For this we will draw not only on our intellectual and intuitive grasp of things. We will also have to develop other, deeper aspects of our potential to participate in our own processes in a direct and courageous way, without any fear or resistance. Much of the formal meditative work suggested in this book serves this purpose.

And as our inquiry deepens, it will become progressively clearer that we have not embarked upon a path where we merely struggle with the technicalities of our practice in a cold, mechanical way. Spiritual life is alive as a constant unfolding of our deep humanity. True self-enquiry and self-transcendence is therefore a living process where we realize that we *are* the path we will have to walk. We *are* the living experiment we will be experimenting with. There is no path other than the complexities and difficulties we bring to our lives. From within this rich soil of human potential alone could flower a life founded in the well of our own awakened Intelligence. It is up to us how far we are prepared to walk this inner path of self-discovery and self-transcendence.

The instruments we will develop through the formal meditative and contemplative practices suggested in *Part Two: The Practice* are sufficiently effective to deal with every aspect of our mental and emotional complexities in a coherent and practical way. These will not only allow us to explore many different approaches to our reactivities, inconsistencies, disturbances, emotional dysfunctions and other forms of inner contraction and debilitation, but will also point the way directly to the freedom and emotional equanimity we strive towards.

Perhaps one of the most encouraging elements of the path of self-enquiry is that every new discovery reveals itself as an integral part of a wider liberating process. All we need to do is to find appropriate ways for dealing with our situation. The results will follow by themselves in a natural and quite remarkable way. And as our enquiry unfolds, every aspect of our contracted being will gradually fall away by non-use. When the false, dualistic vision is left behind, only the truth of the wholeness of life remains.

Although *Spirituality Without God* enters into deep and subtle aspects of our entire field of experience, it always endeavors to approach things in a non-technical and non-academic way. Every subject discussed and every practice proposed is explored in the broad context of a quest for wholeness and a truly sane and integrated life. And because this is an enquiry into the *totality* of our human condition, the reader will not find any speculative metaphysics or empty philosophical propositions merely to stimulate the imagination. Such unnecessary elaborations serve only to detract from the urgency and integrity of our investigation.

This is an exploration into the deep potential of human life where we discover many aspects of how we think and feel about things. No area of our inner life is irrelevant to this discovery. And no speculation about it is necessary or appropriate. This gives our exploration a truly humanistic character, devoid of metaphysical speculation in the hope of divine redemption.

Instead of freeing us from our confusion, disorder and bewilderment, our spiritual heritage has served only to complicate our lives by suggesting that we look outside or beyond human life for the ultimate fulfillment of our potential. In this way our spiritual traditions have contributed to our deeply fragmented, dualistic vision and brought us to a point where we have lost all sense of the wholeness in which we already inhere. We may have the rare or occasional glimpses of free Being and undivided reality, yet, more often than not, we practice a style of living that keeps us apart and destroys the deep relational integrity of our lives.

Spirituality Without God proposes an original and radically humanistic vision for discovering the non-dual truth of life and the emotional equanimity we all yearn for. By putting aside the dogmas presented to us as revelatory truths by the spiritual and mystical traditions – where we are instructed either to merge with something presumably Greater than ourselves or realize our identification with some inner Unitive Principle such as Brahman, Emptiness, Consciousness, Atman, God or the Self – the enquiry proposed in this book clearly demonstrates that the path to, and the realization of, the non-dual truth of life lies entirely within our *human potential*, and nowhere else. We need nothing but the integrative measure of our deep humanity for the truth and beauty of our human appearance to be revealed.

Through self-enquiry, self-knowledge and self-transcendence we discover that when every aspect of dualistic presumption within us has been recognized and transcended, we are already free in the great simplicity of Being, which is whole and always nothing other than perfectly human, sane and loving.

For the sake of clarity and to simplify our enquiry, *Spirituality Without God* has been divided into two parts.

In *Part One: The View* we explore many of the misconceptions we have about life and living. These essays form an integral part of the path of self-enquiry, self-knowledge and self-transcendence. They penetrate deeply into many of the themes we may come across in the traditional mystical and esoteric paths of liberation, and endeavor to explain the limitations and confusion that have developed around these teachings over centuries of mere repetition. At the same time we are presented with new and original ways to look at our own lives, directly available to our understanding, insight and experience.

The purpose of this type of enquiry into the human condition as a whole is to sensitize ourselves to the many misconceptions and uninspected *attitudes* we bring to our lives. Although our explorations should always be alive with Intelligence and characterized by a genuine spirit of enquiry, we need to guard against becoming merely intellectual or philosophical. Rather, we should always endeavor to remain *realistic* by never moving away from that which cannot be verified on present, experiential evidence. In this way we always remain true to ourselves by keeping our enquiry within the measure of our present condition. This alone is the basis for true spiritual enquiry.

In these essays we are further sensitized to the fact that no enquiry is complete without allowing for the full development of our true emotional potential to work in resonance with our deeper Intelligence. Everything we explore from the point of view of the heart, as well as from our deeper Intelligence, finally finds its true measure in the direct experience of a deep emotional Intelligence, which could be seen as the functional instrument of the holistic nature of life.

We are also made aware of the necessity for preparing the ground for such an open-minded and open-hearted way of life as well as developing a radical spirit of enquiry by taking a critical look at many of the issues which bind and limit our full participation in life. Once this spirit of enquiry has been well established, we will be sufficiently prepared not to offer resistance to the penetrating insights and forms of direct experience which will become an integral part of our process when we engage in the formal meditative work as suggested in *Part Two*.

In *Part Two: The Practice* we enter into many different meditative practices that give substance, through direct experience, to the issues we have allowed to ponder us in *Part One*. Here we discover how to find our measure in formal meditative practice and to integrate the techniques of meditation into our daily living. We learn in detail how to work with our emotional reactivities and psychological disturbances; we explore experientially how the ego sustains itself through comparison and self-proving; we look at how thought and attention form a finely woven network of inner confusion and illusion; we develop the art of meditation through Passive Awareness and Direct Awareness; we learn how to work with contemplative enquiry to free us from conditioning and mental/emotional reactivities.

And as our practice matures, it allows for the unfolding of a life that begins to lose its separate and fragmentary appearance. We begin to live in the light of our gradually unfolding wholeness and inner wisdom. These are evidenced by the deepening presence of true emotional responsiveness, unconditioned Intelligence and a softness of heart that constantly feels its way into situations in a gentle and sensitive manner.

The final chapter on Integration points us beyond formal practice to the true non-dual expression of life, freed from self-limitation and self-imposed suffering.

PART ONE

THE VIEW

Chapter One

VISION AND PRACTICE

Life is a matter of priorities. Consciously or unconsciously we are motivated toward the fulfillment of what we find more interesting, profitable, satisfying, meaningful or enriching, rather than to the things we consider not to have the potential of adding value to our lives. What is important to us as individuals tends to order itself along a distinct line of priority-potential that determines, conditions and controls much of our daily interaction with life. This is true, not only of our everyday activities, but is also particularly evident in our inward quest for meaning and an integral, holistic way of life.

Because many of us are not merely satisfied with biological survival, but need to find a deeper meaning to life, this inward demand for happiness, emotional equanimity, relational integrity and wholeness becomes an all-consuming passion to seek and find a teacher, teaching, organization or religious institution we believe may deliver us from our inner emptiness.

However, the greater our need, the greater the possibility that we may fail to approach our path with sufficient care and inner clarity. The lure of ready answers, the charm of a charismatic teacher, or a teaching that may merely satisfy our superficial need for emotional and psychological comfort zones often deceive us into believing that we have entered upon a path of true liberation. The indiscriminate urgency with which we seek, dilutes the integrity of our quest and thereby limits our ability to make sound decisions with regard to this critical area of inner investigation. The greater any particular need, and the higher value we place on the fulfillment of any demand, the greater the potential for us to delude ourselves. Need often takes our discernment away.

Need is indeed the mother of invention. But whereas in practical matters invention is a necessary instrument for survival, it could prove to be completely counter-productive if used indiscriminately in areas where a different, more circumspect, approach might have been more practical. Without enquiring deeply into our own situation, we create visions of what human life should be like, and on the basis of these, project answers as to how we should fulfill the integral demands of our born condition. But such visions, if not based in the reality of our present situation, will only obscure the revelation of our potential for holistic living. The questions we ask, and the answers we present to ourselves with regard to the path of inner exploration, have to be intimately related. That is, our path has to serve our quest for freedom in a direct and intelligent manner.

In view of this, we may appreciate the critical importance for developing a healthy skepticism and a penetrating, fearless spirit of enquiry. If we are serious about coming to terms with our human condition we will realize that life is a dynamic process that cannot be approached through dogmas, superstitions, ancient metaphors for truth and beauty, philosophy, religion or metaphysics. None of these can ever touch the direct experience of the living moment. Whatever their origin and validity, these are nothing but concepts we impose onto the truth of life. Whereas life is a *living* process, ideas are stagnant reflections in thought about it. Thought is secondary and ultimately unimportant to the direct experience of the living moment which alone can afford us with unmediated information from which to arrive at intelligent living.

We should thus take considerable care how we approach our enquiry. We should not allow the intensity of our need for meaning and true human fulfillment to be diminished. However, this intensity needs to be tempered by a quiet determination not simply to accept the first culturally available set of 'answers' as

Part One: The View

the measure for our deeply felt need for meaning and truth. Our priority should remain with the intensity of our spirit of enquiry as such, and not occupy itself with an anxious search for answers and ready-made comfort zones. Only then can we protect ourselves from all the dogmas and superstitions presented to us as revelatory truths, which, more often than not, have been based on a lack of insight into our human condition as a whole.

To start our enquiry and then to proceed to practice on the vision and insight of another, however ancient or insightful, is to deny ourselves the opportunity of ever understanding ourselves *as we are*. And to approach our path of self-enquiry and search for truth from a disposition that does not reflect our own living reality will leave us vulnerable to confusion, disempowerment and, ultimately, abuse.

No system can free us. No teacher or teaching can free us. Even we, as bundles of self-contraction, cannot free ourselves. All we can do is to become deeply sensitive to what we bring to the living moment that inhibits the freedom of our natural, uncontaminated humanity and allow our inner Intelligence to do its liberating work. This is the theme that underlies every aspect of our practice as described in *Part Two: The Practice*.

We cannot find what we seek. The fragmented, seeking mind is fundamentally of a different nature to the wholeness it believes it is seeking. Our work is to discover how to allow for the natural and effortless unfolding of integral living. To seek and to find, is to add a mere modification within thought to our lives. It is to add further complications to an already complicated and confused state. Truth, as non-dual reality, and freedom as an open-ended and responsive emotional Intelligence, are already part of our being and therefore cannot be added to life. The fulfillment we seek and hope to find can only be *allowed* to shine through the fog of our culturally and self-imposed values of conformity and self-limitation.

And these values not only include all the culturally acceptable ways of dealing with life in its ordinary functional dynamic. These are profoundly evident in how our cultures have informed and conditioned our search for meaning and truth. Unfortunately these have not delivered on their promises. Having experimented with both inner and outer seeking for many centuries, our cultural 'truths' have failed to bring coherency, compassion and integrity to our lives. We are as bewildered today as we have been during any other era of our history. It is therefore important to question the ways by which we endeavored to solve our natural demands for meaning and relational integrity culturally.

This is where our vision assumes a central role. Self-enquiry is an investigation into the *totality* of human existence. We are not just concerned with ourselves as isolated emotional and psychological beings. What we believe about life is reflected in the total ordering of our lives. It reflects in every aspect of living, including the lives of others. It is therefore important that our consideration of these matters include as wide a spectrum of human potential as possible. Through this we will be able to gain clarity and perspective about how we function and how our interaction with our world often distorts and destroys true relationship.

When we thus enter onto the path of self-discovery, and we become sensitive to how our *vision of reality* determines our quest for truth, we may appreciate how important it is for us to recognize the full extent of our cultural conditioning. Such recognition will alert us to everything our cultures have devised and developed in their attempts to establish inner and outer order through coercion and manipulation. Naturally these will also include our cultural approaches to sane, integral living. And as we have seen, the undertone of both inner and outer rules for social conformity has created a cultural circumstance that makes true, independent enquiry very difficult. We have become totally desensitized to the destructive and sub-human values which society enforces through conditioning and demand for conformity.

If truth is our intent and deep abiding interest, we have little choice but to enquire into, and to understand and transcend every aspect of untruth into which we have been conditioned.

Part One: The View

This, of necessity, will have to include our deeply held notions about God, religion, metaphysics, mysticism and spirituality. What is culturally considered as valuable, beautiful and ultimately true and liberating are often little more than misconceptions about life, perpetuated through uninspected repetition over a long period of time. We seldom question these values simply because they have been presented to us as such 'self-evident', revelatory truths.

Yet, unless we discover the relevancy of these truths with regard to our path of self-discovery, these will inevitably form part of our limitation and separation from the real. So, perhaps as an introduction to some of these forms of social truth, we could look at a few aspects of how the notion of God (in its broad context as the Great Other) has been presented to us from both the Judaic and Hindu perspectives and how these descriptions of the Ultimate determined our relation to it, as well as its relationship with us.

The notion of this Great Other influenced, conditioned and limited our search for truth and human happiness ever since it was introduced by the ancient masters of speculative metaphysics. In some form or another, this God-idea removed truth from our human realm and made it available to us only via a necessary search into the Great Beyond.

However, if we could remain realistic and practical about this matter, and become alive to the deep conditioning power of all the historical propaganda that surrounds this notion of God (or any other form of this metaphorical Great Other), we may remain open to investigate things in a clear and unbiased way. In the process we may discover that we are indeed capable of enquiring into every aspect of our living reality for ourselves, and from within our own human perspective alone. And this free and open-ended spirit of enquiry will ultimately prove to be perfectly capable of revealing the truth we previously imagined to be vested only in God.

Without exception, all spiritual, esoteric or religious paths present us with a vision of the Ultimate or God. And integral to this concept of the Ultimate we always find a set of rules for how to relate to it to fulfill our destiny in a truly spiritual way. And, depending on the direction of our interest and the motivation behind our search, we generally accept the principles of theory and practice as explained to us from the perspective, or vision, of our chosen path.

Part of this vision will generally also include descriptions of the ultimate nature of things. We are taught about the nature of God or Truth. We are offered ultimate explanations for our suffering, our unlove, our disorder. We may be told that this world is of a lesser status than the Ultimate Essence of existence, or that the physical universe is the result of the determinations of a creator-God. Often our world is described as a veil of sorrow and tears, caught in a perpetual destiny-creating web of karmic consequences. We learn about reincarnation, past lives, karma, the wheel of birth and death. Heaven and hell are explained to us. In short, we come across many concepts, explanations and descriptions, all attempting to explain the deeper context of life from the point of view of some presumed First Principle or Primordial Cause. And depending on the style and content of our search, these matters will be explained differently, yet with equal 'revelatory' authority, according to the broad vision of the path we have entered.

From this an interesting picture emerges. If we take a closer look at all this speculative other-worldly 'information' made available to us, we will notice that there is a direct and clearly discernable relationship between the way these teachings have explained the nature of the Ultimate as opposed to the relative, and how we should relate to both of these. That is, we have been given descriptions of God, Truth, and Reality, on the one hand, and human life and our world of experience, on the other. And integrally woven into these descriptions of God and humanity are forms of practice necessary to establish the 'right' relationship between us and our God or, in general, humanity and the Ultimate. Our vision of the Ultimate therefore clearly determines how we will approach it.

To the extent that we accept any path and enter into the practices proposed by such a path, our practice will have as its central theme this relationship between the Ultimate and ourselves. It would therefore be useful to keep in mind that all religious, spiritual and mystical paths which concern themselves with the liberation of humanity in some form or another could be seen as a direct result of the way their underlying philosophies describe both the relative and the Ultimate. Without a vision of the Ultimate in comparison to what has been described as the relative, less-than-Ultimate condition, there would have been no development of religions or mystical traditions. The one requires the other for its existence. One could say that the relative and the Ultimate are mutually dependent visions of reality.

It is thus only in the continued practice and reaffirmation of their underlying metaphysical propositions that these paths have survived. The way things have been explained to us by the great philosophers and spiritual traditions, and the way we practice on the basis of these explanations, could be seen as an integral whole, each according to its own philosophical grasp of this fundamentally *dualistic vision* of Ultimate and relative. And nowhere is this relationship better represented than in the Judaic religions of the Middle East and in the teachings of Indian Hinduism.

In the Judaic-based religions we find that each has its own specific understanding of the role of God, His prophets, His law, afterlife, heaven, hell, sin, the origin of things and the role of the Church which is supposed to represent God's vision for humanity here on earth. In addition to these, each religion has given certain responsibilities, codes of moral conduct and ways of practice (like prayer, going to church, the mosque, the synagogue) as ground-rules to its adherents in accordance with which they should live, ritualize, gather, and generally organize their lives. And although there seems to be considerable variations, modifications and differences in the daily practices of the followers of these three religions, they all share the notion of an all-powerful, omniscient, omnipotent and ultimately benign and fatherly creator-God.

Yet, however benign and omnipotent this God might be, as creator, he remains eternally separate from his creation. This has denied humanity, as one of his creatures, the right to direct contact with him. In an attempt to bridge this divide, and to establish some communication with their God, it was necessary to introduce socially legitimate and recognizable intermediaries who, as fellow humans here on earth, could become channels of communication between humanity and God, and thereby bringing the Creator closer to his creation. In all three traditions we find the appearance of prophets to serve this purpose and, in the case of Christianity, also a Savior for all those who believe in him as the Son of God.

If we now look at the rather problematic relationship between this kind of creator-God and his creation, we will notice that all forms of practice, ritual and symbolism in these religions are directed towards resolving this single problem their followers face: their ultimate separation from God. Instead of feeling nourished from within the God that created them, they can only look up to heaven and meekly ask for help. This form of practice is a direct result of the way in which God is viewed as an all-powerful entity, separate from his creation.

Elaborate attempts have been made to appease this God through prayers and songs of praise, symbolic or real sacrifices and deeds deemed to be of merit in his eyes. Detailed rituals, such as baptizing, circumcision, fasting, going on pilgrimages and so on, have been developed as forms of bonding with the Creator, all in an attempt to bridge the eternal divide between God and his creation. Yet, all these are merely symbolic or, at best, psychologically comforting, because in the final analyses the closest one could ever get to this God is to join him in heaven after death. Until then he remains distinct, and often rather aloof, from his creation.

It is also interesting to note that no merging is possible with the Judaic God. He is a creative and directive power, but because his creation is ultimately seen as separate from himself, humanity can never become God. No part of creation is considered to be an integral part of God. Humanity is destined, even in the after-life, to continue in a dualistic, subject-object relationship with its God where he always plays the dominant, controlling and ultimately determining role.

This necessitated a totally different psychological and emotional relationship with God to what we find in the Hindu Vedantic teachings where God is seen as being directly accessible to the individual through meditation and inner exploration. Although the notion of God as creator also exists, he is not seen, in any ultimate sense, to be separate from his creation. This is especially the case in the non-dualistic teachings of the Advaita Vedanta philosophy: humanity cleared from everything it has placed in the way of experiencing its identity with God, can in fact become God or realize its already existing unity with God, Consciousness or Brahman. In these teachings the relationship between humanity and God takes on a distinctly less dualistic and authoritarian role than we find in the Judaic religions.

To make sense of one's life in the context of a God who has never directly revealed himself to any aspect of his creation, and therefore exists merely as an idea and belief in the minds of his followers, is very different to believing in a God that is perceived to be directly accessible and who could be found 'within', if only we were to look.

In the one we have a Father we have never seen or had any contact with, who has created us, told us what to do and made it very clear that we will suffer greatly if we do not obey his commands. In the other we also have a creator, but one who allows our return after freeing ourselves from our own delusory ways of looking at things. And not only are we offered the opportunity to return to this God, we are also assured that we could merge back into the totality of his nature.

We are not here concerned with weighing up the merits or demerits of these religions, the one against the other. From a humanistic perspective, the entire notion of some God as the Great Other, whether ultimately separate from us or to be merged with in mystic unity, is based on the fundamental error of mistaking a projection of thought for reality. Clearly such a misconception needs to be investigated as an integral part of our path of self-enquiry and self-transcendence. Both Judaic and

Hindu descriptions imply a dualistic vision of God and humankind. And in terms of holistic living, such a vision creates endless confusion and misdirected forms of practice. These will form part of our unfolding enquiry into the nature and manifestation of dualistic living.

For the sake of our present discussion it is just important to be sensitive to how these two notions, or visions, of God condition and determine God's relationship to humanity, and therefore humanity's relationship to God. These mutually dependent relationships tend to limit and define the nature, content and ultimate liberating potential of these paths.

As we have seen, many of us have this yearning for that which is greater, deeper and more meaningful than how we experience ourselves ordinarily. We somehow need to make sense of our lives in a broader context than just going to the office or watching television. We seem to be destined to discover a way of life that is based, not only on our ongoing self-centered activities, but informed by something more holistic and real.

In a most general sense we could call this a longing for something 'other' than the contracted state of self-limitation we dramatize *as* our daily functioning. And how this 'other' is presented to us by the path we have chosen will profoundly affect, determine and condition our quest for integral living. If this 'other' is something fixed, dualistic in nature or separate and divorced from our human potential, such as we find with the God-notion, the very 'other' we seek will become part of our ordinary, limited and fragmented vision.

On the other hand, if we could consider the possibility that what we believe we seek, and into whose 'hands' we are about to entrust our deepest human longing, may be nothing other than our own *undiscovered human potential*, our relationship to the ultimate will undergo a radical revision. It may become evident that if this 'other' aspect of our potential is something we merely need to uncover or allow to manifest, then clearly it cannot be something 'out there' for us to search for, believe in, seek or find. The truth, beauty and fulfillment of human life are enfolded within the total fabric of our being. These need

Part One: The View

merely to be given the space to unfold and to become part of our intelligent participation with the living moment.

We will also begin to appreciate that this deeper aspect of our being is always available to us, if only we could clear away all the obscurations we have placed in the path of its revelation. The reason why we can, and often do, have the deep certainty that there has to be a different way of living available to us, is because we often become aware of the promptings of our inner Intelligence and greater humanity - even in the midst of our confusion. We simply have the deep sense that there is something pure and genuine to our human condition, if only we would become sensitive to its revelation.

But as long as we seek for the fulfillment of our lives in the explanations given to us by the sterile traditions of uninspected living, presented as revelatory truths, will we be steering our search for truth in the wrong direction. We will be dramatizing another form of dualism, confusion and fragmentation, which will negate the truth of the potential wholeness and integrity of human existence.

From this we may see the importance for investigating and fully appreciating the fundamental principles on which our path is based. This becomes especially critical as the subtlety of our enquiry into 'self' and 'other' deepens. As our enquiry matures, and we begin to leave behind the social concepts of religion, the worshipping of a God or gods and the dogmatisms and rituals associated with these forms of exoteric practices, we will also start to appreciate the necessity to take considerable care that our practice and involvement in our path have their roots firmly established in the *observable and experiential here and now*.

Unless we always consider things from the realistic perspective of our present human situation, we are likely to be vulnerable to seek for the true value of life in metaphysical speculations and other-than-human forms of the ultimate. This calls for great clarity of vision and dedication to our search for truth.

Naturally such clarity may not be possible at the outset of our journey. However, we owe it to ourselves to bring to our path integrity of purpose and a vigorous spirit of enquiry. This will prevent us from believing we are searching for truth, while in reality we remain active as seekers for security and mere temporary emotional and psychological relief.

Once we have committed ourselves to the path of liberation, we need to ensure that we remain very sensitive to the possibility that we could be led astray by ways of thinking and practicing which have little to do with a holistic, sane and integrated life. As we have seen, we could be particularly susceptible to this because our need for release from the distress of our own self-limitation is so acute. We tend to seek for paths which may result in mere behavioral modifications rather than affording us with genuine transformative practices which could allow for the unfolding of truly integral living.

We may change from one religion to another; adopt a new spiritual path; change our dietary habits; change our meditative practices; modify our outward behavior towards others; contemplate new concepts about God, truth or reality and so on. And by becoming indiscriminately identified with these we may truly believe we have found a source of new inspiration and *the* path to liberation.

Yet, none of these may serve the purpose for which we entered into our exploration in the first place. We may feel good about both our new path and ourselves for having discovered this rich fountainhead of presumed revelatory truth. But unless we have done our homework very well, and have taken considerable care as to what it is we really seek, we may not in fact find the fulfillment in these we have been looking for. Inevitably such a path will become an integral component of our dualistic, fragmentary vision.

When we have sufficiently been sensitized to the importance of the relationship between the vision our path proposes and the practices it prescribes, we may be considerably better equipped to think/feel our way into this rather complex and difficult form of personal enquiry.

If we observe this process with clarity and insight, we will notice how powerful our psychological demand for security and stability is. We often feel we are fully prepared to let go of the old, painful ways of doing things, yet we want to do so from a

Part One: The View

disposition of complete control. We will only move once a clear alternative has been projected. But such shifts from within the security of one paradigm to another pre-conceived and secure disposition have no transformative power. These are still founded within the same bewilderment and confusion that forced us to seek for security as the main objective of our quest. Truth does not concern itself with psychological comfort zones. We either align ourselves with the movement and truth of life, or suffer our separation from it.

So, unless we remain sensitive to this conflict of interest between our psychological demand for security and the open-ended, rather insecure nature of discovering a new life of wholeness and integral living, we may indiscriminately enter upon the first path that presents itself to us which holds out the slightest promise of deliverance. And we will do this for no other reason but for our inability to endure the relative insecurity which characterizes any true search for freedom.

We cannot hold our spiritual enquiry to ransom. We need to realize that our search for freedom is a search away from the field of the known into the possibility of direct experience. It is the field of identified knowledge that our enquiry will reveal to be the source of unfreedom and unhappiness. Unless we can establish ourselves in the correct attitude towards this enquiry as a whole, we will soon find ourselves back in bondage as a consequence of our inability to live with the discomfort of the insecurity inherent in any form of creative change. In such a case, the path we have chosen to deliver us from bondage will become a mere extension of our suffering.

Once we have established this open-ended attitude, characterized by an alive and vibrant spirit of enquiry, we will be in a considerably better position to discern between the many teachings offered to us, and whether we should enter into any one specific teaching altogether. We could study the offerings of the great traditions, but we need to remain guarded against becoming influenced and conditioned by these teachings before we have given every aspect of our initial motivation our most dedicated consideration.

Over time, we may naturally find our own measure of insight and practice, and may utilize or reject in complete freedom aspects of the traditional teachings we find acceptable and valuable and those we do not. Whatever we accept as reasonable and helpful, we nevertheless need to remain vigilant against the possibility of allowing ourselves to being conditioned by these teachings

True measure pivots on true discernment. And discernment is a direct reflection of our ability to see the false for the false, the limited for the limited and the fragmented for the fragmented. Such is the nature of all recognition based on Intelligence and an open-ended spirit of enquiry. Through such deep and penetrating insight into the world of the known, we gradually regain our confidence, and begin to see for ourselves the depths of both our illusory ways of doing things, and the tremendous potential inherent in the mere fact of being human.

The quest is wide open. There are no rules for self-enquiry. There are only more or less useful ways for approaching our sense of limited being. And as our enquiry develops, we realize that all limitation is a result of a false sense of inner and outer fragmentation. But to investigate our Gods, our saviors and our spiritual traditions as being potentially part of this total field of fragmentation, and not to assume that these automatically fall within the category of revealed Truth, require a very alive and open attitude. Throughout the ages we have come to accept so many things as irreducible statements of truth that we no longer question these. Yet, these have become an integral part of that which obscures the revelation of our true and simple humaneness.

This open-minded and openhearted disposition will soon lead us to a new and more comprehensive vision of the truth of human life and establish our realistic relationship to this. If the insight that guides our path of self-enquiry and inner exploration has the slightest sense of duality woven into it, where the ultimate is explained in Otherworldly terms, we should take great care. Such a path may not yet have developed sufficiently in itself to present us with a true, non-dualistic vision of reality.

Part One: The View

If, on the other hand, we could come to an integral understanding of things, where truth is not seen as something separate from our human situation, we will direct our search not at what we presume is the Great Beyond, but rather investigate what it is we do that obstructs the integration between ourselves and the undivided truth of human experience.

Again we see the critical importance of the relationship between the vision we have of the ultimate, and the influence this is likely to have on the direction and substance of our enquiry and practice. Arriving at a realistic and appropriate initial point of departure could be seen as one of the most important decisions we will ever take towards the spiritualization of our lives. This is why it would prove to be of considerable value to allow sufficient time for pondering over the many philosophies and forms of practice presented to us via the traditions and their proponents - including the work presented here. All that is required of us during this phase of our work is to remain open-minded and openhearted so that we do not allow ourselves to become conditioned and controlled by any of these.

Everything needs our careful consideration and free spirit of enquiry. The more time we allow, the more relaxed our enquiry will be. And the more relaxed our enquiry, the greater the potential for us to come to a sound, reasonable and realistic feeling-sense of things before we enter into the path of our choice.

Chapter Two

SPIRITUAL HUMANISM -
The quest for human-centric spirituality.

The concept of God as the Great Other has existed in the human psyche for thousands of years. It manifested in many different forms and dominated and controlled our lives ever since it appeared in the human mind as a projection of our highest moral and ethical ideals. No other aspect of human creation has had such profound effects on the quality of our everyday experience: from the most sublime to the lowest ebb of the inhumane in us.

Through its long evolutionary path, God has been described in forms which served the particular needs of various social orders, philosophers, religions, propagandists and historical periods: from the homely, personal gods of the people of the Middle East and the Indian sub-continent prior to the recognition of a single God within these traditions, to the mystical, transcendent God of early Hinduism, which, eventually, was transformed into the all-inclusive Essence or Ground of Being of the Advaita Vedanta philosophy. Today these notions of God are as clearly evident within the wider spectrum of modern religious and mystical enquiry as they were in ancient times.

God is still regarded as either the omnipotent creator-God in heaven; or a mystical Being with whom we could merge after following a long, inner path of return - as a drop would merge back into the ocean which is both its source and ultimate destiny; or it is described as the immanent, Essential nature of all manifest existence from which we have never truly been separated. In this instance God is seen as our true Essence, prior to

Part One: The View

the belief in a categorical division between God and his creation, God and humankind.

Yet, in whichever way we have described and explained our gods to ourselves, evident in all these is a view of humanity which suggests that we are not yet within the embrace of the Highest. While alive here on earth, going through our daily routines of responsibility and volitional activity, human life is regarded to be dependent for its ultimate happiness and fulfillment on a Source which always existed prior to, and therefore separate from, all aspects of its creation..

In this we notice a distinct, if rather subtle, dualism: if God existed prior to humanity, it would not be unreasonable to suggest that it has an ultimate existence separate and separable from human life. This would also imply that as humans we need God for our existence. God does not need us. One of the earliest concepts of God was 'One without the other'. Originally only God existed. In religious and mystical terms this implies that humanity is a mere after-thought in the mind of God. So, in an ultimate sense, this implies a distinct form of dualism which none of the traditions have managed to bridge, despite the attempts to do so by some of the great Advaitist (non-dual) philosophers. Where there is a God, there is indeed an other - a human being - separate from the God he/she worships or aspires to merge with in mystical union.

If we investigate this God-concept further, it also becomes evident that we need God for our ultimate fulfillment, whereas God has been projected as an entity or state of Being completely sufficient unto itself. This vision of humankind as the inferior partner, or lesser principle in the creative potential of the Ultimate, has forced a particular mentality of inferiority and disempowerment upon us and greatly conditioned us into a primary belief of our separation from life itself. Whereas the Ultimate has been described as eternal life, the condition of humankind has been relegated to the realms of birth, death and decay – all suggesting our fundamental inferiority relative to the unchanging nature of the Ultimate. This left us with only one apparent course of action: to return to That of which we are presumed to be a modification, creation or emanation. And all traditional religious or mystical paths afford us with means

17

through which we could accomplish our return to, or unification with, the Ultimate. Whether this return will happen after death or during some mystical unity with the Godhead during our lifetime, our path has been pre-determined as a fundamental movement towards the Ultimate. Our only apparent choice is which path to follow and which 'revelatory' description of God to believe in.

If we now contrast this with the kind of secularism developing mostly in the West - and rapidly spreading to other parts of the world - where more people are beginning to question the existence of a God as such, we notice an interesting shift towards scientific enquiry, technological development and the notion that rational thinking can ultimately deliver us from the problems we have created for ourselves. The concept of God as our source of inspiration and ultimate fulfillment has therefore been replaced with the concept that science and rational thinking could serve as instruments for the facilitation of human well-being. What our gods were supposed to have done for us, science and the rational mind now have to accomplish. The atheistic humanist movement therefore moved from a dependence on God to a dependence on scientific rationalism as its sole source of inspiration and information.

This movement, away from the creator-God as sustainer of its creation, towards scientific materialism makes sense if one considers the less-than-accurate information about so many aspects of human life which was forthcoming from the religious schools of thought. However, when the human mind began to question its dependence on its own God-projection and shifted its focus instead to a dependence on rational thinking and scientific materialism, it committed yet another error of judgment: it moved from an uninspected religious certainty to a rationalist/materialist view of things without first investigating the fundamental problems both these styles of human enquiry were attempting to address.

The humanist movement, in its reactive urgency to rid itself from the stigma of the God-paradigm committed the same error which previously led to the error of the God-concept. It moved from the belief in God to the belief in knowledge. Unfortunately both these beliefs are based on an uninspected view of the nature of the unique problems facing us. In addition to this, it failed to appreciate the limited potential of the instruments employed by both rationality and belief to deal with human life in a coherent, comprehensive and effective manner. The movement from God to rationality is therefore a mere *modification* within the projective ability of thought, rather than a radical shift into the exploration of other, more subtle, areas of our human potential. Belief in a God is as much a product of thought as is the belief in rationality as the panacea for all our ills. Both are created and sustained by thought. Without sensitizing ourselves to the inherent limitations of thought, all the steps we take towards solving our problems via the agency of rationality alone will be conditioned and controlled by the nature of the instruments we use.

If Humanism were to become the basis for a truly integral approach to human well-being, it would have to sensitize itself to the vast well of human potential which lies beyond mere scientism and the power of rational thinking. In fact, at some point in its enquiry, Humanism will be forced to re-look at the question of transcendent living, much as the eastern traditions have done, but without any of the religious dogmas and presumed revelatory, mystical 'truths' associated with these ancient metaphors for integral living and the wholeness of life.

Humanism without God needs to look deeply into the entire potential of the human condition before it could describe itself as truly humanistic. Humanism which rejects the notion of a God, as well as not having an ongoing program through which to discover the wealth of ability which exists as transcendent potential within the depths of our human spirit, will fail the high ideals to which it aspires. Humanistic values which do not include the enquiry into our non-dual, self-transcendent potential, will remain immersed in the limited ego-paradigm that produced the illusion of God, and all forms of the Great Other, which it believes it has left behind. It will create a world of relative functional and psychological security within its scientific/rationalist projections, but because these are primarily based in a materialistic, non-transcendent and ego-based view of humankind, they will leave us as bewildered, emotionally disturbed and spiritually barren as we endured as a consequence of the God-paradigm.

We projected ourselves into the dilemma of God, and we may, through right thinking, come to the understanding that God never was. But if we consider that we projected this thing called God in an attempt to deliver us from our suffering and general distress, it may also be clear that the same instrument (thought) that created this delusion, cannot be trusted as the sole instrument through which to transcend the problems it has created for us. As little as God, as a projection of thought, ever had the power to influence the course of human life and to relieve us from the suffering we brought upon ourselves, in any fundamental way, equally as little can the instrument that created this God deliver us from the consequences of its own activities. Rational thinking, valuable as it may be, cannot transcend itself.

A new energy has to be brought into the equation of human problem-solving. A new light has to dawn for humanity. A new, different kind of intelligent participation in our inner functioning as well as the instruments we use for this functioning has to be facilitated from within our human potential if we were not to repeat our misapprehensions and mistakes of the past.

The speed with which we destroy the natural resources of our planet, the rampant materialism to which we dedicate so much of our valuable human resources, the superficiality of our emotional responses, our unlove and self-interest, the corruption in all our institutions, the devastating wars, our political and religious divisions – these are all direct consequences of our failure to understand our human situation in its functional reality.

Spiritual Humanism suggests that we trace our steps back into the vast well of human ability that have been obscured by all the traditional explanations of who and what we are and how this interpreted version of human life should relate to its world and the presumed Beyond.

Paradoxically this 'new' energy is as old as humankind itself. The kind of enquiry which Spiritual Humanism suggests is therefore not to be associated with a categorical movement away from our ordinary lives into the realms of our gods. Rather, it describes a gradual unfolding of our true and natural condition. In this we simply wake up from all the dreams and beliefs that limit and control our lives. This awakening into conscious awareness of our natural condition has been our potential ever since we started to notice ourselves as human beings. In fact, human life is founded upon a depth of true Intelligence and love, but these have never revealed themselves as the functional basis of interaction and relationship. Rather they have been *obscured* through a lack of self-reflection and self-knowledge.

We have no-one to blame. Not even ourselves. We have simply never been made fully aware of our true human potential. Spiritual Humanism suggests that the time has arrived for us to fall back onto our own human resources, to have faith in ourselves and to discover the functional measure for a truly humane interaction with life. This necessitates a profound enquiry into every aspect of our being – including exploring the vast potential within the transcendent (non-self) truth of human existence. And it is this enquiry which validates the word 'spiritual' as an integral component of Spiritual Humanism. If we do not allow for transcendent living, we will end up with the kind of rampant materialism evidenced in modern living which cannot but lead to nihilism, bewilderment, cynicism, a deepening of fragmentation and inner and outer conflict.

When we put aside the God-concept, we have nothing but our humanity to rely upon. And what Spiritual Humanism encourages and endeavors to facilitate as a practical, reasonable and most urgent quest, is the awakening of each individual to their vast, undiscovered well of human ability, generally completely obscured by uninspected living. As we noticed, one of the pivotal observations that Spiritual Humanism brings to our attention centers on the insight that, as part of our evolutionary process, we made use of instruments to assist us in dealing with the totality of human life before we investigated and discovered how these instruments work. That is, we have used thought, memory, attention, emotional responses, reason and intuition to manage the full complexity of our living environment, before we developed the art of self-observation and self-reflection. Without true self-reflection we will remain unaware of how we use these instruments in ways that more often than not distort our vision and fragment our lives.

As a direct consequence of this uninspected use of these powerful instruments, we created a world which reflects, not our deepest human potential, but rather the results of the indiscriminate use of these faculties which were not designed to deal with the complexity of human life as a *whole*. Instead of resolving the challenges of life by making use of the entire spectrum of our potential, we sought resolution of these by utilizing the same instruments which created our problems in the first place. This suggests that we projected 'answers' for facilitating human well-being before we properly inspected either the nature of our problems or the appropriateness of the instruments we applied to deal with the challenges of life. In this we perpetuated human-created suffering, truly believing we were dealing with it effectively and creatively.

The reference Spiritual Humanism makes to 'uninspected living', therefore, not only suggests that we lack knowledge of ourselves as *products* of thought and emotion, but most profoundly, that we have little or no insight into the functioning of instruments which up to this point in our evolution have mostly been responsible for creating sorrow, conflict and inner and outer disorder. If we are at all serious about a quality of life which reflects our deeper, truly humane potential, it is imperative that we investigate how we are controlled by instruments at our disposal which operate in an inner environment of pure habit and unawareness. No-one, no traditional religion, no guru and no God can correct the error of this unconscious abuse of such powerful instruments. Only conscious living, when explored and allowed to function at its deepest levels of insight, Intelligence and pure emotion, could deliver us from what we unconsciously sanction as an ongoing process of uniformed functioning.

Such self-observation and self-knowledge need to take place in the context of a wider enquiry into the whole matter of self-transcendence. As will become evident as our enquiry proceeds, only when self-transcendence becomes the motivating principle behind our investigations into the underlying causes of suffering and disorder, could the possibility of true integral living arise.

Part One: The View

Holistic living and self-transcendence are thus related in a very special way: the process of self-transcendence facilitates the revelation of the truth of non-duality (wholeness) as it manifests in every moment of awakened Intelligence.

And it is at this juncture where we notice the uncompromising position of Spiritual Humanism relative to the humanist ideal: *to be a humanist is also to be a non-dualist* - not as a separated, self-contracted bundle of knowledge *about* non-dualism gained merely from reading books and informed by those who teach non-dual philosophies, but as a person, in and as whom non-dualism begins to function on an ongoing basis. There can be no true Humanism without the reality of the non-dual truth of human existence to inform and sustain it. On its deepest level the human spirit is both founded in, and an expression of, the experience of the non-dual truth of every living moment. Thus the term: *Spiritual Humanism*.

Without God, we are thrown back onto ourselves, and this could be seen as potentially one of the most creative developments in human history. For once many of us find ourselves in a position where we could discern about these matters for ourselves and to discover who and what we really are without fear of persecution and public ridicule. Spiritual Humanism suggests that at the most subtle level of human experience a natural state of non-dualism becomes self-evident. This is not something 'we' merge with. It is also not some Primordial mystical condition or a God eternally existing in mystical space to which 'we' return. Rather, it is simply that which remains when our inner sense of fragmentation and separation has been transcended through right practice and integral living. Here, inner and outer no longer appear as two separate states of observer and the observed. No clear line can be drawn between the content of awareness and the awareness of content. The two are self-evidently one undivided and intelligent process of present arising.

And the most vital aspect of the uncovering of non-dual living is how this manifests in our ordinary human situation as love, charity, compassion, pure emotion, sanity, Intelligence and psychological well-being. This is why non-dual living is so important for the facilitation of the full expression of the humanist ideals. These truly humane qualities cannot generally manifest in the noise and turbulence of the fragmented 'I'-conscious state, driven and informed by conditioned thinking. We can neither believe nor reason ourselves into the full expression of holistic living. *We can only create the conditions necessary to allow for its gradual unfolding.* We may have unsolicited moments of insight, unitive consciousness and deeply moving experiences of clarity and unobstructed vision, but these are soon lost. The power of conditioning, with its resulting confusion and delusion is still too controlling.

This is why it is important that we attend to every aspect of our lives where we habitually and unconsciously fragment the truth of the living moment. Our bondage is a subtly woven web of inner misapprehension and confusion. We believe so many things which contradict the reality of our living experience, and project so many thoughts onto the simplicity of life, that we find it difficult, if not impossible, to discern projected and transferred 'reality' from the real movement of life itself.

Should it therefore be our deep, abiding passion to live with what is *real*, rather than our projected view of things, we would do well to refine our search into how we function as disturbed and self-contracted human beings to the point where our investigation becomes as subtle as the nature of the confusion we investigate. Only when the intensity and clarity of our enquiry meet the functional, but limited, intelligence inherent in our state of confusion, measure for measure, does the possibility of freedom arise. Before then we will remain absorbed in the clutches of our self-created, destiny-creating vision.

We *are* the path we will have to walk. There is no easy way out of the net of human-created suffering which we alone have woven and which we alone could undo. Few have achieved this, and, as we have seen, the reason for our inability to break free lies not with the integrity and natural ability of the human spirit of enquiry, or the Intelligence within our human potential, but rather because we have neither been sensitized sufficiently with regard to the nature of our problems, nor been afforded with constructive and appropriate ways to deal with these. We are faced with a *human* dilemma, and we alone can transcend the problems we have created for ourselves. Our Gods, in whichever form, have proven to be of little help.

Spiritual Humanism offers us insights into the entire process of inner fragmentation: how it gets established and maintained through unawareness and lack of self-knowledge and how to transcend this finely woven network of misapprehension, confusion and suffering we have created for ourselves. This requires that we re-open our enquiry into the human condition: how we function as bundles of self-contraction; how thought creates and sustains the many illusions which dominate and control our lives; how our emotions are tied into their own network of psychological memory and patterns of reactivity and how the random and habitual movements of attention and thought create a false sense of realness which distorts our vision and obscures the non-dual reality which is our deepest potential and most natural condition.

But if we consider that wholeness is not something to be discovered *within* as some Primordial Essence, but is rather the simplicity of that which remains in any moment of present experience when our inner work has freed our being from the bondage of the self-contracted state, it may be clear that no aspect of human experience could be left out from this enquiry. We have to investigate the way things appear to us *externally* as much as how we create our confusion *internally*. As we have seen, wholeness is not something that binds inner and outer together, it is not of 'one taste', or of one Primordial Essence. Wholeness is simply the direct experience of the non-dual truth of the present moment, which has nothing whatsoever to do with merging the separate self-sense into some Greater Presence, or realizing our presumed oneness with the universe.

The separate one can never *be* whole. Neither can it ever *become* whole. When its presumed inner status has been exposed as mere uninspected thought-projections, and through right practice it is gradually transcended, what remains is the self-evident simplicity of non-dual present arising as it unfolds in each living moment. Spiritual Humanism sensitizes us to this truth of non-dual, present arising, and keeps reminding us that when we investigate the presumption of separation, such work has to include our entire field of experience. No aspect of this field can be permanently by-passed or excluded from our enquiry. That which is not thoroughly investigated, observed and transcended, will remain with us as a potential source for disequilibrium, confusion and suffering.

Our delusions form a comprehensive and very effective barrier between ourselves and the wholeness of present experience, and only by investigating every aspect of these delusions could we create the conditions necessary for this great simplicity to shine through the fog of our misapprehensions. This is why *Part One* of this book looks at so many diverse aspects of how we delude ourselves into the belief of fragmented living. These are serious and vital considerations which cannot be by-passed. They form the necessary mental and emotional orientation towards true self-enquiry in general, which in turn facilitates the success of the inner work described in *Part Two*. Every detail of our uninspected sense of separation has to be recognized for what it is and be regarded as a necessary area for investigation and self-observation. Only when these have been re-cognized from the perspective of our deeper Intelligence as mere illusions, can they finally be transcended.

We are caught in a dream of folly. Mistaking this dream for reality, we are destroying both ourselves and our world. The problems we have created are deeply embedded in the fabric of our limited self-vision, and evidenced by the rather dysfunctional relationships we, as bundles of self-contraction, share with others and the world in general. Spiritual Humanism suggests that we first discover for ourselves the falseness of the ways in which we function, and from there to allow the clarity of our own living reality to lead us from darkness to light – from mere biological humanness, to truly humane living.

Only when the human spirit stands free from any self-imposed limitation and conditional relationships based on this deluded sense of self, can we consider ourselves truly humane. From there the natural order of things will unfold by itself.

Chapter Three

THE THOUGHT-ATTENTION KNOT

Human suffering has been explained in many ways. For thousands of years we have been offered explanations for our sense of unease or discomfort by the religious, spiritual and philosophical traditions of humankind. The reason for this apparent preoccupation with suffering is not difficult to understand if one considers how few of us can lay claim to a completely fulfilled and happy life. We are born into a world where things simply don't always work out according to our needs, hopes, desires and demands. It is as though life has its own agenda that appears to care little for our expectations, however important these may be to us. And not only don't things always work out according to our plans and projections, even our most stable forms of security have shown themselves to be vulnerable to the ever-changing nature of life.

Whereas other living creatures have shown a remarkable ability to live with changes within their environment, we seem to suffer these changes very acutely. We may have the ability to adapt physically to a wide range of environmental and other challenges, yet we display an emotional resistance to all forms of change, both inwardly and outwardly. We somehow have not learnt to live in harmony with change, and this has brought us in direct conflict with life itself.

Life is one continuous process of unfolding, and our resistance to this fluid nature of things could be seen as the primary reason for our emotional distress. We are at odds with the fundamental reality in which we have to function. This creates a living environment that is characterized by inner and outer conflict, disorder, defensive patterns of behavior and a general sense of bewilderment. And because these forms of uninspected living have been with us for so many thousands of years, they have become an integral part of our lives.

If we now consider how the different spiritual traditions explained things from an Ultimate point of view, it may be clear why the suffering resulting from the inevitable conflict between our demand for security and stability, on the one hand, and the reality of change, on the other, has been such a prominent feature in all these teachings. In order to present us with a consistent and coherent picture of creation, these Ultimate explanations had to address also the question of human suffering. Suffering had to be given its legitimate place in the context of these 'complete' descriptions of Reality.

However, not being able to explain human suffering in purely *human terms*, these traditions inevitably attempted to describe it in the same metaphysical language associated with their insights into, and speculations about, the nature and origin of existence. Our suffering had therefore been given a *metaphysical nuance* that divorced it from the human context in which it appears. This removed our suffering from its human ground, and placed it in the realm of metaphysical speculation.

Once described in these Otherworldly terms, and accepted by us as revelatory truths, we were effectively removed from gaining direct insight into our inner disturbances. We were thus left completely exposed and vulnerable to the ever-fertile imaginations of those who offered us explanations and remedies for our inner and outer disorder.

Instead of finding out about these matters for ourselves, we have become totally dependent on the authority of the traditions to explain our suffering, and therefore how to put an end to it. This prevented us from looking at our own situation and discovering to which extent we ourselves might be responsible for our distress as a consequence of having little insight into the totality of our human condition.

Part One: The View

Much of what has been suggested as remedies by those to whom we have entrusted our inner equanimity and outer order, has become part of the problem. This makes sense if we consider that we do not suffer some metaphysical, religious or mystical disorder, but rather something very real and immediate to our everyday experience. Yet, once explained in metaphysical terms – such as the laws of karma and reincarnation, original sin, predestination, an angry or disappointed God and so on – we clearly lost all participatory input to free ourselves from our suffering. These theories attempted to explain an essentially human affair in terms of vague and unexplainable metaphysical propositions.

However, if we were to re-examine these explanations with an open mind and heart, it would be self-evident that there is no reason why these rather extraordinary Otherworldly notions had to be attached to human suffering. Suffering is a human phenomenon and should be investigated from within our human condition. We do not suffer God. We suffer our very own selves. What is real to us when we feel the pain of our own mental and emotional disorder shows no relation to anything we might have done in previous lifetimes where we were supposed to have sown the seeds for our present suffering. Neither has anyone ever found a discernable connection between their suffering and a revengeful God, the Devil, some primordial sin or what Adam and Eve did in the Garden of Eden.

Our suffering is real, painful and disturbing. It is *our* problem and can only be addressed from within the reality of our own human situation. If we want to free ourselves from this dilemma we need to appreciate that we are not struggling with the consequences of some Primordial design over which we have no control, but rather are confronted by destiny-creating forms of uninspected living for which only we are responsible. Once we accept our suffering as a purely human phenomenon, and become fully responsible for it, we could discover ways of understanding and transcending it.

If we consider the tremendous emphasis that many of the traditions originating from the East have placed on the theories of karma and reincarnation, we may appreciate the additional problems these teachings introduced into our lives. Instead of liberating us from our suffering, they have complicated matters considerably and left us more bewildered than before. The way the concepts of karma and reincarnation make sense to the layperson is that all forms of action have inevitable consequences and, depending on the quality and nature of our actions in this life, we will be rewarded or punished for these in future lifetimes. In other words, we could accumulate good or bad karma in this life, and then enjoy or suffer the direct consequences of our deeds in a next life, or even some future lives.

From this it may be evident that the theory of karma only makes sense in the circumstance of rebirth or reincarnation. These traditions have explained reincarnation and karma as a finely woven web of never-ending, destiny-creating dilemma. And as human beings seem to be intent on creating more bad than good karma, we can see how this theory of reincarnating individual karmic patterns could be used to explain human suffering within the broader framework of a divinely-created, or God-manifested, reality.

According to this theory we simply suffer our own misconduct. And not only the misconduct of one previous life, but also the many misdeeds somehow registered in a vast pool of karmic memory stretching over many lifetimes. The way out of this dilemma would therefore be to monitor our actions and modify our behavior to safeguard ourselves against negative future karmic consequences. Furthermore, as good deeds may result in good karma, we are motivated to act in accordance with whatever we may understand by the term 'good', to thereby enhance our chances of more karmically-favorable rebirths.

However, it may be clear that whereas this karmic theory has attempted to explain the reasons for our suffering in this life, it has effectively removed us from the possibility of directly observing, understanding and transcending our present suffering. If what we are in this life is largely determined by what we have done in previous lives, we are left completely disempowered to do anything about our suffering here and now. According to this theory we live a kind of karmic blueprint: almost as though our karma has been imprinted into our genes.

Part One: The View

The way karma is explained, dictates that things are more or less determined for us according to the Divine law that governs it. We seem to have this inherent ability to create karma and, merely by being human, we are destined to remain in the realm of birth, death and suffering with little hope of escaping our reincarnating, karmic consequences. And according to this theory we have been doing these karmic rounds for millions of lifetimes.

However, if we look at this from a more realistic perspective it will be evident that it presents us with little more than an elaborate justification for our suffering. It attempts to explain our unhappiness away, rather than leading us to the light of our own understanding about our present human condition. Once stated as truth, and subsequently restated by millions of eager and uninformed believers, such speculative, metaphysical propositions take on the form of revelatory truth. Being 'revelatory', these become an unquestioned and integral part of the way we believe the Divine orders and controls the universe. And the less it is understood - and capable of being inspected in the light of reason and personal, direct experience - the greater the presumed 'proof' of its Divine origin.

Other than being an interesting theory, and perhaps a kind of misdirected, psychological comfort-zone, the notion of a personal karmic record, stretching over many lifetimes, has failed to explain in which way we, during our present lifetime, may be responsible for our suffering; and what we could do to free ourselves from the ongoing dramatization of this universal human dilemma.

We are not pointing here to the natural destiny-creating ways in which we live, and how the inappropriate actions of one generation are passed on through history, convention and social conditioning to future generations. Nor are we denying the obvious and necessary consequences of our ongoing activities, which may impact positively or negatively at a later stage in our lives. What concerns us during this enquiry is the notion that our present suffering is explained in terms of a theory that makes us the passive receivers of a bundle of reincarnating karmic residues which would seem as far removed from our present situation as the actions of a distant relative who lived a few hundred years ago. This theory simply does not address the pressing issues facing us in our present situation where we seem to continue a life of disharmony, alienation and disorder, without knowing why we are doing it.

A further example of how religious concepts have attempted to explain away our suffering is evident in the Christian concept of original sin. Not different to the way in which our unease, as a result of the painful consequences of karma and reincarnation, has been given some presumed Divine origin, suffering, in the Christian sense, is also described as the result of primordial wrongdoing. Again we see how it is explained as something which has no relation to our everyday lives, other than us suffering its consequences. However, whereas in the case of the karmic theory we are being held responsible for our own deeds in previous lifetimes, the Christian gospel teaches that we suffer because of the wrongdoings of Adam and Eve. Somehow we have all fallen with them into a disposition of eternal suffering and inevitable wrongdoing.

Again we notice how this essentially human dilemma has been explained in terms of an underlying theory of an almighty creator-God whose laws determine that our born-condition necessitates human suffering. We only have to be human to be designated 'sinners'.

Based on this 'evidence' of primordial sinning, the Christian tradition presents us with a ready answer to our problems. Believe in Jesus, and the hereafter will be a place of infinite grace and joy. Little is said about how to free ourselves from the suffering we feel while alive, other than directing our prayers to the very God whose dictates brought the suffering upon us in the first place. Nothing is said for the possibility of looking for the source of our suffering in the midst of our ordinary living.

If those who presented us with all these detailed speculative propositions about the origin of our emotional distress were to have been somewhat more discerning and guarded in their assumptions, they would have been faced with the fact that to come to an understanding of suffering may not be so easy. In

Part One: The View

their attempts to bring coherency to their metaphysical speculations about the origin of things, they had only their fertile imaginations to fall back on. And as we shall discover, thought can project all sorts of images, and then experience these projections as objectively existing truths. In this way, speculative thought takes on the form of reality.

This is the fate of all speculative metaphysics with its grand schemes of gods, saviors, creators, sustainers, destroyers, heavens, hells, karma, and original sin. And while we so desperately cling to our gods, our saviors and the 'revelatory' nature of these religious projections, human suffering is still with us, despite all the attempts by the spiritual traditions to explain it away in terms of some extra-human phenomena.

Another aspect of this enquiry points to the failure of these theories to directly connect the presumed reasons for our distress with the remedies they offer us. In the Christian tradition we suffer because of the misdeeds of Adam and Eve (or because of the works of the Devil, or predestination). The remedy - the belief that Jesus died for our sins on the cross - has no direct connection with the misdeeds of Adam and Eve, not to mention its failure to address the possibility of relief from our suffering in our present situation. All possibility of relief is vested in some presumed afterlife. The Christian system simply does not address the content, structure and human aspect of our suffering while we are alive.

The same holds true for the theory of karma. Our present suffering has no relation to what we presumably did during our few million past lifetimes, or how our destiny is supposed to unfold in any future lifetime. Again, it does not address the possibility for the cessation of suffering while we are alive. Everything gets projected from past to future, as though our present living reality is merely an arbitrary, transitional moment between lifetimes, ultimately of little consequence in the vast continuum of millions of reincarnations.

In both cases, these 'causes' and their remedies point away from our present human condition. These traditions have explained our suffering in such a way that we have no direct connection with either the cause of our suffering or the possibil-

33

ity of doing anything about it here and now. They portray us as mere passive receivers of the consequences of misdeeds for which we cannot be held personally responsible. I cannot change the fact of either the presumed sinning of Adam and Eve in the Garden, or anything I was supposed to have done over many previous lifetimes, and yet these are presented as the fundamental causes of my present dis-eased condition.

The direct consequence of this inherent schism between the way our suffering has been explained and the remedies offered by these teachings (and many other similar traditions) is that they have not been successful in relieving our suffering in any meaningful way. This is an absolutely crucial failing on the part of our spiritual heritage. Unless we critically examine the causes of suffering, here and now, we are unlikely to free ourselves from inner turmoil.

To do this, we need to take full responsibility for how we live, and refrain from depending on the authority of our spiritual traditions, however ancient and well respected, to explain these matters to us. Once we have developed an insight into how we create and sustain our own suffering, it becomes something we could work with in a realistic, practical and sustainable way.

However, before we enter too deeply into such an investigation, it may be important that we are clear what we mean by the word 'suffering' in the context of our present enquiry. Human suffering is so wide and far reaching that it would be misleading to discuss it as a unitary phenomenon, with a common etiology and a single remedy. Physical pain and discomfort, for instance, are of a very different nature to that of emotional and psychological distress. Very often these two are biologically interlinked, so that it is not possible to draw a clear distinction between them.

For instance, a mother experiencing great anguish at the sickness of her child or a husband feeling frustration, anger and disappointment when, as the sole breadwinner in the family, he loses his job, could be seen as natural, biologically-based emotional responses to incidents in one's life which may be beyond one's control. Similarly, many other forms of emotional response – such as fear, anger, sadness, and so on – are often simply part of being human. Physical pain can never be wished away.

It would seem, then, that these are forms of physical and emotional disturbance about which little can be done. These are as part of human nature as hunger and thirst are part of human nature. We may learn to manage them as best we can. We may control, understand, suppress, ignore or investigate them, but these forms of suffering will remain part of our human condition in some degree or another for as long as we manifest as psychophysical beings.

However, had these been the *only* problems we have ever had to deal with, we most certainly would not have needed all the elaborate metaphysical explanations and remedies for our suffering – especially in the modern era where most of our basic needs have been catered for, however modest our lifestyle might be. Unfortunately, from the very beginning of recorded history, humanity has been beset by forms of suffering which have little or no relation to physical survival and ordinary daily necessities. We have been exposed to wars; inept and corrupt governments; confusing, fragmenting and alienating religious systems; unrelated metaphysical prescriptions for living; greed; poverty; nationalistic irrationalities; self-serving, personal enrichment at the cost of others; sub-human social and political systems; emotional deprivation; rampant materialism and a general degradation of the humane in humanity.

None of these could be seen as necessary for survival, or even remotely survival orientated. They are embellishments to the simplicity of our inherent human nature based on a view of life that could only be described as uninspected and thus destiny-creating. All actions have consequences, and if our actions are based on values and standards that contradict the natural order of things, we cannot but suffer the residual consequences of such actions. And most human suffering is of such residual, destiny-creating nature. We should therefore distinguish between human-created suffering and the forms of suffering which could be described as more natural to human existence.

The tragedy is that we have become so used to living in the context of these less-than-human circumstances that we have come to accept these as natural expressions of the way things are. We no longer question the values, principles and structures that support gross violations of our human dignity and inner order. Having lived with these for many centuries, we have become disempowered to the point where we truly believe that there is nothing we can do to relieve us from the destiny-creating consequences of our actions.

And in a way this is true. No individual transformation will be sufficient to effect any measurable change in the momentum of our human-created folly as a whole. However, what is also true, is that, as individuals, we could do much in the way of coming to an understanding of how we personally participate in, and therefore sanction and perpetuate, our own suffering. It is on this individual level of accepting the responsibility of participating in our own destiny where we could become pro-active by approaching these matters in a spirit of open-minded self-exploration.

This is no easy task. Many great students of life have tried to investigate the causes of suffering, and what could be done to relieve humankind from their consequences. This is why we, as ordinary people, often feel such a task to be beyond our ability. In fact, our initial reaction to the mere suggestion that we investigate this for ourselves often results in bewilderment and feelings of disempowerment. Yet, there is nothing written that we cannot observe, understand and transcend that which binds us. All that is required is a determination to find out for ourselves how we really function and to which extent our ignorance of this could be responsible for the dilemmas we create for ourselves.

One way of approaching this enquiry is to look at how thought dominates our entire field of consciousness. Although we may not generally be aware of it, we are really habitual and chronic thinkers. Thought not only interprets all incoming data to establish practical and useful relations with the world, it is also constantly active *as* a form of inward dialogue. In this inner world of thought we talk to ourselves and others; project things into the past and future; participate in the drama of our own story lines and generally occupy ourselves with many small details projected by our imagination. This inward chatter seldom stops. We come to notice it most clearly when, for instance, we sit down for meditation and try to feel the silence within.. Without any apparent necessity, our minds just continue with this endless inner activity: creating, projecting and experiencing their own imaginative outpourings as reality.

Having said this, it is nevertheless interesting to note that, of itself, this mind-stuff is really quite harmless. The ramblings of thought have no *inherent* potential to disturb us. Thought appears in the field of consciousness in no way different to everything else. To have the visual experience of a tree or to create the thought-image of a tree comes to much the same: both are appearances in our field of awareness. Things appear all the time, and part of this ongoing process of present arising are the projections and images created by thought. In the same way as the great diversity of the world of present experience comes and goes, the inner projections of thought are also merely momentary and non-binding appearances in consciousness.

And yet, despite this *inherent neutrality* of thought, our lives are nevertheless determined, dominated and controlled by it. All the problems associated with the specific human dilemmas pointed to earlier, have their origin in thought. Thought is the creator and sustainer of wars, divisive religious dogmas, corrupt governments, greed, materialism, low self-esteem, self-aggrandizement and all other forms of self-centered activity. None of these would be possible without thought.

Thought is also the principal agent in the fragmentation of human experience. Fragmentation inevitably leads to resistance, conflict and suffering. We cannot expect to fragment our world into religious factions, nationalities, self-serving economic policies, power blocks and ideological imperatives without the necessary residual consequences of mutual tension, misunderstanding, disrespect, greed and ultimately war. There is ample historical evidence of how these thought-created distortions have dramatized themselves many times over in the long history of human conflict. And all of these stem from the ability of thought to fragment human experience into isolated forms of thought-created reality.

Yet, can we reasonably blame all human conflict and suffering on thought alone? No doubt, without thought, none of these forms of suffering would be possible. But what is the relationship between thought and the way we experience it? Why do we allow thought its apparent automatic dominance over our lives, despite the fact that it clearly plays such a vital role in the distortion and fragmentation of our experience? If thought is indeed the neutral, rational instrument of the living organism, why has it produced such vast misery in the world? Why can we not simply look into the ways thought works and use it as a functional instrument for survival, instead of allowing ourselves to become completely conditioned and controlled by it? In other words, why can we not see thought as an inner process next to other necessary processes, and simply allow it to inform us intelligently about challenges as they arise so that we may respond to these in an appropriate, sane and coherent manner?

The reason for this is the power of identification. We have become totally identified with thought. As we think, so we are. Identified thinking determines our being – and through identification we have come to mistake the world of thought for reality itself. Without realizing it, we have become so thoroughly identified with thought that there exists no separation between the experience we have of ourselves, and the content of our thinking. In this way we are at the mercy of the content of thought.

Being wholly 'I'-dentified with our thought-projections, our thinking ability has largely lost its neutrality, usefulness and survival-potential, and has instead taken on an existence of its own, which has little to do with its practical function of interpreting, understanding and the ordering of our lives.

Through the process of identifying ourselves with the activities of thought, it no longer *serves* human life, but has mostly *become* human life. Identification with thought means that no separation exists between the human mind (as thought) and hu-

Part One: The View

man life. What we know, we *are*. In this way I *am* my religion. I *am* my nationality. I *am* my war. I *am* the image I have of myself and others. I *am* my political party. I *am* the way I interpret my field of experience. I *am* my morality, social order and social conditioning. I *am* both that which thought presumes to be me and not-me. In fact, I am the entire fragmentary, destiny-creating and uninspected projections of my own thinking. All these are creations of thought, and while I am identified with thought, this thought-world *is* me. In this, there is no other. And it is this projected reality we suffer and enjoy for as long as we are identified with it.

We are indeed born free, but because we have this propensity for becoming identified with the projections of thought, we find ourselves bound within the limitations and conditions determined by the logic and reality created by this identification, regardless of its consequences. As we have seen, we do not suffer the content of our random thinking processes as such: we suffer the content of our thinking because we are identified with it.

This is a very important insight. Yet, to become aware of my identification with thought and to notice how this complicates my life is only the beginning of a considerably more subtle investigation into the causes of suffering. The natural question we may now ask is: what makes identification possible? Which aspect of my inner potential facilitates the process of identification altogether? Here we are faced with a critically important question that requires our careful consideration.

Self-observation will reveal two fundamental facets of the process of identification. The first is that it takes place unconsciously. The second reveals its total dependence on the power of attention to keep it in place. And the reason that the process as a whole could be described as 'unconscious' is that attention operates here in a completely unconscious way. During the process of identification attention associates unconsciously with any idea or emotion and thereby creates a state of *identified reality*. In this way we become that with which we are identified. If attention therefore focuses itself unconsciously on any aspect of thought, we become identified with the content of such a thought. To be identified with any thing, state or thought, is to experience no difference between myself and the thought-created object of my identification.

Because attention is the focusing mechanism of awareness, our consciousness is automatically drawn to where attention focuses itself. From this we may appreciate that if attention associates itself in a random and unconscious manner with the content of thought, our association with thought will also take on the *unconscious nature* of this process. In this way attention binds our awareness into the logic and content of our disorderly and conditioned thinking patterns which create a reality for us that is completely projected by thought, and sustained by the unconscious association of attention with its projections.

Another interesting aspect of this unconscious association between thought and attention is that although we are conscious of the *content* of what thought projects, we are unconscious of the *process* of identification as such. That is, when we are absorbed in this identified world of thought, we suffer and enjoy the apparent reality of our thought projections, yet we remain totally unaware of the unconscious *processes* which facilitate this thought/attention reality. When I sing praises to my God, country or political leaders, fight my nationalistic wars, look down upon those who do not share my religious beliefs, feel myself superior and separate from others who not share my moral or other culturally-created convictions, I am conscious of what I do and think, yet totally unconscious, or ignorant of the processes which make it possible for me to feel and act the way I do. Clearly in such lack of self-knowledge exists great potential for suffering.

This unawareness could be seen as one of the most important reasons why we never managed to come to terms with our suffering. We remained ignorant of the inner functions that are at the root of the symptoms we experience as mental and emotional disorder and suffering. This unawareness left us at the mercy of the projections of thought, while we truly believe there is nothing we can do about our suffering. Being thus unconsciously locked into, or identified with, whatever thought projects, we inevitably suffer the painful and disturbing consequences of this thought-created reality within our psychophysical being.

And for lack of a better description, we could call this specific form of identification between the content of thought on the one hand, and the way attention associates itself with this in a habitual and unconscious way on the other hand, the *'thought/attention-knot'*.

Although we may attach this rather functional description to this inner activity, we should not underestimate the profound effects of this habitual association between thought and attention on our lives. This unconscious and ultimately unnecessary process touches and distorts every aspect of our being. In fact, so deeply-rooted is this inner function, that the thought-reality created by this process established itself in us as a kind of *condition of being*. We live so completely through, and *as*, this thought/attention-reality that it has become like an operating system that conditions and determines almost every activity taking place within it.

The 'ignorance' of which all the self-transcending traditions speak, is nothing but our unawareness of the fact that we generally live on the basis of this limited field of operation determined by only two aspects of our total human potential: thought and attention. And as we shall discover as our enquiry proceeds, this has devastating consequences on how we relate to our world emotionally. Once we enter the dream of this thought/attention-reality, we suffer and enjoy the contents of the illusion it creates in no way different to how we experience our dreams during sleep.

During our dreams we also have all kinds of experiences with deep emotional and imaginative content. Yet, when we wake up from the dream, it becomes perfectly evident that what we have been suffering or enjoying within the dream, was nothing but a reality that was valid on one level, or state of consciousness, but totally invalid and unreal in the waking state. This is exactly what happens to us when we enter the 'reality' of the thought/attention-knot. We enter the dream of this reality while awake, and thereby sacrifice our natural state of open and intelligent awareness to the living moment. Clearly this manifests a state of semi-conscious participation in the living reality of the present moment. The thought/attention-knot shows little or no relation to the reality of existence. It forms a self-enclosed, *thought-created reality*, totally divorced from the world in which we find ourselves. And integrally part of the conscious process of self-enquiry and self-transcendence is to wake up from this dream.

At this point it may be important to realize that we are not calling into question the legitimate and necessary function of attention. Attention plays a particularly important role during all our activities. As we have seen, attention is an instrument of awareness. It not only focuses awareness when we need to become specifically aware of an aspect of present experience; attention also serves the physical body by immediately bringing important happenings to its notice, such as when it is threatened or physically challenged.

In other instances we could consciously focus attention where we choose: for instance, when we want to look at something with intent, when we study, or think about a certain problem and so on. Here attention is relatively under our volitional control. We determine where we want attention to focus and then shift it from one field of interest to another as may be necessary. If used consciously in this way, attention has a natural and useful function of directing awareness. It serves the body in an intelligent and objective manner as a necessary and valuable focusing mechanism of awareness. In this it fulfills its function as one of our most valuable instruments for survival.

However, exactly because attention has the ability to isolate one aspect of the present arising from another to enable us to inspect something in greater detail, this isolating aspect of attention requires further investigation. Attention not only isolates: in the process it also *excludes* much of the rest of the field of present experience from which the particular object has been isolated. This brings about a shift in awareness which is useful

Part One: The View

in one way and less than useful in others, because although we need this kind of exclusive focusing ability when required, when it happens *unconsciously*, as we may notice when the thought/attention-knot is active, we become so exclusively focused that we lose our more primary sense of general awareness which has a very different, vastly more holistic, quality to it than that of any state of focused attention. (For a detailed enquiry into this, see *Part Two: The Practice of Passive Awareness* and *The Practice of Direct Awareness.*)

But to come to a more direct sense of how the thought/attention-knot creates a reality and binds our being into this dream-state, let us take the example of what happens to us when we read a novel. Very few of us have probably given consideration to this strange phenomenon of how it is possible for a novel to cast its spell over us. What makes it possible for us to 'get into' the story and to become so totally absorbed in it that hours may pass without us noticing it? In fact, besides time, much else also passes us by: like the sound of the traffic; the child shouting at his friend across the street; the neighbor's lawnmower making a noise; the smell of food from the kitchen, and so on.

While these are going on around us, we are totally engrossed in the verbal images and storyline presented to us by the author. We become totally identified with the characters, incidents, circumstances and emotional content of what we read. It is the art of the skilled novelist to bring to life a world contained in word-images that appears real and totally believable. And while we are immersed in our book, there is no distance between ourselves and the content of the book. Our identification with what we read becomes total, and it is this identification that makes the success of a novel possible.

Yet, none of what we experience when we read our book is actually happening. Or perhaps we should say that the entire 'reality' we experience when we read our novel exists only in thought. What we experience is nothing but our own imagination. We do not read our book, we dream it. And what makes the whole thing possible and real, is that attention has *uncon-*

43

sciously associated itself with the images thought projects into our field of awareness while reading the narrative of the author. We have entered a world of thought/emotion-reality through the unconscious association of attention with the content of thought. We could also say that novels work because we have the possibility of entering the dream of the thought/attention-knot while in the waking state.

This confirms our earlier observation: we only become what we think when attention is focused on the content of our thinking in an *unconscious* way. The binding power of the thought/attention-reality on our being is only possible during this act of unconsciously allowing attention to associate itself with the content of thought or emotion. While we remain ignorant, or unaware of the way in which this process determines our present reality and, in the case of our real world of living experience, to a large extent our destiny, we will continue to be controlled, conditioned and defined by the content of thought with its profound effects on our emotions. What the spiritual traditions call 'mind' is nothing other than the thought-attention knot. Ignorance or unawareness of this is the *root-ignorance* from which most of our human suffering originates. We are simply unconscious that we are dreaming our presumed dilemmas.

In this regard it may also be worth noticing that ignorance is essentially ignorant of itself. While we dream, we are only aware of the content of our dream, and totally unaware of the fact that we are dreaming. And this is true of every condition created by the thought/attention-knot. While we are caught in the reality of our thought-projections, we only experience the thought and emotional content of that reality. We are completely unaware that the reality we believe we are experiencing is created by thought, and sustained through the power of attention as an ongoing yet profoundly unconscious process.

It may now become clear why the enquiry into this aspect of our functioning is so important. It not only affects us on our emotional and psychological level, but also has had devastating consequences when vast numbers of people respond collectively in this unconscious way to all sorts of conditioned impulses. We are clearly culturally conditioned. But what we often do not appreciate is that conditioning comes with its own logic. When we respond conditionally to any situation, we not only bring conditioned information and emotional reactivities into present awareness. We also bring into play the *logic* that gives meaning and value to the way in which we conditionally respond.

In this way, conditioned responses completely bypass and pre-empt the free Intelligence available to us to meet the ongoing challenges of life. The conditioned response presents itself with logic of its own and thereby gives us the impression that we are really thinking about the issues at hand.

But often this is not the case. When we respond conditionally, we merely unconsciously repeat that which has been conditioned into us at some point in our history. Naturally, this places a tremendous limitation on our ability to respond with Intelligence and open-mindedness to situations. And this specific form of confused 'reality' is possible only whilst we are caught in the dream-state of the thought/attention-knot. Through the activity of the thought/attention-knot, we *become* our conditioning. In this way we merely dramatize forms of conditioning, while we believe we are consciously and intelligently participating in our own present activities.

When we, therefore, collectively respond to challenges from culturally conditioned preconceptions – like our religious convictions, nationalistic identifications, moralistic and ethical values, socially accepted forms of behavior, customs, dogmas and taboos – we simply all dream the same dream at the same time. And if the predetermined logic of the dream demands that the appropriate collective response to a challenge is for us to enter into a nationalistic war, or that one of our gods has commanded the annihilation of a neighboring nation, we mobilize ourselves into action on the basis of these unconscious and un-inspected conditioned tendencies, totally unaware of what it is within each of us that is motivating and informing our behavior. All we experience is the apparent logic and content of our conditioning while we remain totally ignorant of the way in which these have been given life and relevance via the unconscious activity of the thought/attention-knot.

What our generals, political masters, leaders and priests do not tell us when they call us to arms for the benefit of their own, self-serving motivations, is that they are simply relying on the unconscious in us to demonstrate and dramatize collectively some specific aspects of the content of our culturally conditioned potential. And the instruments they use to obtain our 'willing' co-operation are nothing other than the thought/attention-knot and the conditioned, predetermined emotional responses these thought-realities elicit. We completely enter the dream of our nationhood, our religious correctness and superiority, our moral values, superstitions and dogmas. These imagined realities present themselves so real in the context of their own logic that we are often prepared to kill or be killed for them.

Here we have entered a world of imagined reality not unlike the world we imagined while we were reading our novel. Both display the same characteristic way in which a thought-reality is created and sustained by the thought/attention-knot. We gave the characters and circumstances in the novel the same sense of life and reality as we did to the stagnant pool of residual, cultural indoctrination conditioned into us during a time in our lives when we had not yet fully developed our discriminative faculties sufficiently to discern about these matters for ourselves.

Whatever we repeat unconsciously carries with it the seed of potential bondage and suffering. Some of it may be useful and necessary. Much is mere unconscious, uninspected repetition of unrelated, unnecessary and life-negative information. To make the unconscious conscious is not just a process of recalling into the present emotional shadow material from repressed early hurtful memories. This may be important psychological work. But of greater significance is the ability to become conscious of the unconscious activity of the thought/attention-knot.

Thought and emotion, together with the unconscious association of attention with them, form a true unity. It could be described as an almost impenetrable and coherent whole, or, as we have seen, a *condition of being*, which cannot be bypassed or ignored in our quest for freedom. These processes have to be seen in operation and recognized for what they are, and this can only be done when we are ready to inspect every aspect of the way in which we function and how we unconsciously use the instruments available to us in relation to the challenges of life.

It may be interesting and marginally intelligent just to read about these matters and to form a clear intellectual understanding of the truth of these debilitating forms of internal activity. Of pivotal importance, however, is that we observe and feel these processes happening within us. (This aspect of our investigation is dealt with in detail in *Part Two: The Practice*.) There is nothing difficult about such work at all. In fact, it is rather less involved than the profound complications which inform and motivate our everyday confusion and emotional reactivities. All that is required is to allow for an inner quiet to develop in us, and to observe our own functioning in an intelligent and participatory way. This simple, yet direct, approach will soon begin to free us from the unnecessary complexities of our uninspected lives.

From what we have seen, we are both the creators and sustainers of our destiny of suffering. We are responsible for it, and only *we* can penetrate deeply into our own functioning to discover the causes of our discontent by inspecting how we operate. In doing this, we will determine for ourselves how we create our own painful relationships to the living moment. For this we need not rely on the authority of any tradition to inform us why we suffer or to teach us the way out of suffering. By simply observing our own activities, we begin to take responsibility for ourselves and gradually develop intelligent and emotionally fulfilling ways of working with our inner dysfunctions. During this work we will also notice the direct relationship between the causes of our suffering, and how to go about inspecting and transcending it.

When we start engaging directly with our inner world through meditation and Contemplation (See: *Part Two: Working with Contemplation*), we will notice that we will be working intimately with the same instruments which have been responsible for our distress and unhappiness. In this we discover not only how these have facilitated the sense of self-contraction and limitation on our being, but we will also learn how to use these in an intelligent and conscious way to serve our total being in the holistic and natural way for which they were designed.

Freedom from suffering should clearly and unmistakably exhibit a freedom from the thought/attention-knot. As long as we are still, in any way whatsoever, defined, controlled and conditioned by the content of thought, our path is not yet complete. In the final analysis we could say that self-transcendence is nothing other than the recognition, understanding and transcendence of this profoundly complex, devastatingly effective, yet totally unnecessary imposition on our being. This can only be achieved through our dedicated and conscious participation in every internal process that we have unsuspectingly allowed to control and condition us.

(In *Part Two* every aspect of this work will be investigated in considerable detail in the context of relevant forms of meditation and contemplative practice.)

Chapter Four

COMPONENTS OF THE SEPARATE SELF-SENSE.

Eastern and Western Approaches to 'I'- consciousness

At some point during the process of self-enquiry, it becomes evident that the separate self-sense is not just one inner movement or entity. We begin to sense that for us to understand ourselves fully, we have to become very discerning about the processes which are responsible for the notion of the 'I' in its total manifestation. Although both Eastern and Western psychology have paid little regard to the distinctive elements that constitute the separate self, an in-depth enquiry into the mechanisms and processes of the total 'I'-sense is of critical importance if we are to understand the role of this presumed inner entity in both spiritual and psychological work.

For instance, three terms that are generally used to describe the separate self-sense: 'I'-consciousness, the 'ego' and the 'self-image' have often been used as having the same meaning. However, closer inspection will reveal that although they all manifest as a sense of separateness or 'I'-consciousness, they are really three distinct processes, each requiring our careful investigation. And as these concepts constitute the separate self-sense as a whole, it is important that we sensitize ourselves to the fact that they are in fact distinct processes, each with a different history, etiology and emotional feeling-sense.

It would therefore be inappropriate to regard these as a single appearance in consciousness simply because they all manifest as a separative movement within us. To mistake these processes as one unitary movement can lead to considerable confusion - whether our enquiry is of a psychological or self-transcending/spiritual nature.

We have seen such confusion, not only in the minds of spiritual teachers and psychotherapists, but also in their students and clients. Traditional spiritual teachers tend to place little or no emphasis on psychological work, concentrating mainly on quieting the mind and subduing the ego. Therapists, on the other hand, encourage the healthy development of the ego. And whereas the Eastern spiritual traditions show a remarkable insensitivity and naivety towards our inner emotional and psychological processes, Western psychotherapy regards psychological work as primary to their task of facilitating the unfolding of a mentally stable and emotionally mature person.

In Eastern mysticism the ego is described as an aspect of our being that needs to be eliminated, transcended or neutralized as part of the spiritualization of our being. The spiritual path, being purposed either towards the realization of the inherent non-duality of all appearance, or the merging with a unifying factor such as Consciousness, God, Emptiness, Self or Brahman, sees the ego as the most fundamental obstacle in the way of finding Truth. In these teachings the separate self has been presented as the essential principle that separates us from truth. This is why, in most Eastern traditions, the ego/I has been regarded as the root-cause of human suffering: it stands between us and the truth of our ultimate identity with this unitive consciousness of Being.

In Western psychology, on the other hand, great emphasis has been placed on the healthy development of the ego as an integral part of our psyche. Psychotherapy endeavors to interact with the ego in a way that facilitates a transition from its sense of alienation, disempowerment and conflicting conscious and unconscious impulses, to a greater feeling of equanimity and emotional stability in its relations to its world. We could say that psychotherapy is mostly ego-therapy, because its primary function is to heal and re-orientate our emotional/psychological, self-centered being.

Part One: The View

Western psychotherapy, therefore, tends to approach this question of separation and 'I'-consciousness from a very different perspective to that of Eastern psychology. One strives to enrich, strengthen and re-affirm the ego/'I' in its relation to the world. The other sees it as a fundamental obstacle to the spiritualization of our being.

Part of the confusion surrounding these different approaches to sanity and inner and outer well-being derives from the fact that neither of these traditions presented us with a coherent picture of exactly what is meant by the terms 'ego', 'I' or 'self-image'. Using these terms interchangeably as though they imply the same thing or process confused both spiritual and psychological enquiry. This has led to the misunderstanding between the two traditions with regard to the nature of ego-work we saw earlier. However, had the spiritual traditions and our Western psychological investigators been more guarded in their description of the ego/I as a single entity, such confusion need not have arisen. As we shall discover, once we gain insight into the processes and functions which create the separate self-sense, it will become evident that there is in fact a natural resonance between self-enquiring ego-work and ego-transcendence that need not form the basis for any conflict whatsoever.

Another aspect of the misunderstanding between psychological and spiritual work is that while Western psychotherapy is more or less clear about the ego-healing purpose of its work, the spiritual traditions of the East have been rather vague in their approaches to working with the totality of the separate self-sense as an emotional and psychological process. And although the 'self' is the central focus of both traditions, little consideration has been given by Eastern thought with regard to the nature of this 'self' as such.

In its most simplified form, we could say that Western psychology attempts to bring order and functionality to what it termed the 'ego', without any attempt to transcend it as an inherent part of its work. Here the focus is on the healing of the ego, based on the assumption that the ego is the core of our being. A well-adjusted ego would therefore imply a well-adjusted, sane and happy life.

Spirituality Without God

Eastern mystical systems, on the other hand, show little regard for such detailed ego-centered enquiries, and has instead concentrated on eliminating its effects on our being through many different forms of meditative, contemplative and resistive practices such as attempts at willful detachment from the world. Ultimately Eastern mysticism aims for the total transcendence or elimination of the separate self-sense. These two positions would therefore appear to be irreconcilable. Ego-transcending work and ego-healing work would seem to be too far apart not to be considered mutually exclusive approaches to our inner life.

However, this may not be an adequate reflection of the truth of the matter. Much depends on our understanding and insight into the nature of the separate self-sense as a whole and how we approach both Eastern and Western forms of self-enquiry. If we are clear in our view about the spiritual process as forms of practice which facilitate the *humanization* of our being, we will not attempt to bypass psychotherapeutic work. And if we are really interested in a holistic healing process through psychotherapy, we will not neglect the importance of self-transcending work. Intelligently approached, and sensitively applied, these two forms of practice form a healthy and robust interaction along our path of both self-understanding and self-transcendence: psychological and spiritual.

An interesting phenomenon we observe during traditional Eastern forms of meditative work, are experiences of inner joy, unitive consciousness, states of tranquility, inner absorption, bliss, and so on, but which cannot generally be sustained beyond formal meditation practice. This leaves a sensitive schism between meditative experiences and the way we ordinarily live. Our old patterns of emotional and psychological disturbance soon reappear, and together with these, the reassertion of the separate self-sense. This clearly indicates the necessity for appropriate emotional/psychological work to accompany the gradual spiritualization of our being. In this regard the East has shown remarkable naivety and lack of insight relative to the tendencies that create and support the emotional problems associated with the separate self-sense.

Part One: The View

Had these traditions been more sensitive in their approach to the mechanisms which contribute to the separate self-sense, and not merely defined the ego as some kind of inner entity, or mere concept, to be eliminated or forgotten, this problem would not have arisen. Rather, we would have seen a detailed and methodical enquiry into the inner processes that facilitate the experience of 'I'-consciousness with its disturbing effects on our being.

Only when we have developed the ability to observe directly how the separate self comes into being, can we work with it in a meaningful and self-transcending way. Had the Eastern teachers approached the ego/I in this way, we would also have noticed a clear shift into emotional/psychological enquiry. And when this whole separative movement has been inspected, understood and felt through, can the long-term effects of the meditative practices they propose be integrated into our functional reality.

The problem with Western psychotherapy, on the other hand, originates from the perception that ego-transcending work undermines the psychotherapeutic process. That is, ego-transcendence is seen to be in direct conflict with ego-restructuring as practiced within the ego-therapeutic process. Yet, by occupying itself solely with the restructuring and reorientation of the ego as though it truly represents the core of our being, psychotherapy has given credence to something that it has not fully inspected or understood. However much we all deeply cherish our own self-image and self-affirmation, this does not detract from the fact that there is a depth and richness to our human potential that completely negates the necessity for us to feel ourselves so totally identified with the separate self-sense. To regard the ego/I as the foundation of our inner life is to reduce human life to an uninspected pattern of inner reactivity, and thereby deny ourselves the freedom of a truly participatory, holistic and self-transcendent enquiry.

Western psychotherapy, therefore, needs to introduce the principle of self-transcendence as an integral component of its emotional/psychological work, while the Eastern traditions would greatly benefit by recognizing the debilitating emotional/psychological effects of the separate self-sense on the spiritualizing process, and begin to work with these in a methodical and practical manner.

53

Of course this would require a paradigm shift for both traditions. The East would have to realize that no sustainable self-transcendent/spiritual life is possible without understanding and transcending the deep psychological and emotional problems associated with the separate self-sense.

Western psychotherapy, on the other hand, has to look beyond the confines of a healthy ego for true sanity, emotional stability and human well-being. At this point alone we may arrive at a complimentary and harmonious interaction between these traditions of spiritual and psychological investigation.

The Ego-component

In order to facilitate a deep mental and emotional transformation in the way we live, we need to observe, recognize and transcend all inner resistances we bring to the living moment. A thorough investigation of the components which constitute the experience of the separate self-sense - which in itself is nothing but a series of well-grooved, emotionally-reactive resistances to every aspect of life - will greatly assist us in the full humanization of our being.

As our enquiry into these mechanisms of separation unfolds, it will become evident that we cannot limit our investigation to just the *content* of our emotional and psychological reactivities. (For a detailed enquiry into this, see *Part Two: Working with Psychological and Emotional Reactivities*.) We need to extend our investigation into the *processes* of which these disturbing emotional states are mere symptoms. We have to be alive to, and develop sensitivity towards, these inner functions. If we choose to remain unaware of how our inner processes translate into emotional and psychological complexities, we will continue to suffer the complications these unconscious functions necessitate.

To come to an understanding of the nature and function of the ego - as one of the components of the total separate self-sense - it is important that we acquaint ourselves with the processes through which it comes into being. What concerns us in this enquiry is not so much the *emotional content* of the ego, but instead how it arises. That is, this investigation does not concern itself with *how* we feel as isolated bundles of ego-centeredness: rather, we will be investigating the *inner processes* which result in the manifestation of these feelings. For this we could start by looking at some of the characteristic symptoms of the ego-state.

One of the first things we notice about the ego is that it always functions as an ongoing process of inner and outer comparison. The ego is always active as a form of comparison whereby it habitually and unconsciously compares itself to both the expectations it has of itself (its self-image), and in its relations to others. As egos, we measure our functionality, not by standards of competence based on our own insight and understanding, but rather by what we believe others will find acceptable, worthy of praise or objectionable in our performance.

Another characteristic of the ego is that we are totally identified with it. There is little space between the sense I have of myself, and the outcome of the ego's comparative deliberations. What the ego thinks of itself is what I think of myself. In our ordinary, uninspected way of living, there is no separation between my self-sense and what the ego thinks of itself. We are more or less completely identified with the comparative ego-process.

The third aspect of the ego is that it is entirely created and sustained by thought. We cannot compare ourselves with others or evaluate what we believe others might think of us without engaging thought. And as we have seen in the previous chapter, we tend to be completely identified with the content of thought via the agency of the thought/attention-knot. This implies that whatever the ego thinks about itself in relation to its own self-image, or in comparison to others, becomes our total vision of ourselves. The identification we feel with the ego is an integral part of the reality created by the thought/attention-knot. We dream our ego-stuff in much the same way that we dream all the other dramas associated with the thought/attention-knot.

This may explain why we experience the projections of the ego about itself so acutely. We do not experience our projections of inferiority, abnormality, inadequacy, unworthiness, rejection and low self-value as mere objective and unnecessary processes going on within us. We become totally identified with these. And being identified with these comparatively based ego-projections, we literally *become* what the ego thinks about itself.

The ego-process is always active, not only *with* self-measurement, but in a deeper and more fundamental sense *as* self-measurement. As egos, we do not only measure our performance in a realistic and objective manner. The ego-process displays a remarkable tendency for becoming an integral part of this measuring process itself. It seldom stands free from the process of measurement, as it always first considers its own standing in any situation. It is more concerned with self-evaluation than with objective measurement. The ego measures its own responses in terms of the image it has of itself, and how it measures up in relation to others, and this profoundly inhibits our ability to see things clearly and to come to reasonable evaluations of things.

In this our focus gets diverted from the important and necessary task of objectively and intelligently evaluating input, to a subjective, self-conscious appraisal of ourselves. Naturally, this gives us the impression that the ego is a kind of natural, central headquarters from where it directs the flow of things. But if we give a little further consideration to this, it may become apparent that rather than facilitating the flow of life, the ego becomes a *blockage where life is arrested and modified in terms of the ego's self-evaluating demands*. By entering into this habitual and rather morbid state of self-evaluation, this process often becomes so self-critical that it turns into negative and destructive self-judgment. This leaves us vulnerable to develop a chronic and deeply disturbing sense of negative self-worth.

This is why our reactions and responses to many life-situations are often out of context. We may get challenged on a simple practical, technical or emotional issue, and we respond, not with the Intelligence and openness of heart that would be appropriate to the situation, but rather in defense and maintenance of a psychological structure I call 'myself'. In this, ego-survival has taken precedence over biological survival and this could be seen as one of the most destabilizing factors in the establishment of an integral way of living.

Part One: The View

At this point it may be worth mentioning that our enquiry into the comparatively based functioning of the ego does not call into question the healthy and necessary comparisons we need to make when, for instance, we have to learn certain skills. From early childhood, through to adult life, we will be greatly disadvantaged if we do not develop our ability to learn through observation, imitation and conformation in the context of intelligent, participatory comparison.

In fact, to learn any skill, requires that we make use of our ability to compare our development to the standards set for us by the teacher or instructor. Technical, artistic, scientific, mathematical and most practical skills can generally not be learnt in any other way. We need interaction with others in order to learn. Even the geniuses amongst us require instruction, and develop their talents by testing their development against the level of proficiency of their teachers. The art of necessary and useful comparison should not be underestimated.

However, being human, we are not only internalizers of factual information. We respond to the learning process in a very personal and emotional way. Our successes are often met with self-congratulation, and our failures with a sense of having failed ourselves. This is because for every success there is a positive emotional response, and for every failure we experience the relative pain or discomfort of negative emotional reactivity. As we proceed with our individual development, these emotional memories of past successes and failures remain with us and form a kind of residual emotional background from which we tend to operate. And because learning is fundamentally a process of correcting errors, often many times before we succeed, we tend to be vulnerable to develop a larger residue of negative emotional reactivities than positive ones.

Over time these become part of a complex of emotionally charged interference-patterns, which lay the foundation for inner turmoil, uncertainty and disempowerment. The reason is that we are forced to learn many new things in the early years of our lives when we have not yet developed the necessary skills to make positive and practical use of our failures and mistakes.

This is especially true in relation to our moral and ethical learning where often our inner sense of right and wrong comes into conflict with the things we are taught and expected to do or believe in. This results in profound feelings of uncertainty and failure exactly because they address the deeper, more intimate aspects of our being. And not only are we expected to think and act along the demands of those around us: during the process of socialization our emotional responses are manipulated and interfered with to the point where they become deeply conditioned and externally controlled.

And it all comes at a price. The demands to become different to what we feel and know to be true and real about ourselves, make us extremely sensitive and alert to what is expected of us. The inevitable price we pay for our readiness and need to conform is the loss of intelligent participation in our own decision-making processes. And this sensitivity to external demands to conform becomes an ongoing inner process of chronic comparison or self-evaluation we call the 'ego'.

This brings us back to the ego-process as an integral part of the broader separate self-sense. The existence of the ego necessitates the feeling of separation, and although we cannot define the total separate self-sense within the borders of the ego alone, this comparatively based ego-awareness is one of the most pivotal components of the 'I'-conscious state.

Being comparatively based, the ego inevitably experiences itself as fundamentally separate from everything to which it compares itself. Having contracted into a laager of its own comparative disposition, it views life with suspicion and fear. And to fear any aspect of life, is to feel ourselves separate from it. This is the dilemma of the ego in the ego-conscious state, and it is this disconcerting view it has of itself that makes it one of the most potent sources of fragmentation, separation and alienation within human consciousness.

The 'I'-thought component

The second component of the separate self-sense manifests in a rather different way to that of the ego. The 'I'-thought is the result of an uninspected presumption based on certain observable mental processes. Whereas the ego is dominated by its own emotional reactivities in its endless quest of self-evaluation, self-proving and self-judgment, the 'I'-thought is entirely a product of thought, founded in nothing but the uninspected and unconscious use of the instruments which create and sustain it.

To come to an understanding of this aspect of our dualistic, self-centered vision, we need to look at the interaction between sense-perception and attention on the one hand, and the way thought interacts with these processes to create and sustain the idea of the separate self-sense.

In ordinary sense perception the feeling of separation appears to be most real. The tree is always perceived to be 'over there'. The sound of the dog's barking clearly comes from a distance away. The aroma unmistakably comes from the kitchen. Whatever we may sense, always appears to come from a source that is separate from us. To our ordinary understanding, the world of the senses presents itself as something that exists categorically separate from me as the observer. There always seems to be 'me' and that which is 'not-me', subject and object, the perceiver and the perceived.

If we now briefly look at the role of attention during any act of perception, we will also observe an implied sense of separation between 'me' as the one paying attention and the object of 'my' attention. It is almost as though the act of attention necessitates a dualistic relationship with its object. 'I' feel myself separate from the person, thought, feeling, sensation or state to whom or which 'I' pay attention.

And it is this implied separation from the things we perceive and to which we pay attention that requires us to look at the role of thought during both these processes. It is thought which informs us that because we sense things, and can pay attention to specific aspects of our world, we are necessarily separate from that which we perceive and attend to. Thought arrives at what appears to be a very reasonable conclusion: if what is perceived is not part of me, an observer *has* to exist to notice it. And it comes to the same conclusion about the act of attention: if attention can be focused on any aspect of present arising, there *has* to be someone directing attention. Thought therefore projects an experiencer/observer as well as a doer behind the acts of perception and paying attention where in truth there are no such entities. The 'me' noticing, and the 'me' paying attention, are evidently nothing but projections of thought mistaken for reality. There are always just the movements of attention and thought doing their rounds.

And because this thought-projection of the observer or the 'me' unconsciously confirms its own supposition during all acts of perception and attention, we soon begin to believe that this 'I' is something permanent. We begin to intuit the separate self-sense as a kind of central headquarters, and different in quality and substance from the thinking process that creates it. The 'I'-thought loses its 'thought'-aspect and takes on the appearance of a separately existing entity called 'I'. In this way an inner 'actor' is allowed to establish itself as a permanent 'witness' and 'doer' that believes it notices things, objects, inner states and emotions as well as being the active principle in everything that happens. Clearly these are mere presumptions created and sustained by thought. This is why we can correctly refer to it as the 'I'-thought'.

If we recall how the thought/attention-knot gives reality to the projections of thought, we may appreciate why the 'I'-thought appears so real to us. We don't experience the 'I'-thought as a mere thought amongst other thoughts. Rather, as an activity within, and an expression of the thought/attention-knot, the 'I'-thought *becomes* me. It becomes reality and integrates itself into our lives as one of the main components of the total separate self-sense.

And so real is this 'I'-sense that we truly believe that it exists *prior* to all forms of perception and all acts of attention. This thought-creation presents itself (and is experienced by us) as the constant and central figure behind all forms of experience. Everything may change around 'me', yet 'I' seem to remain as the permanent 'witness' to this changing environment.

This leads us to an interesting observation. In the process of creating this inner actor, thought displayed a unique ability for projecting the 'I'-thought as separate from itself, and then experiencing its own projection as though it has true objective existence. The 'I'-thought is clearly a creation of thought. Yet, we somehow do not experience it as such. Our experience of this inner projection is that the 'I' really exists independently from thought. Most of us believe beyond all doubt that somewhere inside us dwells this 'me', the 'observer', the 'doer', as something categorically different to the imaginative and projective ability of thought.

This is further evident in the sense I have of 'me' being in relationship with aspects of 'myself'. For instance we say, 'I' think, feel, experience, see, hear, taste and so on. This means that 'I', as the 'doer' or 'experiencer', feels itself in relationship with other aspects of 'myself', such as the feelings and thoughts which it believes it is 'observing'. We also describe how 'I' feel disappointed, angry, proud or contented with 'myself'. Again we notice how the 'I'-thought sets itself apart from other thoughts, as though it exists categorically separate from the thinking process that produces both the 'me' and the content of 'myself': the observer and the observed.

These different terms we attach to the 'I' are not mere semantic devices for the sake of verbal communication. When I say 'I think', I truly mean just that. I really believe that it is this 'I' that 'thinks'. We have the sense of this inner actor that we believe resides at the center of our being. We are therefore inwardly divided into the 'me' and 'not-me', where the 'me' is experienced as the observer of everything it presumes to be 'not-me' and the 'doer' of everything that gets done.

Thought, therefore, does not only project and transfer its own images outwardly onto things and people. It does the same inwardly. As we have seen, it can create and project an image, which it calls 'me' and then experiences its own projection as though it has an existence categorically separate to itself. We could also say that thought has projected and transferred an aspect of itself onto itself. Both 'I' and 'myself' exist only in thought. 'I', and any thought about 'myself', are two aspects of one thought-process believing they are staring each other in the face.

However, these are mere deceptive plays within the projective potential of thought. And like all forms of projection and transference, we remain unconscious of the mechanisms by which these states appear, as well as the fact of it when it happens. We are generally only aware of the content of these projections. 'I' am always only aware of 'my' inner feelings and thought-projections about 'myself', without being conscious of how this 'I', as the presumed observer of these states, is created and sustained by the projective potential of thought.

From what we have seen, it may be clear that the 'I'-thought has a very different character and etiology to that of the ego-process. Although these are both creations of thought, it is important to draw the necessary distinctions between them in order to sensitize ourselves as to how these differences impact on our emotional and psychological being. The complexity of the separate self-sense as a whole demands that we become sensitive to its different components so that we could work with these in a conscious and methodical way to relieve ourselves from their debilitating effects on our emotions and psychophysical being.

The Primal Recoil- component

A further way in which the separate self-sense gets informed about the presumed validity of its own existence, is through an early individuation process based on emotional recoil from what we perceive to be a lack of love or human warmth. This recoil takes the form of a compensatory activity within our being, based on the perceived need for defending ourselves against our own emotional vulnerability. And the direct consequence of this primal recoil from vulnerability manifests as a subtle self-contraction or defensive gesture deep within our emotional being.

To compensate means to counterbalance or to make amends for a perceived loss or unfulfilled need. And to need is to have or develop a capacity for something. The specific capacity which needs fulfillment at this early stage of our lives is the demand for love. We are born with a capacity for love or nurturing. The need for love is the most primal, and primary, demand of our human condition. It is the one emotion that is with us from the moment we are born, and that remains an integral part of our being, whether fulfilled or not, for the rest of our lives. If love is fulfilled, our deepest inner need is fulfilled. If love is left unattended and unfulfilled, we will display the vast range of emotional disturbances so characteristic of our present human condition.

Love tolerates no sacrifice, or even compromise. A life which is not informed by the constant presence and nourishment of love, becomes emotionally barren, psychologically disturbed and contracts into an emotional defense structure against the pain of perceived unlove. And sadly, this is exactly the way we live. As 'self-conscious, 'self'-contracted and 'self'-dominated creatures, we are not only ignorant of the wholeness which is our unique human potential, but, exactly because wholeness is not yet our present realized disposition, we are unable to facilitate the flowering of love in our lives. However sincerely and hard we may try to imitate love through socially acceptable and religiously conditioned versions of it, the presence and living reality of love will elude us until we become established in the wholeness of life which naturally and unselfconsciously manifests love as an inherent aspect of itself.

The demand for love is with us from birth. At this early stage of our development this demand is completely unconscious. In the same way as we get hungry, thirsty, cold, hot, and show signs of emotional activity, such as crying, smiling and so on, in a totally unconscious way, the need for love, care and bonding is also present as an unconscious demand. And as we cannot but suffer the physical consequences of being deprived of food, warmth, water and general physical care, similarly we will be emotionally affected if the need for love is not fulfilled.

Because this need, and capacity, for love is so sensitive and vulnerable to the effects of its environment, its response to the slightest feelings of neglect or deprivation immediately elicits a defensive reaction deep in our emotional being. We then recoil from that wide open position of complete and unguarded vulnerability into a subtle state of contraction and self-protection.

This primal contraction of our emotional being could be seen as the first stirring of the separate self-sense. And to a greater or lesser extent this is what happens to all of us in the course of our development – something that will remain with us for the rest of our lives, unless it is inspected, understood and transcended.

Our first and abiding capacity is that of being loved. Love is the food of the human spirit. But once we have recoiled from it, and become identified with the defensive position of emotional self-contraction, the need for love becomes corrupted by this contracted state and begins to manifest debilitating forms of self-protective strategies. Long before we are even aware of this happening within us, we already become identified with these emotional reactivities that embed them into our developing psyche. These show themselves as a growing inability both to give and to receive love, which in turn increase our feelings of alienation, separation and bewilderment. In this way, the primal contraction away from love forms an integral part of the separate self-sense.

From our emotionally defensive disposition we nevertheless all yearn for something few of us are prepared to give and allow ourselves to feel and share. We grow up in a world where there seems to be conclusive evidence for our deeply felt conviction that we need to maintain our defensive position relative to the feeling and sharing of love. We interpret our position of unlove as a state where any sign of emotional vulnerability is bound to be abused or ridiculed by those around us.

And to stand outside of love is to stand outside of life itself. No compensatory activity can bridge the gap between our state of self-contracted unlove and our inherent capacity for, and ability to, love. And as we have seen, it is this unfulfilled schism between our capacity for love and our inability to both give and receive it, which manifests as emotional contractedness, separation and 'I'-consciousness. From here we are destined to seek for meaning and fulfillment in things *other* than love. And this makes us materialists as we now direct our search for emotional fulfillment and integral living to objects, ideas, religions and socially acceptable forms of behavior while we remain bereft of that which alone has the ability to fulfill us.

An interesting and fundamental question presents itself which is worth considering: if we recoiled from love in the first place, and entered into compensatory activities of seeking for

Part One: The View

the fulfillment of love, is there anything the separate, contracted self-state can do to relieve itself from the burden of its own condition?

The answer is no. The 'I'-conscious state, as a movement in defense against what it perceives as unlove, is itself a state of unlove. That which presumes itself to be separate from love, cannot become love. As love is an inherent aspect of the non-dual truth of life, any state that is identified with unlove is part of our fragmented, dualistic vision. The fragmented state of unlove can therefore not transform itself into love or wholeness.

As a manifestation of unlove, the 'I' always stands in the way of the very thing it is desperately in need of. Seeking for the fulfillment of this need from within the state of unlove can thus only deepen our sense of separateness. The 'I' can only strengthen itself: it cannot relieve itself from the plight of its own existence. All effortful attempts by the 'I' to go beyond itself simply enhance its sense of alienation and fragmentation. In this way the separate self-sense is given further substance and validity.

In view of this it is therefore imperative that we discover how to re-align ourselves with the energy of love and compassion *without strengthening the 'I'*. Human life, although capable of alienating itself from this nurturing energy, was not meant to exclude itself from the Intelligence of love. And whilst the separate self-sense cannot transcend its own contracted state of unlove and self-consciousness, there is nothing written which prevents us from experiencing the complete fulfillment of love and compassion as part of our ordinary functioning. How to allow for this is the work of self-observation, self-knowledge and self-transcendence. With right practice, the natural order of things will no doubt establish itself as our functional base for living which will draw us back into the full expression of love.

In '*Part Two: The Practice*', we enter methodically and experientially into meditative practices which allow for the complete transcendence of the presumption of the 'I'-conscious state.

Concluding remarks

Self-consciousness is always unconsciousness. We cannot be identified with deep residual patterns of unconscious reactivities and at the same time consider the 'entity' (the separate self-sense), which is the presumed holder of these disturbances, to be existing in a state of conscious awareness. Not only are we generally unaware of the hidden emotional and conditioned content which manifests as the separate self-state, we are generally also totally unconscious of how the different components of the 'I' work together to strengthen and maintain this separative movement within ourselves.

And as we find ourselves in the state of 'I'-consciousness for most of our waking hours, we could say we are seldom fully conscious. *Our work is to discover how to be fully conscious without being self-conscious.* As we shall discover, all contemplative and meditative work is for the purpose of creating the conditions for us to wake up from the dream of subjectivity and its separate 'I'-conscious shadow in all its forms.

Chapter Five

INTELLECTUALISM AND REALITY- CONSIDERATION

*T*he path of self-transcendence is fundamentally characterized by the recognition and transcendence of all aspects of limitation on our being. Where there is a sense of 'self' to be transcended, there is limitation. And where there is limitation there is resistance. The separate self-sense is an ongoing process of resistance to the ever-fresh revelation of the living moment and consequently to life itself.

It is therefore of critical importance that our path should address all aspects of resistance in whichever form these may manifest in our daily living. But before we can recognize and transcend the limitations we bring to life, it would be useful first to establish how to approach this matter in a realistic and intelligent way.

Perhaps the most important consideration we can bring to this enquiry is to ensure that the investigation into the fragmentation of life *does not in itself become an integral part of the fragmentary process.* As we have seen, thought and attention have fragmented our experience into the observer and the observed, the 'me' and the 'not-me', self and other. From this initial fragmentation, our lives have taken on the form and quality of a world-view that believes in the 'me' as the permanent center of experience, with everything else separate from it.

If we are thus to enquire into the limitations and resistances we bring to life, we need to be sensitive to the way we approach such an enquiry. Should we, for instance, hold the view of 'self' and 'other' as two categorically separate forms of manifestation as our point of departure, we would limit and condition our enquiry from the outset within the very fragmented frame of reference that needs to be investigated and transcended. Yet, as self-contracted beings, this is exactly what we would do, unless we sensitize ourselves to this possibility and remain vigilant that we do not allow ourselves to fall into this trap.

One way of assuring that our path of self-transcendence remains free from influences that may dilute the quality of our enquiry, is to establish a clear distinction between 'intellectualism' and 'reality-consideration'.

Intellectualism is essentially a product of the intellect which has its base in the unconscious logic of thought, memory, learnt behavior, acquired knowledge, habitual responses and conditioning. In its broadest sense it could be described as a movement in fragmentation because it lacks the coherency of the natural order of things. It is essentially based in thought and memory and often becomes absorbed in the reality these create via the agency of the thought/attention-knot.

Reality-consideration, on the other hand, endeavors not to fragment life into clearly defined categories of predetermined responses. Rather, as it is founded in our deeper, more comprehensive Intelligence, it always considers the wider picture. (See *Part Two: 'Contemplation and Reality Consideration'*). This makes our enquiry sensitive to all forms of fragmentation and prevents us from thinking in a separative way.

But as the investigation into these two processes is so important for the success of our enquiry as a whole, it may be worth looking at them in some greater detail.

The intellect is a sophisticated and complex instrument for physical survival. As humans we respond and operate on many different levels from one moment to the next, and often it is required of us to look at a particular challenge from more than one perspective. Here the intellect plays a vital role as it can refer to previous solutions for the successful negotiation of our way through life without each time having to re-invent the wheel.

Memory, knowledge and the logic that functions in relation to these have a necessary and practical role to play in our successful interaction with our environment. This broad-based instrument is therefore necessary in the practical ordering of our lives, as well as in the maintenance of the kind of relative order for which it is naturally and legitimately responsible.

And to give effect to the psychophysical being's demand for order, this instrument created an extensive range of socially acceptable forms of behavior, thinking, feeling and emotional responses which appear to satisfy many of our needs for physical security, outer structure and social organization.

However, integrally part of any ordering-system are the effects it has on us, as the creators of this order. By bringing order to our environment, we subject ourselves to being modified, influenced, controlled and limited by the borders we create for ourselves. To establish order is to create borders and limitations, not only on our present functioning, but, more importantly, also on our ability and potential for exploration, risk-taking and openhearted inner enquiry. And these borders often present us with an impenetrable barrier between ourselves and the fulfillment of our full potential as human beings.

The psychological, ego-based, social environment has become a condition for living in no way less real, demanding and controlling than the natural environment into which we have been born. As individuals we are always confronted by the broad social-psychological reality in which we function and through which we are expected to fulfill our destiny. And although the social order in many ways sets us free from having to negotiate certain existential challenges for ourselves, the price we pay for the psychological and physical security the system offers, is often disproportionate in its negative effects to the good it might bring.

Yet, because these influences have been with us ever since our birth, they have become so integrally part of our internal sense of things that we seldom allow ourselves the freedom and give ourselves the opportunity to challenge the standards, rules and dogmas by which society orders our lives. We simply continue to function within the limits and presumed logic of what has been presented to us as correct and responsible forms of behavior. And it is this 'logic' inherent in all social order that forms an integral part of intellectualism.

Intellectualism is fundamentally ignorant of its own limitations. The intellect has a limited intelligence which functions around deep patterns of social and personal conditioning. It can only repeat, either verbatim or in modified form, what it knows, and does so with the 'logic' and apparent reasonableness with which all conditioning convinces us of its inherent value and truth. We generally remain unaware that this process is incapable of bringing anything new to the table. The intellect can only present us with modified versions of its existing emotional and mental memory base. Little or no insight is possible while we are exclusively functional in this mode. This is how we transfer these uninspected prescriptions for living from one generation to another, including all the ideas we inherit as religion, politics, economic orders, philosophical notions and moral values. It is the function of the intellect to make sense of these, but this 'sense' is always from within the limitation of its own preconditioned and pre-conceived borders.

As our present enquiry centers on the possibility of freeing ourselves from all forms of limitation, it would be useful to sensitize ourselves to a rather specialized form of intellectualism where we mistake conceptual understanding for reality. It seems strange that we should allow ourselves to be deceived in this way. Yet, this is a mistake we all tend to make. Being caught in the mechanics of thought via the thought/attention-knot, it is not always easy to discern between thought projections and reality.

To appreciate this, we just have to consider how beliefs have become irreducible facts for many of us. For instance, for many of us, our God is 'out there', either in Heaven or in some other spiritual realm. He is absolutely real; in fact, often more 'real' than the world of the senses. We repeat all the stories about God's endless struggle with His imperfect creation from one generation to another as though we are relating something we have actually observed for ourselves. The Indian traditions are filled with similar myths about gods and other lesser beings fighting one another somewhere in 'spiritual' space, and these have been told and retold, *as fact*, for thousands of years.

If we follow this same line of enquiry into the modern era where much of the non-dualistic teachings have become available to us through books, tape-recordings and the teachers of these traditions, we find much the same happening. Many of us fully understand the non-dualistic descriptions of these teachings. There is logic to it and, once this logic has been grasped, it is not difficult to construct very clever and subtle arguments for oneself in confirmation of one's understanding. Once we have convinced ourselves of the irreducible truth of such a non-dual philosophy, we truly believe that there is little else to do. We become so totally identified with the *thought* of non-dualism that we can no longer distinguish between our mental understanding and the living, experiential reality of the non-dual truth of life. We literally mistake the finger pointing to the moon for the moon itself.

In the same way as we mistake our gods for reality, we also mistake our intellectual understanding for reality. We talk about the wholeness of life, non-duality, unitive consciousness and Advaita (not two) as though we know exactly what we are talking about.

And, interestingly, this is precisely the case. We talk only about our *knowledge* of these things. What we generally do not recognize is that this is *all* we are talking about. We merely repeat what we have heard, and relate it to others, or think about it, as some immutable, experience-based truth. We sincerely believe we are talking and thinking about the real thing. But as we have seen, knowledge is not the thing. In this instance, intellectualism could be seen as our inability to discern between that which is created by thought, and that which is not.

We could therefore ask whether there is an alternative way that may not only bring more clarity to our lives but which could also facilitate the natural unfolding of our inherent Intelligence and greater humanity. In this way the truth towards which our words point might become our own revelation and living experience. The system of the intellect has clearly failed us. Intellectual humankind has been around this planet for thousands of years and, looking at what we have achieved in terms of a truly humane way of life, little could be accounted for.

However technologically advanced we may be, the fact remains that what we dramatize every day in terms of human relationships, both within ourselves and projected outward to others, display only rather crude and very elementary forms of human development. Underneath the veneer of intellectual stability, order and social tolerance, lies great potential for violence, disharmony, war, disorganization and general relational dysfunction. This is because we have become identified with an aspect of our being which was never designed to deal with the totality of our human functioning. The intellect no doubt has its place. However, when it endeavors to address the totality of the challenges of life, and we allow ourselves to become completely identified with the way it thinks about things, it cannot but miss the mark. Through this the intellect becomes an instrument of disinformation, disorder and unhappiness.

This points to perhaps one of the most unfortunate errors we have made: we have *specialized* in the intellect, which, as we have seen, is dominated by unconscious and uninspected thinking processes. Valuable as thought might be, it is not the instrument that can allow for the revelation of our deeper Intelligence and true emotional well-being.

Nobody can teach us how to love, be compassionate, considerate, openhearted, generous, ethical, moral, just, intelligent and whole. We may read many books about these subjects, and yet, at the end of it all, we will be as bereft of the actual, living reality of these inherent human qualities as before. These are qualities which live in us as potential, and which have to be awakened as part of our total human development. They cannot manifest through conditioned forms of knowledge and response. Our work is to learn how to distinguish between these two sources of information – the intellect and living experience.

Should we attempt to correct the error of fragmented living from within the borders of our fragmented thinking patterns, we will merely be committing another error. The intellect can only modify itself within its own limited field of operation. As we have seen, thought cannot transcend itself. The error of trying to live the fullness of our human condition through the limited and conditioned activities of the intellect cannot be corrected by any further activity from within this instrument which is integral to the error itself. Another way of dealing with life has to become our possibility if we are at all interested in the development of our human potential and the establishment of relational harmony in our lives.

Part One: The View

For this we have to become *realists*, rather than idealists, and develop ways of recognizing the difference. We have to learn to consider things from a realistic perspective and feel our way into the categorical difference between that which is real, and that which is unreal. That is, we have to discover the difference between that which is created and sustained by thought, presenting itself as reality via the agency of the thought/attention-knot, and that which is not. Unreality, or illusion, is to mistake the creations of thought and the limited intelligence associated with it, for reality.

Reality-consideration is a process of intelligent, feeling-discernment based on clear observation. Reality-consideration refuses to be deluded by the apparent reality of the projections of thought. Here, enquiry into life proceeds on the basis of direct personal experience and present evidence, rather than thought-creations mistaken for reality.

Reality consideration is a twofold process. It not only investigates things from a realistic, non-idealistic point of view, but because it is founded in inner quiet, (See: *Part Two: Contemplation and Reality Consideration*) it is informed by a totally different quality of Intelligence than that which normally functions as the limited and conditioned deliberations of the intellect. Not based in memory with all its emotional and mental reactivities, this intelligent feeling-presence is capable of looking at things afresh and presents us with a considerably more realistic, and therefore, holistic view of life.

Operating from within the movement of Intelligence, the consideration is always how to respond to things both mentally and emotionally in a realistic, life-positive and empathetic manner. The Intelligence that makes these responses possible may make use of memory, attention, conditioned thinking and emotional response-potential, but because it is always informed by a different quality of insight and understanding, it takes a more comprehensive view of matters. Our awakened Intelligence literally 'reads' the scripts presented to it by the instruments operating within the intellect, and discern when and how to make use of these forms of information.

To be a realist is therefore not to deny any aspect of ourselves. Rather, it means that we are able both to transcend and to know when to make use of those aspects of our accumulated past, including our habitual patterns of thinking and feeling. Reality-consideration is therefore the most open-minded and openhearted approach to any situation.

For freedom to be real and active in our lives, the process by which such freedom is allowed to manifest should already show signs of the integrity and realism that are inherent in our unfolding wholeness. This calls for an unmitigated adherence to realism: not the cold and fragmented, materialistic 'realism' of the intellect, but rather the realism born from a fearless, integrated and holistic approach to things. Through this we will align ourselves with the living experience of our free human condition: mentally as well as emotionally.

Freedom, not founded in such absolute realism of unconditioned Intelligence and participatory, non-reactive emotional responses, can only be an illusion created by the fertile imaginings within thought. And conceptual freedom is a contradiction in terms. Freedom cannot be contained within the borders of the known. For the very reason of it being conceptual in nature, and not an expression of the free Intelligence associated with the non-dual experience of the living moment, it will remain vulnerable to becoming corrupted by conditions, circumstances and the ever-changing fickleness of the human mind. Clearly, conditioned freedom is at best merely an *image* of the genuine article.

Once we are able to appreciate the difference between that which is created by thought and that which is not, it will also be evident that reality-consideration can never be speculative. It concerns itself with our observable and experiential human condition, and not with metaphysical theories. To consider reality is to consider that which has been seen, felt or intuited or is presently being observed and experienced. And if thought does enter into this field of observation in a speculative way, the Intelligence associated with this process clearly sees it for what it is. Such recognition gradually transcends all unconscious conditioned thinking and feeling.

Because reality-consideration is also a conscious process, (See: *Part Two: The Practice*) it does not allow itself to be drawn into the unconscious state whereby we become the reality of our thought-creations. Rather, it pre-empts unconscious identification with any aspect of thought. It becomes aware of the content of thought the instant it arises, and remains sensitive to the tendency for the unconscious association of attention with such a thought. In this way reality-consideration cannot become part of our fragmentary, dualistic thinking-patterns. It serves the conscious process of undermining all forms of fragmentary presumption and thereby aligns our thinking with the wholeness of life.

But to be real takes courage. Not the courage of our conviction - for our conviction may often still be based on the same uninspected untruths we have come to live with - but rather the courage and open-heartedness to stand free and to observe, to question and enquire, and to begin to live our lives on the basis of our own truth, instead of following the confused light of another. Truth does not present itself to a heart and mind full of certainty. It flowers when there is the prior understanding that all certainty needs to be investigated, explored, observed, and recognized in the light of a completely open-ended approach. That which reveals itself in the light of such recognition will then become the realistic, unconditioned basis of our interactions with life.

Through this we grow along the path of our own investigation, insight and clarity. Nothing can be too high or too low to be included in this enquiry. In reality-consideration there are no taboos. Every aspect of our lives remains open for recognition, investigation and change. Nothing is fixed. Nothing is solid. Our lives become one long, fascinating journey of self-enquiry informed by our own inner wisdom. The intellect as both cultural product and instrument of the known, can never teach us how to become open and responsive to the living moment. And it is the living moment alone which allows our deeper humanity to become the directive principle of our lives.

As we have seen, compassion and all our truly humane qualities cannot be learnt. From the point of view of the intellect these qualities can, at best, only be *imitated*. And because such learnt behavior is not born from within the clarity of our own living reality and founded in the light of our own Intelligence, it will become conditional upon circumstances whereby we display our humanity strategically and selectively: often merely to impress those around us or to convince ourselves of our inner spiritual refinement.

Deep down we know we are vastly less complicated than what the convoluted world of the intellect has convinced us to believe about ourselves. In the natural order of things we are also vastly more capable than what conditioned living has allowed us to think and feel about ourselves. Once we have become sensitive to the profound value of reality-consideration, we will be well positioned to leave behind the uninspected and unfulfilling promises of the intellect. This will gradually allow our lives to be informed by a deep and comprehensive source of emotional Intelligence which is an aspect of human living uncontaminated by the compulsive activities and reactivities of the intellect. From here our humanity could develop in a realistic and integral way.

Note: For a comprehensive, practical and experiential enquiry into Reality-consideration please refer to *Part Two: Contemplation and Reality Consideration.* Here we explore Reality-consideration as a process of intelligent investigation into many aspects of conditioning and other forms of self-limitation.

Chapter Six

ON SENSE-PERCEPTION

Wholeness and the generally accepted view of sense-perception are mutually exclusive experiences of reality. When wholeness is the case, all feelings of separation disappear. Wholeness is therefore free from the dualism implied in the relationship between the observer and the observed In the revelation of wholeness there is just the present arising of 'What Is'. Here we do not experience an externally-existing reality to be sensed as though it has just been waiting out there for us to notice it.

Our traditional view of sense-perception, on the other hand, implies a reality to be noticed as something categorically separate from us noticing it. By further implication, this reality exists *prior* to any perception of it. In this view, things are simply out there, awaiting our becoming aware of them. Sense-perception, as is conventionally understood, therefore always implies duality. In this there is a fixed world that is noticed, or reflected as in the mirror of our awareness. This vision of sense-perception of necessity implies the dualistic notion of the observer and the observed. Wholeness and the sense-perception model therefore represent two categorically different visions of reality.

The question which this enquiry endeavors to address, is whether, in fact, there is such a process or act of sense-perception at all? Clearly, there cannot be two realities. There cannot be the world of the 'senses' as it is conventionally understood, and at the same time and in the same space, the world of wholeness or non-dual reality. Things are either dual or whole. Or to use the Vedanta terms: Reality is either Dvaita or Advaita: two or not-two.

And as our investigation into the wholeness of life necessarily includes all aspects of what appears to be fragmented or not-whole, the question of sense perception has to be seen as an *integral* part of this enquiry. If the path of self-transcendence is going to reveal the *undivided nature* of all present arising, we will have to enquire whether there is in fact such a process active within the human experience as the perception of independently existing objects categorically separate from the presumed perceiver. Things cannot have complete independence from us as the observer if the truth of our living experience is to be equated with non-separateness or wholeness.

Conventional wisdom teaches us that we have five 'outward' senses and also some inward receptors which register bodily positions, balance and so on. Through these 'inward' sense-faculties we become conscious of movements and sensations within the body in the same way as we would become conscious of a tree out there. In this model, 'we', as perceivers, are presumed to be separate from the things we perceive, inwardly or outwardly, and get informed of the existence of these via the agency of specialized sense organs.

And because this explanation of how things appear to us has become such an irreducible point of departure for both scientific and ordinary investigation into manifest reality, few have questioned the model on which this assumption is based, especially in the context of non-dual experience. We simply assume that we have five outer and some inner senses which account for our entire field of conscious and unconscious experience.

However, if we observe the actual processes involved when we become aware of any aspect of present arising, it will become evident that this is not the case at all, and in addition to this, we will notice that we also become aware of many kinds of experience in a very different, more direct way. The world we experience does not only appear to us via the agency of our senses. In fact, many of our most important faculties and vital human abilities become evident *without any discernable sense-organs with which to notice these.*

Part One: The View

For instance, although we become acutely aware of many inner states and subtle processes, there is no sense-organ (or organs) with which this inner world can be 'perceived'. We have no sense-organs for our ability to become aware of thoughts, logic, reason, artistic appreciation, paying attention, memory recall, will, emotional states such as depression, joy, compassion, love, jealousy, fear, anxiety, anger, falling in love, and other inner states of mind and non-mind such as intuition, insight, the state of calm, inner silence, meditative absorption, bliss, wholeness and so on.

All these simply appear in our field of awareness in a mysterious and inexplicable way. We do not 'sense' these as we presumably sense 'objective' reality. And the reason is that we have no sensors in place with which to notice these states as we have been told is the case with ordinary sense perception. We do not 'sense' our thoughts or our emotions: they simply appear, without any mediation of a specialized sense-organ. Yet, despite the fact that we have no identifiable 'sense-organs' for these inner states of mind and emotion, they are nevertheless no less real - and play no less an important part in our experience of reality - than the information we believe we obtain through the five senses.

A reasonable and perhaps obvious question now presents itself: if the more subtle and important aspects of our field of experience present themselves in a direct, non-sensory way, is it not possible that the information that we have conventionally assumed to come to our notice via the sense-organs could also present itself in the same direct, non-sensory way, despite our belief to the contrary? After all, the only evidence we have for how our senses are supposed to function is based on little more than a supposition. No one has ever seen, felt, intuited or scientifically verified the actual workings of our sense-faculties or the *manner by which reality appears* to our waking, conscious state of awareness as a direct result of our so-called sense-organs.

Many scientific and medical textbooks still present us with the naive realistic view of these matters. According to these, things are 'out there' waiting to be noticed via the agency of our five senses. They are seen to exist in themselves. Light reflected from these objects is said to reach the retina of the eye, modified into electro-chemical processes which then reach the brain through a specific nerve where the 'object' of perception gets reconstructed to conform to the original 'perceived' sound, sight, taste and so on. Outside of quantum physics, the notion of an objectively existing reality has seldom realistically been scrutinized and questioned – at least not within the scientific community.

Yet, however much we may find comfort in the presumed stability of a world awaiting our arrival and welcoming our noticing it, the fact is that present evidence does not support such a view. Not only does it not find this presumed world-out-there as a truly separately existing reality, it places a serious question mark over the notion of whether we in fact have such faculties as our conventionally understood five senses at all.

No doubt, without the eyes we cannot 'see', without the ears we cannot 'hear', without the skin there is no sensation of touch and so on. But does this necessarily mean that we *see* with our eyes, *hear* with our ears, *smell* with our nose, *touch* with our skin and *taste* with our mouth? Not at all. These faculties are just part-players in a *mysterious process* of present arising which cannot be linked to any causal event or series of causal events in the process of the appearance of things.

The functioning of the eye is as integrally part of how things appear as are the source of the original stimulation on the retina, the nerves carrying the electro-chemical impulses to the brain, the specific area in which the impulse lodges itself in the brain, and the mysterious way in which the object appears 'out there' only after this specific area in the brain has been stimulated. Ultimately, absolutely nothing can be said about how our world appears to us, despite our tenacious belief that we sense an already existing reality via the agency of our sense organs. What the so-called sense organs register, and what we 'perceive' as reality 'out there', clearly have nothing empirically verifiable in common.

This is not a philosophical proposition or merely an intellectual enquiry. *The way we believe the senses operate is most fundamentally a spiritual/self-transcending matter.* Our enquiry is not into philosophy in order to prove or disprove statements of other philosophers. Our enquiry into sense-perception is of vital and critical importance if we were to make any headway along the path of the gradual revelation of the non-dual nature of existence. Nothing, not even something as conventionally 'evident' as our senses and the way in which they are presumed to register and reflect reality like a mirror, should be left out of this enquiry.

Our understanding of the manner by which we experience the world through the senses fragments our world into the 'observer' and the 'observed'. Such a division is not true of the state of wholeness, and so cannot be true of our 'sense' world – not if non-duality is the inherent living reality of all experience.

This is why we have to sensitize and align ourselves to the fundamental non-dual truth of our condition. As long as we truly believe in the division between the observer and the observed, or the reality of a separately existing world out there to be recorded by our sense-faculties, for just as long will such a belief inhibit and undermine our ability to allow for the revelation of the undivided nature of present arising.

In reality we can say nothing about the ultimate nature or function of any aspect of the world as it appears via the 'five senses'. We know as little about how the senses present reality to us as we know about how all the other manifestations of direct experience appear in our field of awareness.

We cannot deny the appearance of things. What we could, quite legitimately question, is whether our world appears to us solely via the agency of our senses, or possibly in a different way altogether? And it would seem that this 'different way' might very well also be the way of direct experience such as the manner in which thoughts, feelings, emotions and other inner states come to our notice. This may suggest that we may not have two systems by which we become aware of our field of experience, but only one: direct experience. This 'system' of direct experience is ultimately unknowable to our human understanding. And neither does it have to be understood. The appearance of things simply happens. No ultimate explanation of how this takes place is necessary or even appropriate. As we have seen, understanding often imposes its own functional limitations onto what it considers. In this way it creates misconceptions and confusion.

However, to get a more direct understanding of the problems associated with a world as experienced through the senses, let us take the feeling of physical pain as an example.

Conventionally understood, pain is 'sensed' in a specific area in the body and this message is carried by a nerve to the brain where it gets registered. The brain then makes us conscious of the pain in order for us to notice that something is wrong in that particular area so that we may attend to it. We are told we have specialized sensors for pain placed all over the body so that these could immediately detect pain for the purpose of our attention and care.

This is not only the conventional view but also the way we seem to experience pain in the body. No doubt our pain is real and needs our immediate attention. We also clearly experience the pain in a particular area of the body. However, it is not so clear that this sense-model explains the appearance of pain in any area of the body. If we were to follow the sequence of events that could be detected physiologically we will find that there are some unexplained aspects of this model which in fact make it impossible to understand physical pain in this way.

Say I cut my finger and thereby disturb the normal functioning of the area I have damaged. This disturbance is noticed by the relevant nerves which immediately carry a message to the brain informing it via an electro-chemical impulse that something has happened somewhere in the body. While the impulse moves along the nerve, *there is as yet no pain* in my finger. In fact, if the nerve or nerves serving these impulses were to be cut or interfered with, so that the impulse gets interrupted, I would feel no pain at all. Pain only happens when the impulse reaches a specific area in the brain. Before then, no sensation or pain is felt.

From this it may be evident that the nerves do not register pain as such, but rather just greater or lesser forms of disturbance to the normal functioning of the body, which they relay to the brain. Even the nature of this initial impulse is not understood, and must be seen as part of the mystery of the process as a whole.

Part One: The View

However, for the sake of our current investigation, let's accept that this impulse runs along a nerve and finally reaches a particular area in the brain to which this nerve is connected. At this point the nerve has done its work. It has brought an electro-chemical impulse to the brain and immediately after it has reached its destination, we experience the sensation of pain in the damaged area of the finger.

Significantly, though, we have no nerve impulse running back from the brain to the finger sending it the message that it should feel pain. Pain simply appears in the area of disturbance with no verifiable contact between the brain, which received the electro-chemical message, and the area in the body where the pain is felt. It is almost as if the brain *projected* the pain directly 'out there' into the damaged finger without making use of any physiological or electro-chemical means. Pain simply appears in the finger as a *direct experience* in a way no different to how all other directly experienced forms of reality (such as thoughts, feelings, emotions etc) appear.

And similarly to how pain just happens 'out there' in my finger in a rather mysterious and unknowable way, *all* aspects of our presumed sense-reality happen 'out there' without any connection between the brain receiving an electro-chemical impulse from any of the 'sense'-nerves and the appearance of the sounds and sights we believe we sense as objective, self-existing reality. What the senses register and translate into electro-chemical impulses and send to the brain via a network of nerves, in no way resembles that which finally appears to our human vision. Here we are faced with nothing but complete and utter mystery regarding the nature of our world.

Physiologically the last trace of activity that can be detected during the process which facilitates the appearance of our world is when the nerve-impulse arrives in the brain and discharges itself in a kind of electrical happening. How the world appears to the human vision from that point onward is simply mystery and not only unknown, but ultimately unknowable.

From this an interesting observation could be made. When the appearance of things is explained in this way, it becomes clear that we do not have two different systems for becoming aware of the diversity of the field of experience. We do not 'sense' some pre-existing objects, sounds, smells 'out there , and then employ a different system for becoming aware of our thoughts, feelings and emotions. Our whole field of appearance is really just one unfathomable and mysterious process of present arising, and there seems little else we could say about it.

The arising of things in any moment is one undivided process where the perceiving 'subject' and the perceived 'object' simply cannot be separated into two categories of existence - the 'perceiver' and the 'perceived'. The moment the object appears in our field of perception, we become aware of it. And our becoming aware of any object *is* the appearance of the object. The content of our awareness and the awareness of the content is one process of undivided present arising. On present evidence the 'two' cannot categorically be separated into the observer and the thing observed.

When we enter into the meditative practice of direct experience as described in *'Part Two: Working with Direct Awareness'*, the simple truth of this proposition becomes evident as our own directly-felt experience. It will also become demonstrably clear that it is only when we introduce thought into the process and start dissecting present experience conceptually that thought divides the wholeness of experience into presumed subjectivity and objectivity – the observer and the thing observed.

It is at this point that we conceptually, and falsely, separate consciousness and the content of consciousness and begin to believe that these dualistic projections of thought present us with a more fundamental truth than the simplicity of the living, undivided moment of present arising. And it is on this belief that our conventional view of sense-perception has been founded. Once again we notice the deluding power of thought which mistakes its own conceptual versions of things for the reality of things.

Of course, this truth of the mysterious and non-dual nature of present arising may be somewhat bewildering to a mind caught in its own demands for knowledge and security. There is something satisfying and quite charming in being

Part One: The View

able to explain everything in the greatest detail – even that which defies description and explanation. But all certainty is the death of enquiry. To know, often means to become desensitized and therefore insensitive to the open-ended nature of true self-enquiry where all certainty is suspended to create space for the energy of Intelligence to become active as a directive force in our lives. The belief in knowledge as the only tool for human survival and inner discovery destroys our ability to remain openhearted and open-minded to the totality of life. Certainty of knowledge and true self-exploration are mutually exclusive. Once we know, and have become identified with our knowing, all enquiry is arrested.

And when the spirit of enquiry gets short-circuited by the apparent certainty contained within the field of knowledge, we lose our ability to allow for the great simplicity of direct experience. We therefore need not be too perturbed if our self-enquiry leads us to the mystery of things. The sense of true mystery quiets the mind, and this allows our deeper Intelligence to do its liberating and insightful work.

There is tremendous potential in the recognition of true mystery. As we shall discover when we enter into the practice of Direct Awareness, (see: *Part Two: Working with Direct Awareness*) a deep sense of mystery, based on direct experience and insight, arrests the ever-fertile imagination that is always active in producing and projecting a stream of certainty that in many instances bears little relation to reality. Often it serves only to obscure the experience of the undivided nature of things.

In Chapter 4 where we enquired into the different mechanisms which serve as the most fundamental supports for the separate self-sense, we noticed how thought chronically interprets the way the senses work. It first accepts the apparent reality that the senses perceive a world 'out there', and then comes to what appears to be a perfectly reasonable conclusion that because the world is 'out there', there must be something 'in here' noticing it. This 'something in here' is the notion of the observer or the presumed perceiving 'I', believing itself to be categorically separate from that which it 'perceives'. In this way thought fragments the non-dual reality of all present arising. It literally creates an 'out there', by *assuming an 'in here'*,

85

where in fact neither 'there' nor 'here' has any foundation in present experience. And it is this confusion within thought which has led us to believe so firmly in the senses as instruments for perception.

From this it may be clear why it is of such critical importance for us to enquire into the nature of sense perception. As we have seen, wholeness, and the assumption of sense-perception as we ordinarily understand it, are two very different propositions. The belief that our senses are instruments for becoming aware of a world 'out there', could be seen as one of the most fundamental and abiding notions supporting the illusion of fragmentation and duality.

When it becomes clear that we, as previously presumed separate observers, are an integral part of all forms of present arising, our minds gradually modify their dualistic vision and begin to ponder the non-dual reality of experience. This is how we bring thought in line with reality. It begins to realize that we are an integral part of that which we experience. And it is this realization which affords us with the correct frame of reference to enquire *experientially* into the wholeness of life. To be human is to be our *total* field of present experience. And in this wholeness the notion of us as separate observers of our world via the agency of the senses gradually falls away by non-use.

Chapter Seven

THE DESTINY OF 'I'-CONSCIOUSNESS

The separate self-sense suffers the consequences of its own presumed existence in a rather predictable and characteristic way. Feeling itself separate from the totality of its entire field of experience, the 'I' goes through a kind of evolutionary process whereby it gradually transforms itself from the mere sense of its own separate existence into a profound complexity of emotional/psychological interference patterns.

For the 'I' in the 'I'-conscious state this is a necessary and inevitable process. Once established, it can only grow in complexity. And while it believes in itself as something very solid and real, the separate 'I' positions itself for confrontation with its living environment where one fragment, the 'I', experiences itself as the constant, permanent feature of our lives, with everything else as its separate objects. This fragments our experience by divorcing us from it in a most fundamental way. And where there is this presumption of division, where in fact there is only wholeness, conflict is inevitable.

In truth, life is an ever-fresh, non-dual movement from one living moment to the next. Yet, the 'I' has defined itself in its own psychic space as something permanent and fixed, and therefore finds itself out of touch with the moving, and ever-changing, character of the living process. And what makes the confrontation of this presumed fragment with the undivided nature of things so problematic, and even pathological, is that in reality, this split is based on a misunderstanding that has no basis in reality at all.

The 'I' is real only insofar as we are identified with the thought processes that project it. Outside of thought, the 'I' does not exist. But as we are deeply identified with the content of thought via the thought/attention-knot, this projection, being part of the content of thought, becomes very real and solid. And once the 'I' has taken on its presumed status as the permanent, central basis of our lives, it develops a remarkable range of profoundly debilitating and enervating behavioral patterns in a characteristic and rather predictable way. All of these are symptomatic of the one fundamental error in human consciousness: our unshakable belief in our essential separation from life itself in the form of the separate self-sense.

All error shows symptoms of its own non-alignment with what is real. In whichever way error manifests, it always creates a tension between itself and the context or reality in which it has to function. We have developed the error of a separate self-existence in the context of that which cannot be divided. Life is whole, and as humans we are inherently part of this one undivided process of present arising. To experience ourselves as something categorically separate from this wholeness is to be identified with an error of judgment in one aspect of our being: thought.

As we have seen, to be 'I'-conscious is to be unconscious of the condition in which it arises. And much of our suffering could be found in the struggle of the 'I' to relieve itself from the inevitable symptoms of suffering and discomfort its presumed separation from life has brought in its wake.

The 'I' can never just *be*. It is destined always to *do*. Once identified with the fragment, the inherent discomfort of this situation forces the 'I' to seek relief from the symptoms associated with its own condition. As seekers we become human *doings*, and can never just be human *Beings*. And so powerful is the sense of separation in our state of presumed isolation from the totality of life that we can never come to rest in our search for ways of relieving ourselves from the agony of our own self-consciousness.

While identified with the 'I' we are driven by the *logic of separation* to seek a wholeness we deeply sense is possible, but can never find. The fragment can never become whole. All searching by the fragment to find wholeness is futile. And yet, this is exactly the plight of the 'I' which is always actively seeking ways of relieving itself from the agony of its own presumed separateness. But because it is always doing this from its own disposition of separateness, it can never succeed. And it will be these futile and contradictory attempts by the 'I' to find relief from the painful symptoms associated with its own alienated state which we need to explore in order to become sensitive to the impracticality and ultimate futility of this aspect of ourselves.

One of the main attempts of the separate one to free itself from itself is through identification. It uses identification as a means through which to experience a sense of unity and wholeness. Once the 'I' has identified itself with a thought, an emotion, an object, a philosophy, religion, nationality, spiritual path or any other state of attentive absorption, it *becomes* that state. This gives us a sense of wholeness, of having overcome the feeling of separation inherent to our 'I'-conscious state. In this the 'I' appears to have successfully bridged the gap between itself and its world.

However, as our self-enquiry develops, it will become evident that when the 'I' uses identification in this deliberate - if mostly unconscious - way, it is really busy with little else than a form of imitation. It *imitates the true wholeness of life through identification* because in the identified state the 'I' has the false sense that it has transcended itself into wholeness.

However, all that has happened is that it has merely allowed itself to become temporarily absorbed in a state of attention. Here it literally forgets itself while absorbed in its state of identified 'wholeness'. But as we know, such states of absorbed attention never last indefinitely and we soon find ourselves back into the discomfort of our own separate self-sense. Yet, driven by the need to relieve itself from itself, the 'I' will immediately start afresh with its search for something new to become identified with. The process never stops. This identification could take the form of watching television, joining a new religious group, discovering an exciting philosophy of life, being bored, over-actively indulging in some 'meaningful' activity and so on. The 'I' is destined to seek in identification with objects, inner states, thoughts and emotions for a wholeness it senses is always presently available to our being, but which, as a bundle of self-contraction, its very existence cannot allow for. As we have seen, the fragment cannot become whole. No attempt by the 'I' to relieve itself from itself can ever be successful.

Self-fulfillment is another form of identification, where the 'I' seeks to fulfill itself through all kinds of anxious, and often completely indiscriminate, activity. Of course there is nothing wrong with seeking and finding pleasurable and deeply rewarding things to do with one's life. But true self-actualization has nothing in common with the compulsive search of the 'I' in its attempts to escape from itself through compulsive forms of doing. In our desperation we seek out any conceivable new age concept, lifestyle, activity, circumstance or course of action as sources of possible self-fulfillment. We often enter into profoundly destructive activities such as wars, suppression of people, destruction of the earth's resources, mutually mutilating interpersonal relationships, life-negative religious practices and so on, for no reason other than hoping to find in these identifiable forms of self-escape or self-fulfillment.

The 'I' cannot discriminate between life-positive and life-negative ways of keeping itself occupied. This is an integral aspect of the destiny it creates for itself. Once the 'I' has attached itself to these forms of self-indulgence, it will defend its identification with them as though it is a matter of life and death. And this is what makes the 'I' such a dangerous and volatile creature in the broader context of life. It is always vulnerable to the possibility that its identified unity may be disturbed, threatened, taken away or destroyed.

Once identified with any aspect of life, the 'I' must of necessity hold on to it, protect it and defend it. For to lose it would again mean to be exposed to the pain of separation inherent in the naked 'I'-conscious state. This makes the 'I'-state violent, reactive and ultimately less than human.

Another interesting phenomenon within the 'I'-state to observe is that we become as attached to our inner world of disturbed psychological states as we do to anything else. Having divided myself into that which is 'me' and that which is 'not me' – such as 'I' and 'my' thinking, 'I' and 'my' emotion, 'I' and 'my' inner experiences – the complexities and problems associated with 'my' psychological being serve equally as potential for identification as any other projection of thought. We tend to be as reluctant to let go of inner disturbances with which we have become identified, as we are to readily abandon all other aspects of identified existence. The 'I' would much rather have some kind of emotional or psychological issue with which to keep itself endlessly preoccupied, than being without it, and feel the emptiness inherent to its very appearance.

Whether I hold the thought of my high status at work as my object of identification or the projection of my inferiority, inadequacy or negative self-worth, makes no difference to the need of the separate one for identification. As long as the 'I' has something with which to identify itself – whether positive or negative, pleasurable or painful, good or bad, healthy or unhealthy, practical or unpractical, true or false – its all-encompassing need to lose itself in something is always the final arbiter. This unconscious drive towards identification totally destroys our ability to think clearly and objectively with regard to our involvement with things, thoughts, emotions and activities. We are mostly driven and controlled by an unconscious demand for a unity the 'I' cannot but seek and, yet, cannot but not find.

And as we shall observe in the next chapter, where we enquire into the struggle of the 'I' in terms of attachment and detachment, this urge of the separate self-sense to merge itself through identification and attachment, leaves it extremely vulnerable. Life has its own agenda and cares little for the attempts by the separate self-sense to find security and stability in the things with which it has invested identified unity. Stability in objects of identification is a dream the 'I' always hopes will be fulfilled, because if everything were to remain stable and unchanging, its objects of identification would also remain stable. Such stability would offer great security for the 'I'. Its objects of identification would never be threatened. The 'I' could come to rest in its illusion of identified wholeness.

However, the ever-changing nature of life does not allow for this. Change is therefore a major source of bewilderment, anxiety and unhappiness for the security-seeking 'I'. This fundamental yearning of the 'I'-conscious state for security and stability, finds itself in direct conflict with the changing nature of reality. And as this law of change is more real and fundamental than the struggles of the presumed 'I' to seek and find security, it could only be the separate self-sense that would suffer in its mortal combat with the ever-changing nature life.

The destiny of 'I'-consciousness, in its search for objects with which to identify is thus symptomized by a complicated system of acceptance and rejection. It indiscriminately accepts that which it believes it could identify itself with, and rejects that which appears to lack this potential. It can therefore only move within the predetermined categories of these opposites. But it may be important to note that any such rigid and predetermined value-structure is of necessity limited and will always produce fragmented results.

By its nature the 'I' is very conservative. In its fear of losing its carefully constructed world of identified unity, it allows for little exploration and risk taking. Being destined to search for stability and security, the separate self-sense has inhibited our ability for openness and self-exploration, and has thereby placed a profound limitation on our inner growth and the true fulfillment of our human potential.

As we prefer to live in the presumed security of our own identified world, we become mechanical, conditioned, fragmented and thus totally insensitive to the ever-fresh nature of the living moment. While we are absorbed in our attempts to arrest the flow of life in our search for forms of identification, life gently passes us by. Instead of our destiny taking on the *form and character of life itself*, the activities of the separate self-sense necessitate that we live in enclosed pockets of identified construct, completely out of touch with the living moment. And this is part of the inevitable destiny of the 'I'-conscious state.

In conclusion it may again be worth noticing that the process of identification takes place unconsciously. We are always only aware of the *content* of this play of identification. We are generally not aware of the *fact* of it taking place. The act of identification is in essence of the same unconscious nature as the presumption of the 'I', which informs and motivates it. All activities and extensions of the 'I' are processes that take place unconsciously. There is nothing truly conscious about the 'I'-state. The moment we try to bring the 'I' into the field of conscious awareness, it vanishes. No one has ever seen their 'I'.

The 'I' is an illusion. And from this illusion separation arises. Separation gives birth to feelings of loneliness and alienation. From these the need for wholeness and belonging is established. And, as part of the deluded state in which the 'I' finds itself, it then attempts to become whole from within its own fragmented state through identification with aspects of its field of experience. In this identified state, the 'I' is totally unaware and ignorant of the delusion of 'wholeness' it finds itself in.

Should we then mistake this delusion of wholeness for the non-dual truth of the living moment, we are generally totally unaware that the wholeness we believe we are experiencing is in fact nothing but a reactive thought-construct. Only thought can put together that which cannot be put together. The logic contained within the presumption of separation endlessly drives the process of falsely seeking unity from within a disposition of fragmentation.

If, through right practice and right living, we begin to gain insight into the falseness of this movement of the separate self to seek wholeness through the fragmentary activities of thought, we could devise forms of practice which could address the problem at its root. That is, we could begin to enquire into the processes by which the 'I'-state manifest, and to discover means for transcending them.

It is really only at this level of self-enquiry where we may realistically neutralize the inevitable karmic consequences of the self-state by *inverting our enquiry back upon the 'I' as process*. And only when we feel our way into these subtle practices of self-observation and self-transcendence will the necessary destiny-creating consequences of the 'I'-conscious state cease.

This aspect of our enquiry is dealt with in considerable detail throughout *Part Two: The Practice*.

Chapter Eight

ATTACHMENT AND DETACHMENT

*I*n the previous chapter we noticed how the problems associated with the 'I' develop along a rather predictable path. In its quest to heal the schism between itself and its world, the 'I' tries to overcome this dilemma of separation, but always fails, because it does not recognize the impossibility of the task it has set itself: seeking unity through separateness; wholeness through fragmentation.

As a separate, and separated, creature, the 'I' tries to overcome the suffering of loneliness and alienation inherent in its existence by attaching itself through identification to all aspects of life, inner or outer. We noticed how any attempt to correct the error of the 'I'-conscious state from within the categories and predetermined definition of the error itself only exacerbates the problems associated with separateness.

This flight from itself could be seen as one movement within the attachment/detachment game which the 'I' dramatizes as part of its inevitable destiny. What concerns us in this chapter with regard to attachment and detachment is also of vital importance on the path of self-knowledge. Firstly, there is the traditional religious view of these concepts, and secondly, another more unconscious form of attachment which arises through naming and categorization founded in projection and transference.

As we know, the religious traditions have placed considerable emphasis on the transcendence or neutralization of the 'I' as the main source of separation between itself and God. To these traditions it became evident that the tendency of the 'I' to attach itself to objects and ways of living which divert its attention away from God, greatly inhibited communion with the Ultimate.

Their argument against attachment to the world was unambiguous: while the 'I' actively seeks aspects of manifest reality with which to identify and to attach itself to, it simply cannot seriously consider any suggestions that God-realization, rather than self-fulfillment, attachment and identification, constitutes the true path to happiness and human well-being. In short, one cannot serve both the false god of materialism and the true God of the religious traditions. This outward need of the separate self-sense to attach itself to objects, philosophies, nationalities, material possessions, people etc. was therefore seen to be in direct conflict with the traditional notions of unification with God. It was argued that outward attachment strengthens the separative tendency away from God as this results in a kind of 'worldliness' which most mystical and religious movements regard as improper conduct for the truly serious spiritual practitioner. Thus the notion of detachment from the world as a sign of devotion to God became one of the main and abiding features of most mystical traditions.

However, without first investigating the desperate need of the separate self-sense for attachment, the demand for forceful detachment can only lead to cynicism, bewilderment and confusion. It creates a direct confrontation between what the practitioner experiences as a fundamental need within themselves, and their search for spiritual fulfillment. The path of forceful detachment from the world threatens the need for security and stability characteristic of the 'I' in the 'I'-conscious state. This has led to considerable psychological and emotional distress for many sincere practitioners who felt that they passionately want God-realization, yet, equally passionately need their identification with the world to sustain the 'I' while occupied with its spiritualization process.

This rather unfortunate consequence of willful detachment could be expected. Detachment from the world is founded upon a limited view of the nature of the problem it attempts to address. Missing in this proposition is clarity an insight into the nature and function of the presumed entity which is expected to enter into a shift of loyalty from attachment to the world to attachment to God.

As much as the separate self-sense is characteristically a movement in unawareness, and therefore deeply lacking in self-knowledge, the same could be said of the traditional notion of detachment. Had the traditions been more alive to the functioning and demands of the separate self, they would not have proposed willful detachment to bring their disciples closer to God. Rather, they would have noticed that an error cannot be corrected from within the categories of the error itself. If finally the 'I' were to attach itself to its God, it would do so for the same reason it attaches itself to the world. It would seek, in attachment to God, the same emotional security and psychological protection which it sought in all other relationships with its world. Here the 'I' still comes first – not God. Without proper and dedicated self-observation and self-knowledge, it can never become clear to the 'I' that attachment to God is merely another expression of the same deeply felt need to rid itself of its own profound sense of separation and loneliness.

In this we notice the same fundamental strategy for unification through attachment and identification contained within the error which is the 'I'-conscious state itself. The kind of detachment proposed by the religious traditions can therefore not deliver on its promise. Even if God were to have existed, and worthy of being identified with, the strategy of willful detachment would still have been based on a reactive gesture within the very psychological entity that stands between the religious practitioner and their God: the presumption of the separate self-sense. It would therefore be in the *transcendence* of this separative principle within the practitioner that true detachment becomes possible, not in any gesture it makes to merge with its God or falsely seeks unity through identification and attachment to it.

Only by undermining the *presumption* of separation which demands union, attachment and identification can true detachment be established. And such detachment will ultimately reveal itself to be the natural function of right relationship with every aspect of life. When the separate self-sense is not present to demand attachment and identification with each and every appearance in its field of experience, human life could be re-established in the natural order of its own integral being

Willful detachment and self-transcendence are therefore mutually exclusive forms of practice, because all gestures towards detachment are based on a reaction to attachment which is an activity of the separate self-sense. And nothing founded from within any activity of the 'I' can serve the process of 'I'-transcendence. The 'I' itself, as a manifestation of uninspected, unconscious processes, has to be observed, understood and transcended. In itself it can never be free.

From this it may be evident that as long as the 'I' sees itself as the center of our being, nothing this presumed separate entity can do to relieve itself from the suffering inherent to its own existence will succeed. Neither trying to forget itself through identification and attachment, nor attempting to forcefully extract itself from its own attachments has the integrity to resolve the condition of separateness and loneliness the 'I'-state necessitates.

And as long as the 'I'-state dominates our field of experience and thereby interprets the undivided nature of our living reality as something fundamentally fragmented and not-whole, it will remain vulnerable to having to play the attachment/detachment game with itself. And given that we are most profoundly identified with our 'I'-conscious state, no forceful detachment will serve the true spiritualization of our being. The fundamental error has not been observed and appropriately addressed. In this the spiritual traditions have missed the mark, and, rather ironically, in the process created more confusion and misery in proposing detachment from the world as an activity integral to the spiritual process.

The other, considerably more subtle enquiry into attachment and detachment centers on how we unconsciously bind ourselves to a world we construct through naming and contextualization.

We have seen that there is something subjective in every aspect of our human experience. This subjectivity has to do with how we interpret and understand both ourselves and our world, and could thus be explored as an integral part of our experience of our world. We generally do not relate to things as they are in themselves. Things make sense to us only *after* we have invested them with names and qualities, and have ordered them into a general scheme of understandable, recognizable and useable units. This filtered reality becomes the context from within which we prioritize our involvement with our world

We could call this process the 'conceptualization of our world' because the names and qualities we attach to things are aspects of thought that we project onto these. Here our world takes on a subjective form and we begin to relate to it in a secondary, indirect way, while losing touch with the more primary, direct experience of things. Our world takes on the *form of the thought projections we transfer onto it*, and this projected world becomes the world with which we interact. Subjectivity takes on the form of objectivity. Thought becomes reality.

What therefore started out as a practical and necessary process of naming and categorization whereby we attach names to things for the purpose of communication and general functionality, we begin to mistake the world of names for the world of form. We relate to things 'out there' as though our interpretation of them is what they, in fact, *are*.

However, what we believe we see 'out there' as objective reality are often little more than names, images and concepts mistaken for the things themselves. We are generally unaware that what we believe we 'see' are more often than not mere projections, transferred onto the world of appearance by thought. Most of the time we look at nothing but our own brain-stuff. We do not see things as they exist in themselves. We see our *constructed* version of reality and relate to this as if it has true objective status.

And because these interpretations take place completely unconsciously, this unchallenged, projected reality, which we believe we sense and experience 'out there', separate from the mind which creates it, forms a subjective condition of reality, which reflects our own vision of things, rather than what things are in themselves. And it is this projected and transferred reality that forms the basis for an all-encompassing *unconscious process of attachment to our world.*

In view of this, it is important that we sensitize ourselves to the processes whereby thought projects and transfers qualities of itself onto aspects of our world and then to mistake these transferred qualities for reality itself. In this exists considerable potential for confusion, misunderstanding and delusion

If we do not appreciate that what we experience is generally nothing but our own thought-projections which we mistake for objective existence, any subsequent relationship we may enter into with this constructed reality will always be conditioned by the qualities we projected onto it. And as these qualities are nothing but aspects of ourselves, it is clear that each time we enter into a 'relationship' with any manifestation of this thought-projected world, we are, in fact, merely confirming aspects of ourselves to ourselves. From this we can see how we *attach* ourselves through projection and transference to our world of experience. The presumed relationship between 'me' and 'that' is more often than not a relationship between 'me' and aspects of myself. Yet, we form deep and abiding bonds with this self-constructed world 'out there'.

And this leads us back to the question of detachment. In the maze of confusion between what is real and what could be considered transferred reality, we again notice the impracticality of attempting to detach ourselves from our world in any meaningful sense. For if our world consists mostly of transferred thought-projections, how would it be possible to detach ourselves from this world? While we mistake the image which we projected onto things for reality itself, any willful act of detachment would be attempting to get rid of an illusion. Detachment from projected reality is detachment from something that does not exist, other than in the mind that projects it.

This is why self-observation and self-knowledge are such integral aspects of our path of self-transcendence. Without self-observation we will remain totally unaware of the intricate nature of the deluding ways by which thought orders our world.. We have a remarkable potential for deluding ourselves, and find ourselves constantly in situations where the subtle workings of thought do just that. The suggestion that it would be possible to detach ourselves from our projected world before we have thoroughly investigated the mechanisms of projection and transference would therefore be based on mere uninspected conjecture. Self-observation and self-knowledge reveal to us the functioning of the mechanisms by which we mistake illusion for reality. Through self-observation we become conscious of the unconscious functioning of powerful instruments active within us which we have allowed to operate in ways that do not always serve our psychophysical being in the most appropriate manner.

From this we may appreciate that non-attachment has nothing to do with forcefully detaching ourselves from what we may identify as forms of attachment. Until we become sensitive to how we project and transfer names and ideas onto the simplicity of our world, and from the disposition of the separate self-sense attach ourselves to this *interpreted vision of reality*, such attempts at forceful detachment will be completely counterproductive: they will serve to contribute to our confusion, rather than creating inner and outer order.

Only in the clarity of our own self-observation we will discover the illusory nature of both of these. We will gradually awaken to our inner Intelligence which can observe the workings of thought and, in the light of its own lucidity, will gradually undermine the limited and conditioned logic of both the 'I'-thought as the presumed center of our being and the relative, or even illusory, nature of projected and transferred reality. This Intelligence, being of a higher, more subtle order than the logic which mistakes thought-projections for reality, concerns itself with reality alone, and does away with projection and transference; attachment and detachment; self and its objects of identification. It functions in harmony and resonance with things as they are, and does not concern itself with the complexities created and sustained by thought projections.

Over time, our inner Intelligence will make the false fade into extinction due to non-use and non-interest. Once we begin to sense the freedom inherent in our already-existing human condition, prior to 'I'-consciousness and thought-projection, we will show little interest in the binding and delusory activities of

Part One: The View

transference and attachment. Our relationship with our world takes on the *form* of 'What Is'. We begin to live with truth, rather than relating to a reality fundamentally created and sustained by thought.

Chapter Nine

SELF-ENQUIRY, PSYCHOLOGY AND RIGHT ATTITUDE

1) Self-Enquiry and Psychology

The question has often been asked whether there exists any relationship between meditative practices on the one hand, and emotional/psychological work on the other. This is an issue that has been raised mostly in the West, as many meditating therapists are sensing a possible convergence between the two disciplines. Yet, so far, no clear relationship has been identified despite the fact that in the West meditation has extensively been practiced for the last forty years or so.

It would still seem that one of the most unresolved questions for many practitioners and teachers has been the apparent ineffectiveness of the meditative process on our psychological being. To be on a spiritual path and to practice the forms of meditation suggested by the various traditions, often result in rather extraordinary experiences of bliss, visions, insights, absorptions and states of inner beauty. However, these states appear to have little effect on the transformation of our deeply rooted psychological complexities which are often characterized by profound feelings of anxiety, alienation and unfreedom.

It is as though we have here two categories of human potential: the one psychological/emotional, the other spiritual/transcendent. And experience has shown that they do not necessarily have any direct impact on one another.

Whether we display the signs of a relatively healthy self-image and well-ordered psychology, or experience the discomfort of a confused sense of self and a dysfunctional emotional response to things, neither appears to have much effect on how our meditation practice unfolds.

For instance, we could be quite confused and disturbed psychologically and yet experience deep and profound states of inner silence and beauty during formal meditative periods. These states appear in moments when we enter into a meditative state which temporarily sidelines the content of our mental and emotional disturbances. In such instances the meditative process by-passes our negative emotional states and thereby allows for profound experiences of clarity, absorption and often moments of bliss and unity consciousness.

And it is these states which would seem to have little effect on our psychological being. The practice of meditation has little sustainable, long-term effects on many of our deeply rooted psychological and emotional reactive potential. Yet, most of us feel that such positive effects *should* become evident. At the end of our engagement with what we believe to be spiritual practice, a realistic expectation would be for us not only to remain alive to the experiences during our meditation practices, but also to be free from much of our reactive psychological and emotional shadow material. There is, however, no evidence to suggest that the long-term results of meditative practices are consistent with this view. Often people have been meditating for years with little sustainable relief from many of their deeper emotional complexities.

What is also interesting to note is that meditators who display considerable emotional and psychological maturity do not necessarily have any greater access to such states of meditative absorption than someone with many unresolved emotional issues. It is as though meditative states and our psychological status have very little influence on one another. This is why the question of the possible relation between these forms of enquiry has been raised in both spiritual and psychotherapeutic circles. It is a vital question which requires our careful consideration.

The apparent schism between contemplative/meditative practice and psychological/emotional investigation necessitates that we approach our inner exploration from a well founded vision of the nature of the work we plan to engage in. Such a vision should not only be informed by the underlying philosophy and forms of inner work proposed by our spiritual path or therapist. Ideally it should also include the motivations, expectations and attitudes that we, as individuals, bring to our enquiry.

For instance, we often find that we enter upon a spiritual path solely motivated by the pain of some acute existential or psychological crisis, thereby seeking in spiritual practice relief from specific forms of emotional distress which might have been better served by a more psychological approach to our problems. The opposite is equally true: we may consult the wise counseling of our therapist whereas the problems facing us may have a deeper, more spiritual character. In both cases we may not be addressing the problem at the level of the problem itself, and thereby inhibit our ability to work productively with our disturbing material.

Identifying the nature of our disturbance relative to its spiritual or psychological emphasis is vital to our initial enquiry. In this we are often dependent on the considerate counseling of either our spiritual advisor or therapist. Early diagnosis, and clarity within ourselves in this regard, can save us many hours of often unnecessary, and wrongly directed, inner work.

Having said this, it is equally important that we do not make a categorical distinction between spiritual, self-transcending enquiry and psychological work. In fact it is vitally important that we seriously consider the possibility of a close working relationship between our emotional/psychological disturbances and the broader domain of self-transcending work. On the one hand, appropriate psychological work lays the foundation for the development of true spiritual maturity. Spiritual work, on the other hand, cannot find its sustainable measure in an overly confused and reactive emotional environment. If spiritual life were to reflect a stable emotional response-ability, psychological work and meditative practice should be applied in complete *harmony and synchronicity with one another.* Correctly applied, the one informs, motivates, inspires, and ultimately sustains the other.

Much will therefore depend on what we understand by the term 'spiritual'. Often spirituality is equated with mystical union with God or some presumed Ground of Being. This becomes the sole focus of the student's enquiry which often results in deep visions, states of bliss, feelings of unity consciousness, moments of love for humanity and so on. And as God is the main source of inspiration for this kind of meditative involvement, these states are often interpreted as expressions of the Ultimate. This encourages the student to proceed along their chosen path which naturally leads to more such states of attentive absorption. These no doubt are beautiful and interesting experiences one might have along the way but, as we have seen, they do not necessarily have any measurable relieving effects on the deep-rooted emotional and psychological disturbances within the practitioner.

The reason for this is that God-orientated meditative practices are conducted in a kind of emotional vacuum. Every effort is made to still the mind and to subdue the emotions while holding attention stable on some object of devotion such as the name of God or a mantra. This naturally leads to states of attentive absorption and often to even deeper states of Samadhi or deep concentration. During this kind of inner quiet many extraordinary experiences generally present themselves. These are states natural to our human condition when the mind gets quiet. But if such experiences are mistaken for expressions of the Ultimate, the student is usually satisfied that such contact with 'God' will automatically correct their emotional and mental disorder. Little further consideration is therefore given to the vitally important aspects of human dysfunction. But what is often not noticed or appreciated is that such experiences are really *state-specific* and need not effect psychological healing within our psyche.

For instance, long-distance runners may also experience rather profound states of bliss and feelings of well-being. But no long-distance runner will expect these states to last beyond their exercise program, let alone, affect them permanently on other levels of their emotional being. Certain conditions simply elicit certain natural psychophysical responses. But these take place in the context of the kind of practice we involve ourselves in. For this reason such inner states have no necessary healing relation to our emotional shadow material. Blissful states during meditation are of a *different order* to the nature of our emotional complexities. This is why meditation practice *in itself* is not the instrument with which to effect any measurable modifications, or long-term changes, in our emotional/psychological structures.

If we now compare this search for God to the humanistic involvement with meditative practices, we discover a very different relationship between meditative and psychological/emotional work. From a humanistic perspective, the term 'spiritual' refers to those profoundly human qualities such as clear insight, understanding, artistic appreciation, the ability to give and receive love, intuition, compassion, the functioning of an Intelligence not founded within the intellect and the experience of our non-dual identity with life itself. As we have seen in Chapter 2, these are concepts that also describe our notion of 'Spiritual Humanism'. And the unfolding of these deep human qualities is the *essence and heart* of all true spiritual enquiry that is founded in nothing but our deep human potential.

This brings us back to the close relationship that ideally *should* exist between psychological work and truly humanistic spiritual enquiry but which, in the traditional mystical approaches, have been rather neglected.. All psychological complexities are signs of fragmentation within the human condition. To heal ourselves on this level of being is not only to become whole again, but to become more spiritual in the full humanistic sense of the word.

We have seen that self-consciousness is most fundamentally a sign of fragmentation. The spiritualization of our being is therefore the process by which we attempt to break through the spell of fragmentary vision which will allow our natural, holistic disposition to reveal itself as our home-ground. This is where psychological work and spiritual, self-transcending enquiry converge. Emotional disturbances *fragment* our living experience and the transcendence of these is crucial to the spiritualization of our being. *To be whole is to have transcended the presumption of fragmentation.*

Important emotional/psychological work needs therefore to be done for the humanization of our being to be sustainably effected. In fact, the total psychophysical being has to be prepared thoroughly before the subtle non-dual intimations which gradually present themselves during the course of our investigation can become part of our living experience.

Part One: The View

It is absolutely critical that we fully understand the nature of the problems our enquiry needs to address. Most of us start our spiritual path with many unresolved psychological and emotional issues. And as this entire area of psychological, emotional, existential and attitudinal complexity falls within the sphere of either psychological or self-transcending/spiritual work, our path will have to develop appropriate instruments to deal with these. Not dealing with our psychological material adequately will result in an unsustainable, false sense of spirituality that will always leave us vulnerable to the possibility of reverting back to our old patterns of confusion and inner turmoil.

Psychological work and spiritual, self-transcending work, ultimately form one integrated process. Correctly understood and practiced, these two enquiries constitute the basis of all true spiritual practice. Spirituality is a human affair. *Human life is therefore both the path and its fruit.* We can as little afford to by-pass our psychological/emotional reactivities as we can afford not to incorporate self-transcending work as part of the spiritualization of our being. Both explore important aspects of our fundamental human condition.

Seen from a humanistic perspective it is therefore clear that no real dichotomy exists between meditative and psychological work. Rather, they compliment one another and form the sole basis for sustainable expression of our deep human potential.

(For a detailed, experientially based enquiry into this, see: *Part Two: Working with Psychological and Emotional Reactivities* and *Working with Contemplation.*)

For the present it is important that we briefly look at the broader emotional/psychological attitudes and predispositions with which we often approach our spiritual investigations. At the same time we could also identify some of the inherent problems we project onto our spiritual enquiry.

2) Right Attitude

Without thoroughly investigating our motivations and emotional and psychological needs for entering the path, we position ourselves, if not for ultimate failure, at least for the possibility of great confusion and disappointment further down the line. Before we adopt a spiritual path – or even begin to look for methods, teachers and forms of practice by which to free ourselves from our own self-limitation – it may be important first to consider the attitudes we bring to our search.

These attitudes will determine much of the style and content of our involvement with our path. Of course, it is not always easy to determine how we generally think and feel about an issue - especially during the beginning stages of the work. Often we are not even aware that we may be bringing a specific attitude to our search. Yet, we are deeply conditioned in our attitudes, and these greatly influence and determine our spiritual quest, unless we sensitize ourselves to this possibility.

Attitudes could be seen as free-floating mental/emotional notions we have about life, rather than clearly defined, and consciously applied, standards for living. If we were to approach the path of self-transcendence with an attitude, or a series of attitudes, which does not accommodate the kind of enquiry necessary for the work ahead, these will, of necessity, place a limitation on the freedom required for such an enquiry. It will also become evident to which extent they keep us bound within the parameters of the thoughts and feelings they elicit. We will then seek for relief from our confusion in characteristically predetermined ways. Our path, instead of being a vehicle towards freedom and the wholeness of life, will become a mere modified continuity of the same limited and alienated style of living we have known all along. Although much might appear to have changed, little potential for true self-transcendence has been established.

This is why it is necessary to explore some of the attitudinal themes that generally impact on our spiritual unfolding. For instance, we have become so accustomed to the authority implied in our socialization process from early childhood through to adult life that we often feel we have little power and confidence to investigate matters for ourselves. Throughout our lives we have been told what is right and wrong behavior and how we should go about our dealings with others and the world in general. This has limited and conditioned our ability to respond to challenges in a truly impartial and intelligent way. In the process it has established a self-limiting attitude in us that also characterizes our approach towards spiritual enquiry. What holds us back from true self-observation and self-knowledge is not the complex nature of the investigation as such, but rather the *complexity of attitude* we bring to our work.

Although we may regard ourselves as relatively successful participants in our social environment, we generally lack the confidence, and thereby the right attitude, to discover for ourselves where we stand in relation to the deeper enquiries into life. Having been conditioned into the role of one-who-accepts-authority, as well as one-who-is-not-capable-of-discovering-for-themselves about matters concerning our own inner and outer lives, we inevitably seek the authority of some presumed expert, teacher, guru or spiritual/religious organization to guide us, and to lead us from confusion to clarity.

Unfortunately, most of these teachers are as confused as we are. Very often they themselves have not come upon the things they teach us about life and living through authentic experimentation and direct personal realization. Rather, they present us with paths and methods of practice, the truth of which has seldom been revealed to them in its naked simplicity. What we are presented with as revealed truth is often little more than dogmas, given life and continuity by teachers who are still struggling with their own lack of self-transcendence. Yet, moved by the urgency to free ourselves from the confusion and discomfort that we often bring to our lives, we blindly accept the authority of the tradition, guru or teacher. In this way we hope to bring new meaning and content to our lives through the understanding of another.

In this lies a great danger. To embrace any teaching or method of practice without being aware of how our social conditioning and attitudinal predispositions affect the nature of our enquiry, positively or negatively, can have a profoundly fragmentary effect on our search for truth.

Truth can only be revealed in the context of an innocent heart and an unbiased mind. To remain open-minded and open-hearted is to reject all authority and to develop a healthy skepticism towards everything the mass-mind has come to accept as true and valid. By this we free ourselves from the internalized, attitudinal values of the mass-mind, and begin to think/feel our way into every aspect of our human potential for ourselves.

It is part of the mass-mind, *internalized into our own individual functioning,* that assumes that our teachers, leaders, traditions and other teachings of conventional 'wisdom' know something about life, reality and us that we are not capable of realizing for ourselves. We unquestioningly accept that what they teach will lead us from darkness to light. In our bewilderment we truly believe that the methods of practice they offer us will lead to the freedom, sanity and well-being we yearn for. And because these methods and beliefs are accepted on authority, and do not come from the integrity of our own unbiased enquiry, they tend to be little more than mere rules for conformity.

This results in superficial behavioral modifications, which lack the energy and clarity to effect true transformation. In truth, these changes are introduced from the outside, put into practice as a form of uninspected discipline, and will remain part of our dilemma for as long as our participation in these is prescribed by the authority of someone else.

The problems of confusion, disempowerment, unlove and relational disabilities we bring to our quest for freedom are specific to us as individuals. Correctly understood, these form the basis of the path we will have to walk. The suffering and unease that have brought us to our enquiry in the first place are perfectly sufficient to sustain a practical and freeing form of self-enquiry. There is no limit on our inherent human potential. Freedom is fundamental to our human condition. The path is from the darkness we ourselves bring to our living reality to the light of our deeper Intelligence which is always ready to outshine our preconceptions and to assist us in removing the obstacles we have placed in the way of the realization of the non-dual truth of human existence.

From this it may be evident that the path cannot be separated from our own dysfunctional reality. We *are* the path we will have to enquire into, get to know thoroughly, and finally transcend. This is why it is called the 'path of self-transcendence'. Not one aspect of our lives is truly separate from us. Everything we do, think, feel, experience, or even negate, is already part of the life we will have to investigate if we are to free ourselves from the mental and emotional complexities that we are.

The manner in which we interact with reality displays all the forms of separation, alienation and discomfort so characteristic of our pre-inspected and pre-informed ways of doing things. And our situation will remain pre-inspected and uninformed for as long as we base our practice and search for freedom on the authority of another. This does not imply that we do not listen to the wise and caring counseling of a fellow traveler or someone we sense we may be able to learn from. However, none of these relationships should even have a shadow of authority implied in them. To be able to make use of the wise counseling of another is to remain open to one's own inner voice of wisdom at the same time. If there is resonance with the words and intimations another might share with us, such resonance of truth meeting truth will quietly, and quite naturally, do its self-liberating work. Through this we develop faith in our own understanding and feelings about these matters. Gradually this deeper sense of knowledge-less knowing will naturally develop in accordance with its own clarity and insight.

Once we begin to sense that we are capable of approaching these matters for ourselves, it becomes evident that what we previously presumed could only have been achieved on the authority of the spiritual path, the guru, God or his representatives, *now clearly lies within the working potential of our own humanity.* Such a realization shows the first and most fundamental attitudinal shift in our understanding towards reclaiming our human territory and re-establishing within ourselves the inalienable right to our own path of freedom and human dignity.

In addition to the care we should take in blindly accepting the authority of an outside agency, we should be equally careful of our tendency for unquestioningly accepting our own authority. This may seem to contradict the notion of enquiring into these matters for ourselves. Yet, as we have seen, our habitual reactions and conditioned emotional and intellectual responses present themselves not as conscious, intelligent and volitional interactions with life, but rather as a series of predetermined misconceptions. These exert a tremendously powerful authority over how we relate to things. This kind of uninspected inner authority could become as great a stumbling block to our self-enquiry as that of an outside authority.

Not to sensitize ourselves to the influence of conditioning, and the attitudes accompanying such conditioning, would lead to a very superficial enquiry where we will ignore, not only the fact of our conditioned way of life, but also the destiny-creating consequences of these recurring, habitual responses.

Conditioning comes with its own implied authority and logic. The kind of teacher or path we may seek and adopt, the style and direction of our enquiry, the content of the questions we ask and the manner in which we evaluate aspects of our path, all these will be greatly influenced, and often determined, not by the clarity of our own free investigation and insight, but most profoundly by the clouded and nuanced 'reality' created by our preconceived notions of things.

Conditioned reality *is* reality, until it is inspected, understood, felt through, and ultimately transcended. A path of self-enquiry that does not take this into full consideration will remain absorbed in the web of its own projected reality, merely looking at its own projections, however much we may believe we are making progress towards freedom from self-limitation.

This leads us also to look more specifically at the question of psychological conditioning. We are as deeply conditioned by our psychology as we are by the more factually oriented aspects of our psyche. Whereas the view we have of the world, society, religion, proper conduct, morality, ethics and reality in general could be seen as relatively impersonal interactions we have with life, psychology is the residual reflection of our interaction with these in our emotional being. We are not merely a series of factual interrelations with our environment based on objective memories and the projection of these into the past and future. Inherent to our objective view of life is the subjective sense we have of things. On the emotional level, this subjectivity is characterized by the accumulative emotional response-patterns we bring to each and every experience.

Similarly to the way in which memory stores factual information, available for recall when required, emotional reactions are also stored by memory and thereby form an integral part of our memory-base and psychological reactive tendencies. This is how it is possible that certain incidents or circumstances might often evoke an emotional response totally disproportional in its emotional intensity to the reality of the challenge presented to us. Such a situation gets associated with some past experience, *complete with its emotional content*, which is then brought to bear on the experience at hand. To a greater or lesser extent, this is the case with almost all experiences as they unfold from moment to moment.

We do not see, feel and experience things afresh. Most experiences are clouded over and given a distorted emotional content, unrelated to the reality of our present experience or the challenge at hand. Such distortion not only affects the factual content of experience, but also often leaves us emotionally bewildered, confused and agitated.

Here we again see the power and authority of our own conditioning: in this case, our psychological/emotional material. Conditioning means that the condition is set. Given a certain circumstance or experience, we cannot but respond to it in a particular way. The intelligence associated with conditioning is not different to the intelligence that was present at the time the condition was set. This is why conditioning often has such a debilitating effect even on the most advanced and psychologically together persons.

Once conditioning takes over, the emotions associated with a particular condition bring an irrational, contracted and Intelligence-binding activity to our being. We are no longer free to assess the situation with an open mind and heart. We get contracted into the conditioned intelligence of the emotional response as it was experienced when the original disturbing incident got imprinted on memory.

An unfortunate aspect of this is that such response-patterns are seldom seen for what they are. We have become so used to the habitual, conditioned way in which we emotionally react to situations that we seldom question whether there may be different ways of emotionally relating to life and experience. For the person standing within the contracted vision of pre-inspected life, reality is generally little other than a combination of predetermined forms of mental and emotional reactivity. We consciously and unconsciously presume what things are and what our responses should, and would, be. Through this we become solidified within the borders of our own predeterminations and tend to view everything that does not conform to the way we see and feel about matters with suspicion and, more often than not, a threat to the integrity of our very being.

As we have seen, psychological disturbances are the residual consequences of unresolved interactions between our mental/emotional potential and our experiences of reality. If life is real for us only insofar as it represents our social, environmental, mental and emotional conditioning, it will be incapable of responding adequately beyond the borders of these predefined reality-structures.

We tend to respond only to that which we value. If all we consciously or subconsciously value is nothing but our mental and emotional conditioning, we will remain emotionally challenged, not realizing that beyond this limited and self-limiting life exists a vast potential for free and unconditioned relationship. This will also prohibit us from recognizing that we may be capable of feeling *beyond* our own reactivities into a fully human and humane emotional interaction with each and every living moment where our emotions come to rest in a field of open experience, no longer determined by the fragmented and limited self/other view that informed our being during the pre-inspected phase of our lives.

But freedom implies change. We cannot remain as we are, limited and contracted, and expect to manifest the freedom that lies beyond the conditioned limitations we bring to the living moment. It would be unrealistic to expect a sustainable form of self-transcendent living while we are caught in the measure of our own uninspected lives. And this brings us to the last, and perhaps most important aspect of the general attitudes we bring to our self-enquiry: *how do we relate to the possibility and necessity for change?*

We often approach the path of self-enquiry and self-transcendence from a rather one-dimensional point of view. We regard the path as something that should rid us of everything we don't like about ourselves, as well as that which brings us pain and suffering. We do not readily understand that the true path of self-transcendence inevitably leads to a *radical revision and transformation* of the total way in which we view ourselves and our world. Neither are we generally aware of how profoundly it will alter our functioning and responses to life in general.

If we are not looking for mere symptomatic changes, or new emotional comfort-zones, we must expect to change and be changed in a most fundamental way by self-transcendent enquiry. We cannot engage the path realistically, functionally and with integrity, while we remain loyal to the same illusions that have informed our lives up to that point. We have to realize that what we presently *are*, is the result of many misconceptions and unresolved mental/emotional issues which have established themselves in us along a well-trodden path of poorly-inspected ways of doing things. Spiritual transformation necessitates and welcomes change and allows it to do its healing work deep inside every aspect of our contracted and fragmented being. We cannot stand free, as openhearted, compassionate human beings and yet cling to a life that still manifests all the old patterns of self-limitation, self-contraction and dilemma.

Freedom and bondage are mutually exclusive states of being. To the extent that we are free and emotionally capable of bringing to any living moment a heart that is not burdened by memories of past incomplete and painful emotional responses, we are no longer defined, controlled and conditioned by such painful memories.

Unconsciously we have come to live both in, and *as*, the limited view we have of ourselves and our world. This view not only includes all the defenses we have constructed against painful emotional memory-responses, as well as an inadequate self-image, but we experience, and have defined ourselves, as nothing other than these defensive patterns. We are deeply identified with the total field of emotional and factual distortions, self-evaluating and self-correcting mechanisms, defense patterns, justifications, hopes and fears that are embedded in our ego/'I'-conscious state. And because of their recurrent appearances in the form of conditioned responses, we have little else to draw on as we approach the path of self-enquiry.

From the very beginning, a responsive *attitude of change* is thus one of the most important components of our path of self-enquiry. As our process develops, it will become evident that we need to remain sensitive to, and aware of, all aspects of ourselves that have become ripe for change, elimination or transcendence. As our insight develops, it naturally abandons that which is either no longer useful or appropriate, or seen to be based in unintelligence and unawareness. Unless we have an open-ended attitude to the possibility and necessity for deep inner change, we will effectively resist, and even block, any real intimations of change that may present themselves.

Often we simply change silently, deeply within the Intelligence of our Being. On other occasions we may become aware that some deeply held notion about an aspect of our conditioning is beginning to fall away or somehow just seems to have become less functional or true. We may sense that some aspect of a previous emotionally reactive pattern of response to specific situations begins to loosen its grip on us. It becomes transparent and no longer appropriate to hold on to.

These are some of the many insights and manifestations of emotional/psychological freedom that may present themselves along the way. However, for these to become active and functional as part of our lives, it is important that they originate within a well established attitude of change.

Change is only a threat to that which resists change. If we positively invite change, and align ourselves to its powerful *transformative* potential, the insights and shifts we experience along the way will do their liberating work quite naturally. In fact, the ultimate purpose of our work is to allow our deeper Intelligence to become the functional instrument that directs the course of our lives. This alone will transform and liberate us.

There is nothing to fear. Once we have discovered ways for opening ourselves to the full potential of our human condition, we will soon find that things begin to fall into place by themselves. For too long we have put complete faith in the fragmented and limited view we have of ourselves and life in

Part One: The View

general. This is the result of years of uninspected living during which we have internalized many patterns of thinking and feeling which are alien to wholeness, sanity and integral living. It is the *logic* contained within the deep sense of security we feel about our conditioned life that prohibits us from even considering the possibility that there may be a different way of living, free from all forms of self-limitation and self-contraction.

Fear of the new is founded within the presumed certainty and security of the known. It is this certainty we will have to investigate with an open heart and mind for it to be recognized as just another form of bondage to be transcended. This will free us from its hold over our total field of experience.

Chapter Ten

THE QUESTION OF WILL

All volitional activity is accompanied by a greater or lesser degree of will. Much of the quality we bring to what we do is determined by the force and urgency with which we will it to happen. Will is active when we gently row a boat on a quiet lake for relaxation. It is also active when we take the same boat out on a race where excellence of performance is critical to whether we win or lose. The only difference is the quality of will we bring to the situation.

Will is active in most of the things we do, from getting up in the morning and getting dressed, to making wars, doing business, parenting our children, looking for meaning in life, securing our survival, entering into relationships, taking part in religious activities, and so on. Much of what we consider to be success in life depends on the quality of will we bring to the things we do. It is not only *what* we do that makes us successful or not, but the willful determination with which we do it, and whether we can sustain it in the face of adversity.

From this it may be evident that willing is an integral part of our lives and, because it plays such an important role in everything we do, it is worth enquiring into. Will is a fundamental factor in the achievement of both happiness and suffering which result from our actions. And as much of what we do often results in disharmony, fragmentation of relationships, feelings of alienation, the sense of separation, unlove and unfreedom, it may be clear that the interaction between what we believe to be the will and our daily activities require our careful attention. If will is the driving force behind all volitional endeavor, it could be seen also to be an inherent aspect of the causes of suffering. We cannot discover much about our own involvement with our suffering unless we gain insight and clarity into the activities of the will.

If we consider the speed with which modern Western society drives itself to ever greater materialistic achievements at the cost of its human values and participatory, relational interactions, it would be in the collective will of society where we may find the motivating principle behind these failures. In our own individual way, we all participate in this system of folly, driven almost entirely by the force of will. We *will* our materialism as much as we will our social disorder, religious dogmas, wars and our general lack of empathy and compassion towards one another. We are not only the passive receivers of a disorderly social, religious, economic and political heritage. Through active participation in these activities we perpetuate these uninspected ways of living, consciously or unconsciously, generation after generation, in a rather deliberate, methodical and willful manner.

We also notice the controlling tendency of will in our relationships with both others and ourselves. Our interactions with others often display a rather strained relationship. This is because we tend to evaluate, manipulate or adjust our relationships by the force of will. Our relationships often become a battle of wills rather than a process of intelligent, mutual participation.

We further use our will as an instrument for inner change where we seldom gently observe ourselves to gain insight into our own functioning. We often judge and condemn ourselves, and then attempt to correct the perceived wrong by imposing its opposite onto ourselves through the force of will. This results in considerable confusion and often leaves us bewildered and no closer to resolving our inner conflicts.

An interesting aspect of this self-critical attitude is that it is always associated with the notions of 'me' and 'myself'. One part of 'me' is always judging, evaluating, controlling, manipulating, fearing, praising, and blaming the other part of 'me' I call 'myself'. Here we have an ongoing battle between one fragment of the mind being at odds with another. 'I' always want to change 'myself' from this to that.

And what drives this process of inner manipulation, modification or change is an act of will. Some of us show a remarkable strong will when it comes to modifying, disciplining and changing ourselves, while others have a more relaxed attitude towards themselves. But whether we are relaxed or forceful in the way we approach ourselves, all *uninspected strategies* directed at inner change are of necessity accompanied by a greater or lesser degree of will.

This leaves our inner lives in turmoil and creates a mental and emotional battlefield where we become self-critical to the point of developing many debilitating and disempowering attitudes towards ourselves. Often our over-anxious self-criticism and self-correction bring us close to self-destruction.

And all these obtain their energy from an act of will. In fact, there is a direct correlation between the forceful quality of will we bring to our inner work and the resulting complications we create for ourselves. To bring our uninspected will into a situation can only lead to further fragmentation and suffering. Inner work requires insight, understanding and intuition. It cannot be forced or expedited by an act of will. Yet, we often attempt to will ourselves beyond the measure of our understanding, and by doing so, we merely exacerbate the situation. Without our deeper emotional Intelligence to moderate our uninspected willful impositions on the way we think and feel about life, we lose our inner measure and in the process obscure our alignment with the inherent sanity and order of the living moment.

What we have called 'the will' is thus not just a neutral and relatively benign force available to us as part of our ongoing search for inner and outer order, a better quality of life or a greater sense of fulfillment. Applied inappropriately, that is, *unconsciously and habitually*, it loses its pro-active qualities and become counter-productive and even destructive.

But what really is this thing called 'will'? What is its nature and functional reality? Is the will something we have been born with as one of our instruments for survival, or is it something we develop along the way as we grow up? Is will a process or a thing? We speak of 'the will' or 'my will' as though there is some 'thing' called the 'will' somewhere within us. In all the examples we described above where we could clearly see the activity and influence of the will on our lives, it was somehow understood to mean a concrete faculty available to us to be used when needed or demanded.

But how correct is this understanding? Is there any evidence of this 'thing' or process called 'will'? Is the will an instrument or functional faculty available to us in its own right; having an existence of its own?

If we inspect this matter through self-enquiry and self-observation, we may discover that there is no such separate faculty that could be called 'will'. For instance, we may find that will is not in the same category as our ability to pay attention. Attention is a clearly discernable human faculty, while what we have come to know as 'will', cannot be found or experienced as something in its own right.

What we *can* observe, however, and have mistaken for will, is an inner tension between what is, and what should be. That is, from our present disposition, we project some desirable goal into the future and then enter into the necessary activities to achieve such an end. The energy, motivating our actions, we call the will. Part of this energy is the tension which is created between where we are and where we want to be.

The potential within thought to project an ideal beyond itself, and its subsequent demand to reach this projected goal, is the essence of what we believe to be the will. Self-observation will show us that when there is any sense of willing, there is always thought demanding the fulfillment of a particular projected desire, goal or need. The energy which thought brings to the fulfillment of its projected goals is the energy we call 'will'. I can (and will) force myself only as far as I think I can (and will) force myself. All willful activity is thus created and sustained by thought.

The desire for power, success, domination, status, achievement, fame, and so on - all projections into the future - exists entirely within thought. Without thought there is no such psychologically based desire. And it is always the tension between the projected object of desire and our present condition in which the realization of the desire is still potentially possible, but not yet realized, that creates and determines the quality of 'will' we bring to our lives.

As long as we believe (think) it is possible to reach our goal, for so long will we find the 'will' to continue in our endeavor. There is no will outside of the determination within thought itself to continue along its chosen path. When, for some reason or another, it becomes clear to thought that it may no longer be necessary or desirous to pursue its projected object or goal, it loses the 'will' to continue.

Here we have not lost the 'will' for achieving our goal, we have only changed our minds about the viability, desirability, profitability or possibility for achieving the projected goal. And in direct proportion to this change of mind, we either lose or intensify the 'will' to continue. When thought is strong, 'will' is strong. When thought is weak, 'will' is weak. In truth there is only thought, not will.

This is an important insight because we often feel a great impulse towards the fulfillment of something we desire or believe we need. This impulse always first manifests as a thought. It gets evaluated within thought and, if successful in its presentation, becomes part of that toward which we strive or feel ourselves motivated. But to reach the goal we have set for ourselves, we also need to make use of other instruments within the body-mind.

To achieve its goal, thought stimulates the rest of the organism in many ways. Thought literally mobilizes the entire psychophysical being to respond to its demand for action. And this is possible because virtually all our ordinary psychophysical responses are under the influence of thought. Thought can mobilize the body into action by sending out signals that excite the nervous system, the hormones and the emotions. These in turn have profound effects on the physiology of our bodies. And although clearly thought motivated, this entire movement becomes part of what we believe to be volitional, willful activity.

However, this is a subtle process, and we are generally unaware that the energy (will) we bring to a challenge is generated entirely by an often uninspected, or unconscious, thought-projection. We just have a sense of rather blindly willing our way through a situation or towards some specific goal without knowing the exact reasons for doing so.

Westerners have placed great value on the power of the will. It is often seen as the measure of one's character and devotion to one's chosen path. We always marvel at the tenacity and 'will-power' of sports persons, business people, great leaders, adventurers and all those who set themselves extraordinary challenges that can only be achieved through tremendous will-power. Ordinary people like us often also push ourselves beyond the reasonable measure of our natural abilities. But, to a greater or lesser extent, all of us are victims of these uninspected thought-projections and the way they dominate and control our lives.

Once we start to notice that the activities on which we spend so much time and effort are energized by nothing other than the tension between a thought-projected goal and the effort to reach this goal, we will become more discerning and intelligent about how we participate in any act of 'will'. Where previously there was just a seemingly blind urge we mistook for the 'will' towards the fulfillment of our goals, we begin to wake up to the reality of our constant thought-created and thought-driven way of life.

A key element in this gradual awakening to the patterns of uninspected living is the discovery that there exists a natural and subtle space between the ongoing demands of thought on the one hand, and the corresponding responses these elicit in the psychophysical being on the other. If, through correct inner work, (see *Part Two: Working with Passive Awareness*) we become aware of the *unnecessary* connection between thought-projections and the responses to these within the psychophysical being, we enter a whole new field of human exploration. We begin to sense that we need not respond to every demand of thought as a matter of necessity.

By becoming sensitive to this space between the demands of thought and the reactions it elicits within the rest of our being, the hold which thought has over us begins to fragment and lose energy. This is an integral part of the path of self-awareness and self-transcendence. No freedom is possible while our psychophysical being is dominated and manipulated by the projections of thought, masquerading as volitional, willful activity.

This enquiry into the 'will' should thus be seen as integral to the processes of meditation and Contemplation which we will explore in *Part Two: The Practice*. The organism as a whole needs to be healed from the residual toxicity it has collected over years of responding to all the indiscriminate and fragmentary demands of willful thinking. These demands have greatly interfered with our natural functioning as a whole. *Our psychophysical being has become as fragmented and confused as thought itself.* This fragmentation is particularly evident when we consider how the natural equanimity of our emotions is disturbed and violated every time it is co-opted into the expectations created by the lure of uninspected willful thinking.

To mistake the forceful, uninspected movements of thought for a faculty of will is to believe there are two processes active within us: will and thought. In reality there is only one. Thought and will cannot functionally be separated. There is always only the content of our thought projections forcing its version of reality onto our lives and creating ever new destinies for us to strive towards and to get ourselves entangled in. Recognizing will for what it is, frees our attention, and therefore our energy, from remaining range-bound and contracted within the projections of thought.

Such recognition or revaluation brings about a natural reorientation to the way we relate to both ourselves and our world. When we realize that 'willing' is an aspect of thought, we no longer blindly follow the dictates of the 'will', but rather begin to think-feel our way into where we are going and how much time and effort would be appropriate to spend on the things towards which thought motivates us.

In this way we awaken to the possibility of real choice. Choice is only possible in an environment of freedom. And as long as we are energized by the blind dictates of the 'will', volitional activity loses its integrity and invariably deteriorates into mere reactivity or blind compulsive behavior. To be free from reactivity is to be free from that which necessitates reactivity. This requires careful observation and dedicated interest in how we function. No aspect of ourselves may be left out from such an enquiry. We are as much capable of standing in the fullness and freedom of our true human condition as we are of deluding ourselves and thereby obscuring the already existing truth and beauty of our humaneness.

That which is not transcended or eliminated through insight and clarity will continue to dramatize itself in our lives as forms of self-limitation and self-contraction.

Only when every aspect of us that is unintelligent, more than human, more than love and more than the singleness of our undivided natural condition, has fallen away by non-use, will the true measure of our humanity shine through by itself. At this point it will become evident that *life has its own regulating or ordering force*. Our challenge is to allow our entire psychophysical being to begin to resonate in harmony with this will of life as it presents itself to us in each living moment. There is only one true will that is not a consequence of thought, and that is the way things are.

Chapter Eleven

THREE FUNDAMENTAL STATES

The way of self-transcendence typically manifests three distinct stages of development that we are most likely to encounter along our path of self-observation, self-knowledge and self-transcendence. These demarcate three visions of reality, while at the same time serve as points of reference for the gradual unfolding of our insight into the nondual reality of life.

For practical purposes we could call these the states of 'what things are', 'that things are' and 'What Is'. These are not so much stages to be recognized along a continuum of progressive development, although this is often the case: rather, they may appear at any point along our path. It is, however, important and useful to know of their existence and to recognize them, both for how they manifest, and their value as pointers along the way. Although we may shift from one to the other during the course of a day, or even during one meditation practice, these are nevertheless three distinct states of being, each quite different from the other. We could also say that they represent three substantially different insights into our human condition, and therefore into our experience of life. And as much of our relationship with the world depends on our vision of things, will it be useful to consider how these states of awareness determine and influence our lives.

Our enquiry always starts from a position of knowledge. As we have seen, we generally live in and as the thought/attention-knot. This creates a condition of reality within which we could best describe ourselves as 'knowers'. We simply know 'what things are', and this field of the known becomes the point of departure for everything we do and participate in, and therefore also tends to form the basis for our initial enquiry into life, ourselves and the possibility of freedom from that which binds us.

In the state of 'that things are' we have moved from this world of the known into the clarity of a kind of non-conceptual, uninterpreted view, where things are seen in their suchness, devoid from all mental impositions, interpretations, evaluations, and all other forms of projection and transference. In other words, here we move to a state of relative clarity and direct, non-conceptual observation, where we look at things, not from within the field of the known, but rather from a pure-perception point of view. In this state we are merely concerned with the appearance of things as they are. Here we could say we have moved from 'what things are' (or our knowledge of things) to the more primary experience of 'that things are' or the mere sense of things prior to projection and transference.

In the third and final stage, our enquiry leads us into the non-dual reality of 'What Is'. Here we transcend the non-conceptual 'witness' disposition, where we observe things in their 'suchness', to allow for the feeling-sense of the non-dual reality of life.

But to acquaint ourselves better with these three concepts, let us consider them individually and in somewhat greater detail. As we have indicated, in themselves they represent three different , and rather important, stages in our development.

The first state of 'what things are' creates a condition of living where our world is nothing but a field of projected and transferred knowledge. This state is dominated and almost completely informed by thought. From within this field of the known we spend most of our energy trying to fulfill the demands of the ego, social pressures, conscious and unconscious motivations, and our psychological and emotional dramatizations.

It is also in this condition of knowledge where we learn what the world is all about and how to deal with the reality presented to us by our psychologically controlled and conceptually dominated social environment. Here we get to know ourselves as having certain strengths, weaknesses, emotional inconsistencies, problematic psychological material, a healthy or inadequate self-image, a socially agreeable personality or, perhaps, showing the symptoms of a problematic relationship with others. All of these form part of the known aspect of the condition of 'what things are'.

In this state we further have expectations of ourselves; project our successes and possible failures into the future; carry with us the memories of past emotional hurts; react, rather than act; get ourselves tied in knots over socially conditioned forms of moralistic, religious, ethical and lawful practices and generally believe that correct thinking will always produce appropriate responses to the challenges of life.

Our religions, being based on nothing but the imaginative ability of thought, are integrally part of the world of 'what things are'- even though we believe them to be of a revelatory, non-thought nature. Our philosophies are based on the logic of language and the skilful art of adding words upon words in such a way that they appear fresh and directly related to reality. But words, and the logic of word-use, are creations of thought. Our metaphysical speculations are also nothing but thought-creations and, together with religion and philosophy, could be seen as an integral part of this broad category of 'what things are'.

While we are entranced, fascinated, and also bewildered by the remarkable display of the creative and imaginative powers of thought, we generally remain totally unaware that there exists, in the midst of this dream, a reality of the simple suchness of things, and beyond that a wholeness which our remarkable instrument of thought, as a movement in itself, can never imagine, get in touch with, or in any way whatsoever, comprehend.

As our enquiry into this state of thought develops and we begin to sense the absoluteness of our bondage within this limited field of awareness, we may ask ourselves whether this state truly represents our total human potential. Becoming aware of the tremendous isolation, separateness, alienation and suffering contained within this limited thought-version of reality, some of us may wake up to the possibility that this world of the known cannot solve the problems it has created for itself. Nothing that this thought-world can present as remedies or counter-strategies to the dream-reality of its own projections can bring us respite from the consequences inherent in this world of 'what things are'.

And when this crisis matures and becomes really acute, and we are forced by the circumstance of our own distress and suffering to look deeply into the nature and function of what may be at the root of our discontent, we may realize that the entire play between us as knowers and that which is 'known' is merely a reflection or duplication in thought of a world of experience that exists *prior* to it.

Gradually we develop the sense that things exist in themselves before they get interpreted, categorized and nuanced by the projective and transferring ability of thought. And this insight marks the beginning of a new potential for relating to both ourselves and our world. It becomes evident that there may be a more direct way of interacting with present experience where we allow things to speak for themselves and to re-introduce themselves to our understanding as they exist prior to interpretation, contextualization and naming. We could also say that here we begin to relate to things as they exist *before* thought, or in their suchness.

This enquiry establishes in us the ability to perceive things without the necessary interference of thought. Through this we learn to distinguish between subjectivity and objectivity. We begin to sense a clear distinction between the world as projected and interpreted reality, and how it appears when perceived as it is, prior to the filtering activities of thought. Here we have moved from the thought-state of 'what things are' into the simple, observational and experiential disposition of 'that things are'.

This is a significant step forward along our path of self-enquiry and inner clarity. Whereas our world was previously dominated and controlled by the single thought-state of 'what things are' it now gradually reveals itself as having a prior, more fundamental existence. While we are exclusively focused in the world of 'what things are' we are out of touch with the suchness of things where we engage with our field of experience in a much more direct, objective and clear way. We begin to see things as they are, and learn to recognize the limitations inherent in the exclusive state of knowledge.

Spirituality Without God

It is not that we develop a negative attitude towards the importance of knowing 'what things are', or attempt to live without thought. What the movement into the state of 'that things are' brings to our notice is that here we establish different relationships with certain aspects of our experience which otherwise would have taken on just the single color of thought-interpreted reality.

This is particularly evident in the more subtle experiences of our interaction with one another. In the openness that allows for seeing things in their suchness, we develop the ability to see others in a more realistic light, and not as we think they are, or project them to be. By being completely open to others, our emotional responses to them change, because we begin to see a very different person. Whereas previously we only looked at our own projections, we now see the other as he or she really is.

Moving from the state of 'what things are' into the state of 'that things are' is part of a conscious process whereby we observe our own inner functioning that enables us to utilize that which is useful, and to leave behind those forms of doing which create confusion and distress. This aspect of our enquiry is dealt with in detail in *Part Two: The Practice*. There we discover forms of practice which consciously enable us to relax out of the contracted state of the world of knowledge, into the simplicity of non-conceptual perception whereby we free ourselves from the apparent necessity of having to translate everything into the known.

This practice of non-conceptual perception opens us up to a new kind of experience where we become sensitive to mere sensations and where we progressively feel ourselves more at ease to let things be when it is not necessary to translate an experience into knowledge.

And because the practice of perception prior to thought enables us to stand free and open-hearted in relation to what we experience, paradoxically, this also allows thought to make more practical and realistic sense of things when it has to interpret our world. In this way thought becomes a useful and necessary instrument of the body and is allowed to function in its own natural way without us becoming completely absorbed in its projections. We assume a kind of witness position from

Part One: The View

where we observe things in a passive, yet very alert way, without the unnecessary, habitual interference of thought.

It is important that we appreciate that these two states function in a *mutually exclusive* way. From the perspective of the state of 'what things are' we have no sense of the suchness of things. Experientially the one excludes the other, despite the fact that things are always present in their suchness, even while we are absorbed in our state of exclusive knowledge. While our field of experience is dominated by thought and knowledge, we are totally unaware of the existence of things in their suchness: only our thought-world exists

For instance, when thought projects certain qualities onto someone we meet while we are absorbed in the world of 'what things are', we will undoubtedly experience and react to the other as though these qualities were in reality present in that person. However, the person we believe we are looking at, and experiencing as having these qualities, may not possess any of the attributes we believe we are experiencing in them. What we believe we notice in the other are often nothing but aspects of our own creative thought-projections, transferred onto the person in front of us.

Should we, however, open ourselves to the more direct, non-conceptual experience of the other person, we will notice how the projected view starts to fade. It is almost as though an entirely new person steps forward from the fog of our concepts or projected 'reality' of them.

What is also interesting to observe during this movement into the witness state of 'that things are' is how this broader vision transcends the lesser state of 'what things are'. The state of 'what things are' is clearly based on a rather limited aspect of our human potential: the limited intelligence associated with the operations of projection and transference. When we move into the field of clear perception, and start to see things as they are, we open ourselves to the possibility of relating to things in a much more realistic and intelligent way. And part of the function of this Intelligence is to see into the nature and limitations of the previous state. By simplifying our perception of things we have also simplified our world, and in this simplicity we notice the functioning of an inner Intelligence which transcends our ordinary conditional way of looking at things.

If we now consider the even more subtle state of 'What Is', we will again notice a clear shift from the previous state of 'that things are' into the state of 'What Is'. During our practice and experimentation with these states (See: *Part Two : The Practice of Passive Awareness*) one of the clear insights that comes to us during the state of 'that things are' is that any sense of relationship is still based on a subtle, but very marked feeling of separation from our field of experience. Even a relationship of non-interpreted perception has therefore still the sense of the observer as distinct from that which is observed. The witness is still experienced as separate from the person or thing it sees in their suchness.

So, whereas the state of 'what things are' (the state of knowledge) is evidenced by the *outward* projection of thought onto things, thereby creating a reality imagined and sustained by thought, the state of 'that things are' still shows an *inward* projection of the 'I'-thought.'

What distinguishes the witness position from the condition of 'What Is', is evidenced by the fact that in the state of 'What Is' there is neither inward nor outward projection which fragments our field of experience. Neither is it created and sustained by thought and attention. As we have seen, thought fragments outwardly by creating the world of the known, and inwardly by creating the world of the witness or the separate observer. Clearly, both are created and sustained in their respective realities by the projective and transferring power of thought, held in place by the unconscious focus of attention. The condition of 'What Is' exists *prior* to both these forms of fragmentation. Although wholeness or 'What Is' is always the present, living reality of everything that arises, it is seldom given the space to reveal itself because it gets obscured by the domination of thought and attention over our entire field of experience.

So, whereas the first stage is completely created and sustained by thought, and the second stage of the witness is still greatly influenced by the inner projection of the 'I'-thought, the condition of 'What Is' owes its existence to nothing but the reality of non-dual experience itself. It exists neither exclusively *as* thought, nor because it is presumably observed by an inner witness. There is nothing truly 'out there' for us to observe as categorically separate from ourselves. The observed and the presumed observer is one undivided process. As we have seen, things exist because we *are*. Nothing can therefore be divorced from our human condition. Our arising is part of the arising of everything else and no clear distinction can be made between us as the presumed observers, and the world we falsely experience as objective to us. Consciousness and the content of consciousness is one unitary process and could be described as 'What Is' or the wholeness of Being.

All present arising has a sense of awareness as an inherent aspect of itself. We always have the sense of being aware. And as our enquiry into the practice of non-dual experience deepens, it will become our living experience that awareness and the appearance of things are a joint-phenomenon. Our awareness of things and the content of our awareness cannot experientially be separated into two distinct categories. The apparent distinction between appearance, on the one hand, and the notion of the observer on the other, is a failure on our part to distinguish between that which is created and sustained by thought, and that which is not.

The world of 'What Is' transcends the reality of 'that things are', not by negating the suchness of things, but rather by leaving behind the *one who believed it was observing things in their suchness.* In this way duality is transcended and wholeness becomes self-evident. Again we see how the more comprehensive condition both includes and excludes useful and useless aspects of the previous, more limited stage. What is seen to be useless and unnecessary simply falls away by non-use in the light of the more subtle Intelligence that functions in the condition of 'What Is'.

One sign of this new Intelligence is not only what it *does*, and can do, but perhaps even more importantly, how it *prevents us from doing things which complicate our lives* and destroys our equanimity. The Intelligence active in the state of 'What Is' works both actively and passively, and knows when to apply itself appropriately in either way.

Not being centered in the content of thought alone, the state of 'What Is' is free to evaluate things in the light of its unconditioned Intelligence. Having left behind the separate self-sense as part of the compulsive, habitual domination of thought over our total field of experience, we are left free to live from the totality of our human potential. In the condition of 'What Is' there is no urgency to fulfill the demands of the ego, the 'I'-conscious state, the psychological being, the conditioned intimations from the mind or the dramatizations of our emotional shadow material.

Wholeness allows us to feel freely, think freely, enjoy the world of sensation, love and human relationships and to come to rest in our own full humanity without the need either to be something else or somewhere else. *As we are* reveals itself to be a disposition in which things have settled into their own simplicity and quiet beauty. There is nothing holy, mystical or esoteric about this. It is simply to be fully human.

To this nothing can be, or need to be, added. The condition of 'What Is' reveals itself to be the fulfillment of human life, a fulfillment that no longer creates destiny because in its simplicity it does not allow for the fragmentary elaborations and complications which the dualistic 'I'-conscious state necessitates. All the instruments that have been the authors of our distorted, destiny-creating vision remain fully functional, but in the state of 'What Is' they are informed by an Intelligence that allows them to function in a coherent, non-fragmented and holistic way.

Whereas before we have allowed thought, attention and emotion to work in an uninspected, random, undisciplined and uninformed manner, they now operate in the context of, and are fully informed by, our deeper Intelligence which, together with compassion, expresses itself as an integral component of undivided human living.

Chapter Twelve

SPIRITUALITY, SCIENCE AND ART

Many of the great realizers are born with a delicate gift to be transparent vehicles for non-dual reality to shine through them with little or no obstruction. As instruments, their psychophysical being offers little resistance to this artful expression of life. However, for those of us not as gifted in this way, dedicated practice may be necessary to allow for the gradual unfolding and realization of the non-dual truth of life.

Truth, like most forms of artistic potential requires the right conditions to manifest and to become our living reality. Without being given the right conditions, neither expressive art nor artful living can flower. Yet, it is not only art which requires specific conditions for its expression: science shares with art a demand for structure and order before it will reveal its secrets to the enquiring mind. Although we have tended to divide the arts and sciences into two apparently distinct disciplines, they nevertheless have in common this one underlying demand: they both require exact and very specific conditions in which to reach their full potential as forms of human investigation and expression. The art of living is as much based on clear observation, dedication to minute detail and recognition of the subtle order of manifest existence, as any scientific enquiry demands in its quest for a deep understanding of things.

One of the great enduring problems scientific enquiry has to solve is to create instruments subtle enough to track as far as possible the detailed discoveries made through the use of mathematics. It seems not unreasonable to suggest that in the

Spirituality Without God

final analysis no instrument could ever be devised capable of measuring or registering the subtle realities which the scientific mind investigates without becoming itself part of the experiment, and therefore of the results it produces. Here we notice how the instrument that is used to reveal, verify and express the scientific enquiry could become an obstruction to the enquiry itself.

This is the exact dilemma for the spiritual enquirer. We do not use objective instruments of measure to monitor our progress along our own humanizing process. Neither can we develop mathematical equations and hypothesis which may accurately predict the happenings of things not yet seen or experienced. We just have the subtlety of our own inner world and the sensitivity of our psychophysical being as a whole to measure, and to stand witness, to which extent we have aligned ourselves to the natural order of things. No-one, and nothing outside of our own intelligent inner measure, can inform us about this.

The most fundamental problem that spiritual, or self-transcending, enquiry therefore faces, would be much the same as we find in science. But whereas the scientist could legitimately, at least up to a point, proceed with the apparent objectification of their scientific investigations, the spiritual enquiry is both objective and subjective right from the start. We can never divorce the instruments of spiritual enquiry from the enquiry itself, because the enquiry always takes place in the context of our psychophysical being. We are always both the enquirer and the object of enquiry.

The *total* condition of our unenlightened psychophysical state is therefore the focus of our self-enquiry and self-understanding. Our entire being is the path we have to travel. There is no path outside of our own psychophysical condition. *Yet, it is through this very same instrument that the enlightened condition of non-dual reality will gradually manifest and integrate itself consciously into our lives.* In other words, it is the same instrument which in the unenlightened state measures and reflects the pain of separation and alienation that will also be reflecting and manifesting the non-dual condition of life.

Part One: The View

If, through the agency of our own body/mind we were to allow for the expression of the art of non-dualistic living, we would need to prepare the instrument as a whole and monitor its sensitivity on an ongoing basis. Not to do so would result in the instrument itself becoming an obstruction to the gradual manifestation of our clarity. Artistic expression is fundamentally a struggle between the artistic impulse and the medium and instrument through which it has to manifest. The artist is as much part of the medium of expression as are their instruments, i.e. paint, brushes, techniques, musicality, knowledge, ability, logic, writing skills, sculpting tools, marble, and so on. These all offer necessary resistances to the artistic impulse until the artist has learnt to use them in complete resonance with the demands for expression of this impulse.

Only then can the artwork become a flawless manifestation or representation of its original insight. And where this harmony and inner resonance are lacking, we inevitably find mediocre art. Similarly, great art comes about when a great impulse meets no or little resistance from the medium through which it has to manifest.

The impulse needs to become form. Before form there is only non-manifested impulse. Artistic impulse is therefore always only *potential and non-existent* until it takes on form via our human agency. In terms of life and living we could say that prior to our confusion there exists, also as *unmanifested potential,* inherent clarity, beauty and Intelligence within us. Until we allow this Intelligence to express itself as our living reality, only our confusion will be evident in all we do, *while the clarity of our deeper Being remains enfolded as mere potential.*

The path of self-transcendence is therefore nothing but a sensitization of the body-mind to make it available to the subtle impulses of artful and humane living. From this it may be clear that the path concerns itself in a most fundamental way with the removal of that which obscures the expression of our non-dual condition. This discipline of removing and transcending that which obscures or inhibits the unfolding of our true nature is no different to the way we work within the limited context of artistic unfolding. However talented they might be, artists with little skill will produce mediocre art. *The artistic impulse cannot be forced through an unprepared instrument.* For the artistic impulse to reach its full and abiding expression, the instrument has to be sufficiently sensitized and prepared.

Similarly, any gesture on our part, from within our state of confusion and disorder, toward that which is unconditional, non-dual, compassionate and intelligent, would lack the integrity to allow for the revelation of these. In fact, such forceful activity would remain an integral component of fragmentation and limitation. We simply cannot move from confusion to clarity without observing, understanding and transcending the nature and limitations of our present uninspected condition. Not to prepare the instrument in order for it to allow for the complete manifestation of the art of living would mean that we endeavor to come upon order and wholeness by using the instruments of confusion and fragmentation. This would be counter-productive and ultimately futile. Once we discover what it is that fragments our vision, we may begin to work with less resistance and fear in full resonance with our gradually unfolding clarity and inner Intelligence.

Through this, the raw impulse of our non-dual potential will begin to take on the *form of human existence*. It is only when we allow for the manifestation of our deep, human qualities that the artful process of non-dual revelation has fulfilled itself. At this point the original self-transcending impulse and its expression as non-dual reality present themselves as one undivided, non-fragmented movement of wholeness.

And only then will our lives take on the artistic form of humane and holistic living which has always been there as our inherent *enfolded potential*, but which had effectively been obscured by our inability to allow for its complete expression.

PART TWO

THE PRACTICE

Introduction

In *Part One* we enquired into some of the most important aspects for understanding the overall background and principles of the way of self-transcendence. This work of think-feeling our way into that which limits our potential and inhibits our free participation in the undivided presence of the living moment must of necessity precede any serious practical enquiry into formal, self-transcending practices.

This does not imply that it is of no value to engage in contemplative work or to begin to feel our way into our own inner silence through meditation before we have mentally grasped all the facts surrounding our limited self-state. We may freely participate in our own inner silence. It can only be helpful.

We will discover, though, that practice, not born from an understanding and appreciation of our own fragmented, separated and alienated human situation, will lack the integrity, direction and coherency necessary for dealing effectively with the embedded mental, emotional and psychological problems associated with our dualistic way of life. Also, as our practice develops, we will realize the importance of having a clear grasp of wholeness as something inherent to human existence. This will prevent us from seeking for the unity of life in metaphysical, Other Worldly projections of mind.

Such understanding, although not yet fully founded in experience, nevertheless already contains within it the seeds of insight and clarity. When we approach ourselves with deep interest and a dedicated heart, we soon gain a new understanding of both ourselves and our world which gradually aligns our thinking with reality. This shift is of vital importance as it facilitates an ever-diminishing mental and emotional resistance to the unfolding of the non-dual experience. And as our practice begins to inform the way we think about ourselves and life in general, we will realize the importance of the preliminary work of clearly understanding the many aspects of our self-contracted state.

A mind entirely absorbed in, and convinced of the validity of its own dualistic vision, has great difficulty to concede to the intimations of the non-dual nature of things. But if we have done our preliminary work well, and have developed a sufficiently open-minded disposition to all aspects of what we believe we and our world are, our mind will be considerably more agreeable to accommodate the gradual unfolding of the undivided nature of things. Through this, one of the most deeply rooted obstacles to self-transcendence becomes transparent and gradually falls away by non-use.

Practice, as well as a sound understanding of our own situation, can therefore not be divided into two categorically separate components. Rather, we need to appreciate the importance of getting a clear understanding of the terrain in which the specific work of contemplation, meditation, insight and self-transcendence will operate.

We cannot, for instance, believe in a God in heaven, and expect such a belief to be verified by the intimations of the non-dual. At some point our enquiry and insight will come to an impasse where we will find it difficult to proceed along our path of self-transcendence unless we let go of the dualistic notion of a God as some Thing or State categorically separate from us.

Had we, however, allowed our understanding to find its measure in the view of ourselves as inherently non-separate from our entire field of experience, and became sensitive to the fact that our work is always directed towards the removal of that which obscures this experienceable, non-dual truth, little or no resistance would come from the mind when our practice begins to reveal this truth. Correct understanding facilitates the movement from our dualistic vision to the direct experience of non-dual Being. And it does this not in an aggressive manner by attempting to push intellectually into the 'beyond', but rather to approach our unfolding passively by not offering resistance to that which will be new and challenging to the mind's conditioned ways of dualistic thinking and feeling.

Part Two: The Practice

Having said this, it is nevertheless important for us to appreciate that all forms of understanding and insight, however subtle and penetrating, are always only pointers. Understanding cannot translate itself into Being, because it cannot go beyond itself. The instrument, thought, which facilitates mental understanding is not the instrument through which the revelation of the non-dual can become evident. Non-duality does not have its reality within any aspect of thought. It reveals itself as a *living experience* and not as a result of any thought process.

However, it is also important to appreciate that when we start our journey, we have often only the light of our intellectual grasp of things to depend on. Understanding ourselves and our world is an important aspect of our path. At this early stage our deeper Intelligence and ability for insight and inner clarity have not yet become the functional instruments of our ordinary interaction with life. A delicate balance will thus have to be maintained between thought and understanding on the one hand, and the gradual transcendence of these processes, on the other, to reveal the living reality towards which they point. This will ensure that we do not remain trapped in understanding alone without replacing such understanding with living truth.

Our path is to allow for a gradual shift from understanding and insight to the direct experience of the non-dual. To use a Zen metaphor: we should not mistake the finger pointing to the moon for the moon itself. Thought can only point beyond itself, it cannot transcend itself. Understanding, however subtle and true, is not yet truth: it has to be transcended through appropriate forms of practice for wholeness to be revealed.

If we do not allow for this gradual shift from understanding and insight to the direct experiential truth of non-duality, we will remain vulnerable to merely modifying our behavior in the light of our intellectual understanding. This outward gesture may give us the feeling that things have fundamentally changed for us, yet the deep emotional/psychological tendencies, as well as our mental conditioned responses, will not have been removed.

Spirituality Without God

Used correctly and in its appropriate measure, knowledge, and the understanding that functions around knowledge, is an extremely useful and necessary instrument for survival. However, mistaken for the things it points to, thought becomes the great slayer of truth, as it will finally form an impenetrable barrier to the experience of the non-dual.

Practice is what we do to get ourselves out of the grip of the illusion of duality created by thought and to wake us up from the dream of mistaking thought-projections for reality. It is also to free us from the binding emotional/psychological tendencies which are deeply embedded in our psyche.

During the inner work suggested in *Part Two* we discover ways of relating to our inner lives which allow us to see things clearly and in an unbiased and open-minded way. Only when we present our deeper and more comprehensive Intelligence with clear facts of how we tie ourselves into knots, and thereby create all the forms of self-limitation we suffer, can this Intelligence begin to do its work of recognizing these for what they are and gradually relieve us from the illusions they create for us.

As our practice develops, we will notice how our path always leads from fragmentation and separation to greater integrity and wholeness. Once we have understood that the fragmented state cannot move beyond itself into the wholeness of life, it will also be clear that our path is not a search for truth by the separate self-sense. *Rather, the path is a thorough investigation into that which obscures truth.* Such an investigation, of necessity, will include deep, experiential enquiry into the nature of all aspects of fragmented living, including the presumption of self. By bringing our full awareness to such an enquiry, we will learn not only to allow for the gradual relaxation of all forms of contraction which support and apparently legitimize our dualistic vision, we will also gradually awaken to the truth of our non-separation from every aspect of life.

The argument which supports this form of enquiry rests on a single observable fact: once every vestige of presumed fragmentation has been left behind, Advaita or non-duality, which is most true of human life, will simply be self-evident.

Part Two: The Practice

We cannot positively seek the non-dual, because the very instrument with which we seek will ultimately prove itself to be part of the fragmentary process. This will become clear as our enquiry unfolds. Only thought can seek and find. Thought can therefore only seek and discover that which is an aspect of itself. And reality, as non-dual, present arising, is not of the nature of that which can be sought and found.

And as our enquiry into non-dual experience deepens, it will be evident that only the *path* is within. It is here where all our mental and emotional blockages dramatize themselves as series of resistances to integral living. It is also here where our work lies. *It is the 'I', as the most pivotal support of the illusion of fragmentation and duality that is within, not the non-dual truth of life.* Non-duality is neither exclusively within, nor without. The true non-dual is a manifestation of our entire field of present experience as it unfolds from moment to moment. Truth or 'What Is' is simply that which remains when the presumed dividing principle between inner and outer; me and not-me; observer and the observed, has been completely transcended.

When the practice of self-observation has sufficiently simplified our inner complexities, we will begin to sense a new possibility of practice that no longer concerns itself with observing the detailed functioning of our inner world, or the way thought and attention bind us into self-limitation. Rather we come to rest in the practice of Direct Awareness (See: *The Practice of Direct Awareness*), which could only be described as no-effort or non-doing. Here we move into a greater sense of awareness, where the division between me as the 'observer', and the content of my inner and outer world, as the 'observed', gradually melts away. We learn how to allow both ourselves and our world to remain untouched as non-dual reality with no attempt to move away from the feeling-sense of our present experience.

But for these subtle forms of practice to become our possibility, we need to do much preliminary work. It is not possible to jump in at the deep end in the hope to achieve a sustainable, integrated life, instantly. We are indeed already fully human, but only as *potential* or partial revelation. During the early stages of our practice we are still immensely complex and this obscures the simplicity of our natural condition.

Preliminary work is therefore self-simplifying work. And this is a gradual and arduous task that cannot be accomplished overnight. If we attempt to go too far before we have the proper instruments in place to deal effectively and comprehensively with our inner disorder, we will soon discover that we have not moved at all. Rather, it will become evident that we have merely imagined that we have done so, and thereby created yet another illusion to be observed, recognized and transcended.

One of the most rewarding aspects of our involvement in this way of life is that we always have our living reality as a measure of how real and effective our participation in this process is. Life itself is always the final arbiter. We may still delude ourselves into believing that through having attained high and subtle states of bliss and unity-consciousness during our formal meditative practices we might have reached the 'other shore'. We somehow remember these states and begin to feel secure in the *knowledge* that things have changed for us. But such a memory of any inner state or experience is as dead as any memory of yesterday.

This is when life mercifully intervenes and wakes us again out of the dream of knowledge, certainty and our sense of achievement. The self-delusion is shattered by our inability to integrate the insights, experiences and inner shifts which we have experienced during our practice into the rest of our lives. We again realize that the path will only have fulfilled itself when we sense an ongoing emotional equanimity that is continuously sustained by the living reality of the undivided nature of existence.

When life itself becomes our disposition, no delusion is possible. At this point of our enquiry there remains nothing to remember and nothing to seek. The reality of the living, non-dual truth of Being is perfectly, and self-evidently, sufficient unto itself.

Chapter Thirteen

THE PRACTICE OF PASSIVE AWARENESS

1) General Introduction

Much of what we enquired into in *Part One* centered on gaining insight into the whole field of separative living based on the notion of the separate self-sense. We saw how this most fundamental component of our dualistic vision distorts, conditions and restricts our creative and joyful interaction with others and life in general. What also became apparent was the subtle complexity of this presumed inner structure. The 'I' is not just a single thought that keeps reminding us of our feeling-sense of separateness, isolation and alienation. Rather, we realized that it is founded as much in our thinking, as it is reflected as emotional disturbance, psychological reactivities, mental conditioning, memory, physical and physiological defense-patterns, relational dysfunctioning and wider social disorder.

The separate self-sense could thus be seen as a total *condition of living* that affects and controls our entire field of experience, both inner and outer. This results in a complexity of psychophysical disturbances *which have to be considered individually, and worked with in different ways*, if we are to free ourselves from the consequences these have on our being.

For instance, we would not enquire into an aspect of thought, such as projection or transference, in the same way as we would when we work with some emotional disturbance. We would approach these differently so that we may understand how each functions individually in the way they create inner conflict and disorder.

It would be equally inappropriate to work with our conditioned, mental responses in the same way as when, for instance, we attempt to hold attention stable in a specific form of meditative practice. Likewise, we cannot introduce the advanced and subtle forms of effortless practice (see: Chapter 14, *The Practice of Direct Awareness*) before we have sufficiently quieted down the instruments we will be working with in such a relaxed manner. Each aspect of our contracted state, as well as each stage of development along the path, requires a different and appropriate approach.

Although we may have a sound intellectual understanding of the deeper aspects of the path, or a clear mental grasp of the liberated state of non-duality, each step requires its own form of practice to complement, inform, and ultimately to reveal the living truth behind mere description and understanding. While we are immersed in the relative world of our dualistic and confused sense of things, we have to employ *relative* methods of practice that could address these *relative* conditions. The same holds true when we start to work on the subtle aspects of self-transcendence. Here more direct methods of *effortless* practice will have to be engaged to facilitate the unfolding of our non-dual disposition.

As much as it would be counter-productive to engage in advanced meditative practices without proper preparation, likewise we cannot expect to work successfully with our deeply-rooted emotional disturbances before we have sufficiently stabilized the inner instruments with which to approach these rather disturbing aspects within ourselves.

And as little as we can bypass our psychological complexities in our quest for sustainable mental freedom and emotional equanimity, equally we can not bypass the important initial, meditative work which will lay the foundation for all future enquiries into ourselves, whether self-transcending or psychological/emotional. The practice of Passive Awareness as suggested in this chapter is ideally suited to this purpose.

Part Two: The Practice

Any injudicious attempts to marginalize these earlier preliminary practices would only perpetuate the many forms of self-delusion we are trying to free ourselves from. This could result in disappointment and a sense of disempowerment, because we are unlikely to succeed with any advanced work, in any sustainable manner, unless we have laid the proper foundations early on during our enquiry.

The importance of approaching our path with thoroughness and care can therefore not be overestimated. We should always keep in mind that all self-enquiry has to reflect our *actual present situation*. We have to work from where we *are* and allow our practice to unfold and develop from there. *We cannot bypass ourselves.* As we have seen, we *are* the path we will have to walk, and this path will be effective and freeing to the degree that we do not ignore what is real and true about ourselves. To bring such integrity to our work may not be easy. Yet, we have no choice. Anything less will be a perpetuation of our deluded state.

To come to any inner clarity, we need to enquire into the instruments we use which keep our bondage in place. Much of our initial work will therefore concern itself with discovering how we use our potential in inappropriate ways which create and maintain our reactivities and inner turmoil. In time we will gradually find our measure and develop practices that will relieve us in a sustainable way from all unnecessary functioning. This is why we have to be very clear about the specific areas of investigation we wish to address at every stage of our practice. Only then will our practice be based on our present reality and could it serve our enquiry in a useful, realistic and freeing way.

Part of this reality is how we understand our path. Once we have established that the movement is always from *fragmentation to wholeness,* everything we do should be in the service of this insight. And for any practice to have real transformative potential, it needs to be guided and informed by our own participatory Intelligence and clarity. We cannot grow in the light and wisdom of another, however well meaning such advice might be. Others may point the way, but each of us will have to walk the path of self-enquiry, self-knowledge and self-transcendence by ourselves. In this way our path will always reflect our real situation and will it not be based on some idealistic, unrelated vision of where we believe we aught to be going according to the dictates of another.

So, before we start our enquiry into the initial work of Passive Awareness, it may be useful to remind ourselves that the most primary form of fragmentation this practice needs to address is the thought/attention-knot. This unconscious state of contracted being is the foundation for all other forms of fragmentary manifestation, including the separate self-sense. The illusions created by this state obscure the undivided, holistic nature of things. This is why we should thoroughly investigate this inner movement of self-limitation. We cannot specialize in one aspect of our being, i.e. the condition of presumed reality created by the thought-attention knot, yet expect to have the demands of our total humanity fulfilled. For this we need not only to enquire deeply into all aspects of fragmentation, but also find appropriate means through which to facilitate the unfolding of the wholeness of life.

As we have seen, we need to engage our practice at the level of the problem. Once we have identified the thought/attention-knot as the area that most critically requires our initial attention, we could develop methods of practice that directly address this distorting element within ourselves. When we begin to observe and experience the problems associated with this unnecessary inner function, will we discover that it is perfectly possible, and well within our potential, to relieve ourselves from its consequences. We are not destined to live with the suffering we create for ourselves as a consequence of the self-serving activities of the ego/I. Unless of course we determine it to be so by choosing to remain unconscious of what we do.

And one way of waking up from the relative slumber of the 'I'-conscious state is to become inwardly sensitive and perceptive to how the *processes which facilitate* our inner confusion and misapprehension operate. We may understand and appreciate the existence of these processes as description. But if we really want to free ourselves from their debilitating consequences, such understanding has to become our living reality, and this is possible only if we actually enter into the work of observing and experiencing our inner lives.

The thought/attention-knot is not merely another interesting form of self-knowledge. Neither should it become just one more conclusion we have reached, based on a clear grasp of its description. It is a *process*, and will reveal its full significance to us only if we enter with a keen perceptual interest into its functioning. Under scrutiny from our inner clarity, the unconscious nature of this debilitating activity will reveal itself to us. At this point during our practice, we will begin to realize the profound significance of the illusory nature of what we have come to regard as the presumed reality of the separate self-sense.

Our path is a movement from unconsciousness to consciousness; from unawareness to awareness; from the presumption of fragmentation to wholeness. We will observe this fundamental inner shift reflected in all self-transcending work. Our work is to make the unconscious conscious, not only as *content*, but as *function*.

The most basic task of our initial involvement with meditation will thus centre on the development of our ability to become and remain conscious, without falling back into the dream of the thought/attention-knot. In the process we will have to stabilize attention, because bringing stability to the random movements of attention prevents it from leading awareness astray. We have seen how attention, as the focusing mechanism of awareness, plays a crucial part in what we become aware of. In our uninspected, preconscious state of the thought/attention dream, attention dominates awareness.

Where attention goes, awareness goes. However, if attention could be *observed and experienced* as it habitually, and unconsciously, associates itself with thought, it will become our own living experience how this tendency restricts our participation in life. And as our enquiry into this life-determining and destiny-creating habit of attention deepens, we may realize the tremendous importance of taking conscious responsibility for its movements.

Without developing this ability into a delicate, disciplined and conscious art, we will always remain vulnerable to the random and habitual movements of attention into thought. Accepting responsibility for the functioning of attention could be seen as the most crucial aspect of our path, not only initially, but especially during the subtle practices of Contemplation and Direct Awareness.

Only when we have managed to stabilize attention appreciably, can we enter into these more refined practices. Stabilized attention will further prove itself indispensable during all future meditative and contemplative work with regard to our psychological and emotional reactivities. Self-discovery is only possible in a quiet and relaxed inner environment.

In the work that follows, we will become sensitive to how the practice of Passive Awareness stabilizes attention. When attention is stable, thought settles down by itself. From there we may proceed with the more subtle aspects of our work from a disposition of clarity and confidence.

2) Beginning the practice of Passive Awareness

Almost all contemplative traditions have suggested that in order to quiet the mind, we need to learn how to keep attention stable on some predetermined object of meditation. By this is understood that we may take a single bodily sensation, a thought, an emotion or a sense object for our object of focus, and simply attempt to hold attention focused on it for some time. In this way we not only interfere with the habitual tendency of attention to associate itself unconsciously with the ever-changing contents of thought: even more importantly, we also create a measure of stillness against which the habitual movements of thought and attention may be noticed. If we become aware that our attention has slipped into its habit of becoming associated with some aspect of thought, we gently bring it back to its chosen object, and again allow it to remain there for as long as possible.

By this we endeavor to gain control over the random and habitual movements of attention, while at the same time develop our ability to become aware of a process which has been happening unconsciously within all of us for most of our lives. During this exercise thought settles down considerably

Part Two: The Practice

while we notice a measurable reduction in its projections of storylines and other unnecessary images.

However, when we attempt to put these rather simple instructions to work, we may discover that in practice they are not so easy to achieve. The human mind, as the thought/attention-knot, has been dominating our consciousness ever since we arrived on the planet. In our lifetime alone this process has been playing havoc with our psychophysical being, even from a very early age. The patterns of unconscious association of attention with thought have become deeply rooted in us. All we *know* is the content of thought. And all we *are*, while unconsciously identified with this content, is this ongoing stream of thought-projections with their debilitating and overpowering effects on our emotions. We will therefore have to bring considerable patience and real interest to our work if we want to succeed in this process of consciously stabilizing attention.

It is important, though, to be clear about the nature of our involvement with this exercise. Although we generally suffer and enjoy the content of the thought/attention-knot, our current enquiry is *not primarily to free ourselves from any specific projection of thought,* or the feeling-content of any emotional disturbance. The early practice of Passive Awareness at this level is mainly directed at *becoming conscious of the unconscious movements of attention.*

The two main secondary effects of this practice are the quieting of the thought-stream and clarity of perception when thought-projections no longer cloud our vision. But the primary emphasis of this early practice should be the *conscious stabilization of attention* so that we may become sensitive to, and responsible for, its habitual and unconscious movements. Only then will we be in a position to observe for ourselves how the thought/attention-knot dominates our field of awareness.

The reason why this particular form of passive, yet conscious, awareness is so effective is that it forms a background of conscious non-movement against which the movements of attention could be noticed. As we have seen, attention serves as the focusing mechanism for awareness. It focuses on areas within our field of experience to facilitate more detailed investigation. However, through unawareness, we have allowed attention to roam around inwardly in a random, habitual and rather chaotic manner. This is why it is of critical importance to counter this unconscious tendency of attention through the practice of Passive Awareness.

As we need to gain conscious control over the movements of attention, our first objective would be to become aware of these. We achieve this by trying to keep attention stable on a predetermined object. We simply choose an object for attention to focus on. This may be an inner bodily sensation, such as the breath; a specifically chosen word; the darkness in our heads when we close our eyes; some bodily part such as the hands or abdomen; the feel of the air as it passes through our nostrils and so on. *The object is not important.* The significance of this exercise is to learn how to stabilize attention by using a specific object for it to focus on.

Once we have decided on our chosen object, we can proceed with our practice. We get into a comfortable position, and simply allow ourselves to feel a soft restfulness coming over us. It is not useful to enter forcefully into any practice. If we find that we are too anxious, or perhaps agitated, to sit quietly, it may be better not to proceed with the exercise and rather to wait a while until we feel more relaxed and openhearted. In this way our practice will become part of our own relaxedness and not be turned into a willful, ego-proving battle each time we sit for meditation.

When we have found our measure, and allow attention to settle on its chosen object, it will immediately become apparent how difficult it is to bring stability to the wanderings of both thought and attention. The reason for this is that attention is so *habitual* in its movements, and *especially in its association with the projections of thought,* that it imperceptibly moves into thought from where it randomly identifies with its ever-changing content, totally oblivious of its given task to remain with its chosen object. Here we have a clear experience of the unconscious and uncontrolled movement of attention in its association with thought.

Often some minutes may pass before we become aware of what has been happening to us. This means that during that period we were *unconscious* of what we were doing, while we

Part Two: The Practice

were totally absorbed in the content of our thinking. Instead of merely holding our attentive awareness stable on our chosen object, attention has done to our object exactly what it has been doing to our total field of experience all our lives: it moves unconsciously, from one object to another, in a completely unconscious and habitual way, and in the process binds our awareness to the content of its focus.

So, although we may not have stabilized attention fully at this level of practice, we have already experientially verified a very important component of our functioning for ourselves. By simply attempting to hold attention stable on an object, we experienced the controlling power of the unconscious movements of attention – mostly into thought.

At this point it may also be worth noticing how often the mind projects aspects of our emotional/psychological being into our field of awareness. Again it does this despite our best efforts to hold attention stable. These projections will arise in the course of our practice and we should be careful how we deal with these during our early experiments with Passive Awareness. Until we have managed to quiet the whole instrument down sufficiently to relate to these often disturbing mental/emotional issues in a useful and transcending way, it would be completely counter-productive to attempt working with these at this stage.

In the chapters where we specifically enquire into our emotional and mental disturbances (See: *Working with Psychological and Emotional Reactivities* and *Working with Contemplation)*, it will become clear that emotionally reactive and mentally conditioned forms of behavior need to be approached in a comprehensive and conscious way for our work in this regard to be effective and freeing. It would simply be premature to delve into our emotional shadow material at the early stages of our practice. We will be well advised merely to take note of these emotionally laden projections and to bring our attention back to its object. Work on these will take place at a later, appropriate stage, when we have been sufficiently prepared for such sensitive inner exploration.

This matter cannot be overemphasized, particularly in view of the advice often given to beginner practitioners on how to deal with emotional material that arises during meditation. Often they are advised to structure their meditation in a way that presumes a separation between themselves as meditators and anything that may arise in their field of awareness. They are told to establish a 'witness' position from where they merely look at aspects of themselves as a kind of disinterested observer. This leads to the presumption of a prior - and premature - mental attitude of non-identification with any aspect of themselves, including emotional/psychological material that presents itself. These instructions are given with the assurance that such a disinterested attitude will relieve them from the implications of these deeply rooted tendencies.

However, we will find that attempts to desensitize ourselves through this kind of premature non-identification with psychological and emotional complexities, can only lead to further repression of the material that may arise. Such rather heavy-handed treatment of deep emotional matters will prove to be completely ineffective and counter-productive.

The reason is that at this early stage, we have not yet established the *right framework of a quiet, inner disposition* to work with these sensitive matters effectively. Perhaps under the guidance of a competent teacher or a meditating psychotherapist such work may have value. But when we have to rely on our own resources, as will be the case for most of us who either cannot afford the professional services of a therapist, or do not have access to a competent meditation teacher with experience in these matters, it will be more practical and realistic to set this deep emotional work aside until we have established the appropriate instruments to work with them in a truly liberating way..

This type of practice has its place as part of a considerably wider and subtler approach of working with our inner disturbances. However, it needs to be intelligently applied and not used as a form of desensitization, temporary relief or as a mere escape-mechanism. Divorced from its wider, more comprehensive context, where we allow our deeper Intelligence to do its natural healing work, such early involvement with our psychological shadow material will be ineffective and will result only in superficial, and ultimately unsustainable, symptomatic relief. It does not, and cannot address the vitally important deep tendencies of disturbance, which manifest symptomatically as emotional and mental reactivities.

Although the practice of Passive Awareness is a rather simplified activity compared to our usual life of inner turmoil, it is strangely not easy to achieve. Perhaps this is due to the simplicity of the exercise as such. Our nervous system is so over-stimulated by all the input it receives from our anxious living environment that it tends to resist inner quiet and restfulness simply because it has become habituated to all the noise and unnecessary stimulation.

Few of us know what it means to be simply quiet. Yet, despite our apparent resistance to silence, we need to appreciate that there is nothing natural about our inner and outer noise at all. It is silence and inner quiet that are natural to our being. And the practice of Passive Awareness shows us that we are indeed capable of becoming deeply quiet and truly restful. This practice is the first conscious step we take away from the debilitating power of habit and habit-forming tendencies, so characteristic of the thought/attention knot..

3) 'Minding?' and the Thought/Attention-knot

During our initial work with the practice of Passive Awareness we have observed how subtly attention slips from our conscious awareness into its old pattern of unconsciously associating with aspects of our thinking. It does this with such cunning that, despite our best attempts to keep a watchful eye on its movements, it defaults into this habitual movement without us noticing. We usually only become aware of this quite a few minutes after we have lost our object and find ourselves 'elsewhere', usually absorbed in some interesting storyline or other thought-projection. And, as we have also noticed, when this happens, we are only aware of the *content* of our thinking, while totally unaware of this *process* of thought/attention-absorption.

So, as the countering of this unconscious movement of attention is the purpose of the practice of Passive Awareness, we could use an effective aid in waking us up from this. Here we only need to appreciate that what the traditions have called 'Mind', is in truth nothing other than the thought/attention-knot with its effects on our emotions and physical state as a whole. Our entire psychophysical being contracts in its response to the intimations and demands of the thought/attention-knot. We *become* what we think, and this thought-reality brings the limitation to our being we have called 'Mind'. It is Mind that clouds our vision and holds us in bondage within its own thought-created reality.

When we therefore use the word 'Mind', we refer to this dream, created and sustained by thought and given life and sustenance by attention. To engage in a practice that facilitates the relaxation of attention away from this thought-state, and to bring its focus back to its object of meditation, we literally make the unconscious process of the thought/attention-knot conscious. We see the interplay between our conscious attempt of holding our object of attention stable, and the force of the unconscious tendency for attention to move into some aspect of thought.

From this we may develop a very simple, but useful, aid to our practice of Passive Awareness. We simply create the word 'minding?', which means that while we are caught in the dream of the thought/attention-knot, we are in fact 'minding'. And because 'minding' is always an unconscious process, we could use this word effectively in the form of a question by randomly asking ourselves, 'minding?', thereby bringing awareness to the situation.

Knowing what 'minding?' means, this question immediately helps to bring us back into the present moment where we become aware that attention has once more been absorbed into the thought/attention-knot, thereby establishing us in the clutches of 'Mind'. This serves as a wakeup call, bringing us back to the *conscious process* of attending to our object of meditation. Of course, this word is not to be repeated like a kind of mantra. It is to be used discriminately, yet deliberately, every few minutes while we do this practice just to call us back to the conscious process of mindfully attending to our object of meditation.

There is gentleness to this process of asking the question 'minding?' which has a rather feminine quality to it. We do not have to use force to bring attention back to our object of meditation. By asking the question, we merely intimate to our Intelligence what it is we are in fact busy doing. And because the full implications of the question are priorly understood, the relaxation of attention away from thought, back onto its object of meditation, happens quite naturally. It is a soft and non-aggressive process of moving from an unconscious state of attentive absorption – i.e. the thought/attention-knot – to the attentive state of conscious, yet Passive Awareness of our object.

Once the practice of Passive Awareness begins to establish itself as part of our potential and functional ability, we could experiment by gently allowing our freed, yet stable, attention to move around in the body, and to focus for short periods on different aspects of bodily sensation. Working with attention in such a conscious and controlled way further breaks into its habit of defaulting back into some aspect of thought. It can be focused wherever we choose and held in focused awareness on any inner object. There is nothing mechanical about this practice. We freely move attention around the body, always guarding against it losing its conscious aspect and reverting back to its habitual association with thought. This conscious movement of attention already shows an encouraging control over its random, habitual and generally unconscious movements.

During this practice we may also open our eyes and bring attention to anything we see, hear or in any other way are aware of. These are all aspects of the same practice of Passive Awareness. In the process we sense a relief from the domination of thought over our total field of present experience. We begin to develop the feeling-experience of a different quality of life each time we wake out of the thought-attention dream by consciously refocusing attention away from thought onto its object.

Soon we will notice that we become calm and relaxed, while we experience a delicate sense of well-being and clarity. These are all natural side-effects within our psychophysical being of this practice of becoming aware of the unconscious processes of thought and attention when we shift attention consciously away from the content of thought.

Again we need to remind ourselves that at this level it is not our intention to develop, or enter into, deep states of concentrative absorption, bliss, listening to inner sounds, having subtle bodily experiences and so on. These may naturally arise at any point during our practice and are never experiences we need to avoid or frown upon. Such states may even be considered as signs that our meditation is real and effective, although it needs to be pointed out that such experiences are neither necessary, nor any sign of 'spiritual' progress. They simply may or may not happen.

Our work at this stage should be to remain conscious of what we are doing and to keep attention stable on its object. All forms of inner absorption are relative states of unconsciousness. Our process is to allow for ever greater awareness. And for this, states of deep concentration are not necessary.

Should we experience some extraordinary states, we may decide how long we want to enjoy or partake in these before we resume our work of being consciously attentive to our object. States of relative bliss often come upon us, and we should not reject or suppress these. Neither should we regard them as signs coming from some deep and profound transcendental Being, or our presumed primordial nature. States of bliss, mental clarity, and so on, at this level are merely psychophysical responses to changes that are brought about by the inner quiet of our practice. However beautiful these may be, we should allow them to take their course, yet not invest them with too much importance.

If, towards the natural conclusion of such states, we were again to ask ourselves the question 'minding?' we will soon re-establish ourselves in our practice and thereby gain confidence in our ability to control the random movements of attention.

Our temptation may be to remember the quality and nuance of these states and to come to the conclusion that we are really getting rather spiritual and that we should do everything in our power to get ourselves back into these. But all such retrospective reflections are futile. They serve no purpose other than to distract us from the simplicity of our practice. As we have seen, all forms of mental reflection are created and sustained by thought. To fall back into such memories of past experiences of bliss and beauty will only again absorb us into the dream of the world of thought and memory.

Thought is not the thing. And neither is the memory of any experience, however beautiful. To be aware of this will help us getting right back into our practice of Passive Awareness.

Perhaps it may be worth pointing out that the reason for the emphasis we place on developing our ability to isolate certain areas of our inner experience, such as remaining conscious of the movements of attention, is that in our future work with our emotional reactivities (See: *Working with Psychological and Emotional Reactivities* and *Working with Contemplation)*, this ability will form the foundation of our enquiry into our deep emotional and psychological reactive patterns of response. During the practice of Passive Awareness we lay the foundation for conscious awareness without which no aspect of our future practice, or human unfolding in general, would be possible or *sustainable*.

Without the ability to become and remain conscious of, and *take responsibility for, the movements of attention*, we will be vulnerable to its unconscious association with the content of thought, and thereby denying ourselves the possibility of ultimately transcending the entire thought/attention-reality, or any other deep tendencies of mental/emotional disturbance.

Passive Awareness will therefore remain the most fundamental aspect of our practice, until we have gained sufficient control over the movements of thought and attention to enter into the subtle, effortless practices of Direct Awareness and finally Integration. And it will be during these subtle forms of practice that we will truly appreciate the value of having established ourselves firmly in the practice of Passive Awareness.

4) Insight

Another interesting and rather important development we may come across during our practice of Passive Awareness is the appearance of insights. When we become well established in this practice, and are no longer completely caught in the images projected by thought, we often experience interesting insights into many aspects of our lives and things in general. We may suddenly have a deep understanding about ourselves or the path we are on, or just gain a new clarity about life in a way we have never seen before. It is as if the thing takes on a new dimension: almost as though this is the first time we have really understood it properly. We somehow just have a deep sense that we have never seen things with such clarity and accuracy.

Insight has the potential to serve us as a kind of inner guide and as a valuable asset to our path of self-enquiry and self-understanding. Through insights we get information about things from a source that was previously inhibited by our habitual identification with the content of our conditioned way of thinking. In the more open, relaxed environment of Passive Awareness we receive these insights from a deeper, clearer source of Intelligence, which, perhaps for the first time, has been consciously allowed to become part of our functional ability.

However, as is the case with every aspect of our path, we need to approach the manifestation of insights with caution and a very open attitude. Because of their often revelatory or even revolutionary content, we should be careful not to accept these random intimations from our deeper Intelligence as the final truth on anything. The reason is that at this stage of our development, our Intelligence is still struggling to find its way through the fog of our deeply conditioned psychophysical being, and often these messages become somewhat distorted, however clear they may seem from the perspective of our ordinary limited and contracted state. Although they often represent a clear shift towards more intelligent living, insights need to be handled with considerable caution.

We have seen that for our deeper nature to reveal itself, the instrument through which it has to manifest, should be well prepared. The less obstructive the instrument, the clearer the insight. This will become more evident as our progress towards simplifying experience unfolds. The more open we are, the less obstruction we offer to the intimations of our deeper Intelligence. And as our practice develops, our insights will become progressively clearer, more accurate and often reflective of the non-dual nature of things.

So, as part of our general investigation into ourselves, insights could be seen as a clear sign of the effectiveness of our practice. They do not generally present themselves in the bewildered circumstance associated with the random movements of thought and attention. Rather, their appearance is the first sign of our inherent ability to think clearly and accurately about something without our thinking being clouded by conditioning of the past.

However, although insights have a clear and fresh sense about them and often present us with new and challenging ways of looking at things, it is not necessary at this stage of our practice to work deliberately toward the development of insight. No harm will result should we do this, yet, experimenting too intensively with insights at this early stage of stabilizing attention and thought, could easily distract us. It is more important that we allow ourselves to return to the inner quiet that facilitated the insight in the first place. Our time for working directly, consciously and effectively with insights will soon present itself. (See: *Working with Contemplation* and *Contemplation and Reality Consideration*)

There is, however, another aspect of the appearance of insights which may be worth keeping in mind. When we become established in the relative quiet of stabilized attention, we often have insights that may not present themselves to our consciousness in the form of clearly defined thought images. Although these particular kinds of insight *might* be reflected in thought, their true value lies in their subliminal effect on our being, even before we become conscious of them. In fact, this form of insight often affects us without us becoming consciously aware of their presence.

These are real transformative insights which have the effect of changing or modifying aspects of our inner being, thereby effecting long-lasting behavioral changes in our psyche. For instance, we may become aware that we are more relaxed in a situation where previously we might have felt anxious or nervous. Or we just hear ourselves speaking in a more accommodating way, or feeling more open to others where previously we might have been somewhat abrupt or contracted and uncaring. The same happens in our relation to ourselves. We may find a greater acceptance of who and what we are and feel a willingness to work with ourselves where previously we might have resisted any deeper exploration because of fear or self-judgment. The effects of these deeper insights could be quite profound and transforming, especially on the relative level of our psychological and emotional functioning.

These are real intimations from our deeper Intelligence. And although rather random in their initial appearance, they are clear indications that we *do* have an inner Intelligence that is always ready to become an active participant in our lives, if only we would allow it.

But, as we have seen, until we are well established in the practice of Passive Awareness, where we have gained considerable control over the random and habitual movements of attention and thought, it may be somewhat premature to attempt to make use of this kind of inner expression. The time for doing so will soon arrive.

5) *Attention and Awareness*

We have already alluded to the valuable and practical distinction to be drawn between attention and awareness. Although attention and awareness work in harmony and close proximity to one another during the practice of Passive Awareness, we need to look at these separately, so that we do not mistake one for the other. Furthermore, such an investigation will indicate how these affect us in rather different ways. For our present enquiry, we could start by looking at some of the more salient features of the functioning of attention.

During the practice of Passive Awareness we use attention to focus awareness on one thing at a time. When it does so, it excludes much of the rest of the field of present experience. In this process it always diminishes our total field of present awareness in order to focus on a single component of this open field. So, although attention may assist us in becoming more focused in one specific area of interest or necessity, it also places a limitation on our overall awareness of things, as it excludes from our field of experience all but that to which it has drawn our awareness.

Although attention, therefore, brings greater awareness to a particular aspect of present arising, by the very fact that it focuses exclusively on a single object, *it is also a factor of unawareness.* All acts of attention as applied in our normal functioning have this exclusive, and, therefore, relatively unaware (or unconscious), aspect to them. We become more aware of the specific area of focus and less aware of everything else in the total field of arising.

The more determination we bring to the act of attention, thereby establishing a state of sustained concentration, the greater and more complete the exclusivity of our practice. For instance, we find a very strong emphasis on the exclusive power of concentration in many meditative practices where the meditator deliberately attempts to exclude all sense of their external world to gain access to other states of inner experience such as Samadhi, deep visualizations and other subtle realms of manifest existence. Sometimes we find that these meditators could remain in such states of concentrative absorption for long periods of time.

However, for our enquiry into the wholeness of our *living reality* it is not necessary that we specialize in this type of exclusive concentrative meditation. On the contrary, it may be clear that any state of exclusivity would be just another form of fragmentation, and therefore, in itself, not in resonance with the undivided, non-fragmented wholeness of the present moment. We should be clear about this from the very beginning, otherwise we might pursue forms of practice which could lead us into states of meditative absorption which do not serve the *conscious process* of waking us up from the exclusivity of our attention-based, waking dream-state.

Attention should thus be used with considerable discretion. Although it serves the psychophysical being as an instrument for the focusing of awareness it can also become a devastatingly effective instrument in the creation of the illusion of fragmentation and separateness. This is because attention does *not require our conscious direction and intelligent application* for it to do its work as a focusing mechanism of awareness. Nature has allowed attention to operate freely, and unconsciously, within our field of experience and to direct awareness wherever it focuses. This is a useful survival mechanism.

For instance, if suddenly we were to be confronted with a life-threatening situation, attention would unconsciously and immediately do its focusing work which alerts the body that something threatening is happening. The body responds long before we become conscious of what is going on. There is just this immediate, and unmediated, defensive response. Clearly in such circumstances our conscious involvement with attention would have been unnecessary and far too slow to be of any real use.

However, it is exactly *because* attention has been given this natural, survival-oriented freedom to act unconsciously when a situation calls for it, that this unconscious aspect has made it possible for it to become such a critical factor in the creation of the thought/attention-knot. The movement of attention into an aspect of thought has become mechanical and habitual. Its unconscious focusing on the projections of thought *isolates our awareness* and thus restricts it to a very limited field of thought experience. Clearly this could be seen as a rather misdirected use of our ability to pay attention. By defaulting unconsciously into the projections of thought in a completely habitual way, attention serves the exclusive dictates of the mind and not its natural function as a focusing mechanism of awareness. Through this, human experience becomes little more than an expression and continuation of thought.

We have also seen how these random and unconscious movements of attention extend themselves into every part of our lives. Like a scavenger, attention is always habitually in search for something to focus on. There is no necessary survival-based need for this, yet, through habit and our unconscious demands for stimulation and identification, this is what attention generally occupies itself with.

Part Two: The Practice

This is why it is imperative that we gain conscious control over the activities of attention. Where attention goes, awareness goes. And as we are most fundamentally identified with awareness, it is of vital importance that the correct relationship between attention and awareness is established.

This brings us to the enquiry into awareness, and how it functions in relation to attention. As we have seen, attention exerts a subtle, yet profound, control over the process of awareness. It would seem that in our ordinary functioning, awareness not only follows attention in a biological, survival-orientated way, but does so also in a *habitual* way. In other words, when attention focuses on an aspect of present experience in its usual unconscious and habitual manner, awareness is drawn to the same area of focus, in a similar, *rather unconscious and mechanical way*.

This is a vitally important observation, because we generally do not associate the functioning of awareness with the notion of unawareness. We would expect all activities of awareness to be of a conscious nature. But this is not quite the case. When awareness follows the dictates of the unconscious and habitual movements of attention, it seems to sacrifice its overall sense of awareness to become specifically associated with a single object. It becomes specifically aware of the object, but generally unaware, both of what it is doing, and of our wider field of experience, thereby sacrificing its fully conscious expression.

The unenlightened human condition is fundamentally characterized by a profound sense of unawareness, or ignorance. Ignorance is always unaware of itself. To be ignorant is first of all to be ignorant of ignorance. We go through the so-called waking hours of our day, participating in many activities, yet, although we may be somewhat aware of the outward manifestations of what we do, we are generally totally unaware, or ignorant, of the processes which are involved in these activities. For instance, we may think many thoughts, and act mechanically on the images they create, yet we are generally completely unaware of the processes of which they are mere manifestations.

Spirituality Without God

There always seems to be this dual, simultaneous process of being both specifically aware and generally unaware going on within us. In its association with the unconscious movements of attention, awareness takes on an unconscious quality, which makes it ignorant of what it is doing.

This explains why the thought/attention-knot is such a difficult process to become aware of and so tenacious to free ourselves from. To work with it, we need to become aware of an unaware process, or to put it differently, to become conscious of our unconsciousness. This is tricky, yet perfectly possible once we have established ourselves properly in the practice of Passive Awareness. As we have seen, here the emphasis is on waking up from the unconscious states of attentive absorption. We do this by becoming conscious of the unconscious act of attention.

Through this practice we restore the natural order of things in this limited field of being consciously aware of our object of attention. This order suggests not only that attention is an instrument of awareness, and therefore *secondary* to it, we also become aware that awareness is an inner activity which always takes place *prior* to any act of attention. Here the relationship between attention and awareness gets re-established to its natural order.

We are always first aware of the total field of present arising before we can pay attention to any specific aspect of it. The practice of Passive Awareness demonstrates this in a clear and unambiguous way. We can only focus attention on something that is already part of our field of awareness. This practice, therefore, does not introduce any imposition on the natural functioning of our being. On the contrary, it merely restores an innate order where attention begins to function in a conscious relationship to awareness. Passive Awareness brings attention under our *volitional control*, thereby re-establishing it as a useful and important instrument of awareness.

So far we have only enquired into awareness as it relates to the practice of Passive Awareness. However, to understand the nature and functioning of awareness most comprehensively, we need to appreciate that it is a multi-faceted process that cannot be divorced from our entire field of present arising. From this perspective it may become clear that we will not do justice to awareness as a whole by describing it merely in terms of its more outward functioning in its association with attention. The whole matter of awareness deserves a much deeper and subtler investigation if we want to find its true measure as a functional and inseparable component of the totality of human experience.

In the next chapter: *Working with Direct Awareness*, we will discover the profound non-dual nature of awareness/Being. There we will enter directly into the non-dual expression of awareness as an integral component of present arising.

For our present enquiry, it is important that we just remain sensitive to the conscious and unconscious aspects of both attention and awareness as we experience these during the practice of Passive Awareness. The distinction we have drawn between attention and awareness will prove to be of critical importance once we begin to explore the meditation of Direct Awareness.

The last aspect of the practice of Passive Awareness could be seen not only as the natural culmination of this exercise, but in fact leads us to a very important inner state of attentive absorption called Samatha or the quiet state.

6) *Samatha*

When we hold attention stable on a predetermined object, thought and attention could become so deeply silent and free from any compulsive movement that we enter into a profound state of attentive absorption. Traditionally this state has been referred to as Samatha, also known as the 'quiet state'. In an ultimate sense, Samatha could still be seen as a state among other states. Being a state of attentive absorption, where attention is deeply focused on its object, its mere exclusivity would disqualify it from being regarded as the ultimate, non-dual fulfillment of our path.

Spirituality Without God

Yet, Samatha is perhaps the most important state to experience during our practice of Passive Awareness. The reason for this is that from the deep quiet of this state, Samatha affords us with the most useful platform from where to launch the next stage of our work: Direct Awareness.

When we touch upon the deep quietude during the experience of Samatha, we have indeed reached a point in our practice that has real value, and, as we shall discover, affords us with a perfect point of departure into our non-dual work, which quite naturally follows on from the exercises described for the practice of Passive Awareness. Samatha could thus be regarded as the last of our preparatory work before we enter into the formal practice of Direct Awareness.

It may be worth reminding ourselves that all forms of practice, other than the final practices of non-doing or no-effort, are preliminary work within the relative field of experience and should not be bypassed with the intention of arriving sooner at our destination. If we do not prepare the terrain sufficiently for the total openness of the more subtle forms of practice, our enquiry will always remain vulnerable to revert-back to the beginning stages because of the habitual pull of the unconscious, random and uncontrolled movements of thought and attention. The experience of Samatha constitutes an integral component of this preparatory work and should be regarded as the only practical and realistic point of departure for the practices which will facilitate the non-dual experience.

To arrive at this meditative state of Samatha, it may be useful to continue our practice from the point where we have gained control over the random movements of attention.

For the purpose of allowing for the state of Samatha to become our experience, we will find that working with inner objects of meditation, rather than outer ones may serve our objective better. Whereas any object would do for the general practice of Passive Awareness, it will become evident that working with *sensations* such as our inner darkness when the eyes are closed, or the silence we experience when we sit in a quiet place for meditation, will serve this kind of meditation better. *Silence and inner darkness are excellent objects of meditation as they are already effortlessly present within us.*

Part Two: The Practice

If we were to use other kinds of inner objects such as visualizations or the repetition of a mantra, we will discover that the effort to keep producing such a visualization or mantra may somewhat detract from the subtlety required to hold attention stable on the object in a completely conscious, yet soft and gentle manner. Using our inner darkness or silence, we will be working with objects of focus that are already present within us. We need not first create our object of attention. In this case our objects of inner darkness or silence are already part of our own inner condition. No force is necessary. We simply work with aspects of ourselves which are already quiet, present and perfectly stable.

When we have allowed attention to become stabilized and relaxed, we can now gradually deepen our attentive awareness to our inner darkness. In other words, for the purpose of the practice of Samatha, we become more *one-pointed* in our focused attention by very slightly intensifying our ability to remain almost completely absorbed in our object of focus. As a result we will be more exclusively aware of our object without *entirely losing our overall sense of awareness*. Although attention marginally dominates the sense of awareness during this exercise, we still allow for an element of conscious awareness despite the deep identification between attention and it object. We do not get totally 'lost' in the inner quiet of our being.

Soon we will begin to sense a kind of merging with our object of inner darkness in a relatively conscious way. Although we remain absorbed in this state of deep attentiveness, the *residual free awareness* gives this experience a very alive and conscious feel. At this point we enter into the experience of Samatha.

Samatha comes about when there is a deep feeling of *almost* effortless association between attentive awareness and its object of darkness. Such focused attention can never completely merge with its object, but there can be a very refined sense of settled harmony between the two. In Samatha there is no movement of attention as it has relaxed and stabilized into its object. In this we notice how attention and awareness work together to create this state of conscious, attentive absorption.

Spirituality Without God

And whereas in our ordinary unconscious state of the thought/attention-knot, attention is clearly the dominant instrument as it directs awareness unconsciously to the contents of thought, during Samatha this is different. Here awareness and attention support one another in a relatively well-balanced way, although, as we have seen, attention still holds the more dominant position. In this we notice a clear shift away from experience controlled by the unconscious focusing of attention, to a greater sense of conscious, attentive awareness, stably under our volitional control.

This results in a very quiet state of absorbed tranquility that brings a deep relaxation and profound quiet to our whole psychophysical being. During the practice of Samatha we find that our breath slows down, the heart rate drops, thought settles down in harmony with the non-movement of attention and we are almost completely unaware of anything other than this great simplicity of inner attentive quietude.

At this point, a rather important question may be asked: why allow ourselves to move into Samatha if this deep state of exclusive attentive absorption seems to have no direct relation to the vision of wholeness which, as we have seen, should always inform every aspect of our path? Why not simply remain active within the practice of Passive Awareness and continue to develop our ability to remain free from the unconscious habits of thought, attention and focused awareness?

To understand this, we need to remind ourselves that the practice of Passive Awareness serves our self-enquiry in more than one way. During this practice we discover not only how immersed we are in the thought/attention-knot, we also learn how to bring stability to the random and unnecessary movements of attention by holding it stable on its object. In addition to this, Passive Awareness shows us how attention, although an instrument of awareness, tends to dominate and control the broader, overall sense of awareness while we remain active within the dream of thought/attention. The practice also often leads to deep insights and clear comprehension. All these are very valuable results of this practice.

Part Two: The Practice

These insights and experiences will yet prove to be of critical importance as our practice develops.

In addition to these, we also discover that during the practice of Passive Awareness we develop the ability for deep modes of attentive absorption such as states of bliss, inner joy, feelings of great compassion, clarity and so on. These are natural by-products of the practice, and, although not necessary for the primary purpose of Passive Awareness, we could enjoy such states, as long as we do not make these the central focus of our endeavor. They have their place, but should not distract us too much.

However, when Passive Awareness leads us to the state of Samatha, we deliberately spend time with this state of attentive absorption. The reason is that Samatha could be regarded as the most *secure disposition from where to launch our enquiry into the open field of direct experience* and the practice of effortless, center-less awareness. When our inner being has quieted down to the level of Samatha, this indicates that we have reached a point in our practice where the random and unconscious movements of thought and attention have come under our volitional control. It also points to the important fact that they have settled down so significantly that they could be *trusted to remain quiet and relaxed while we proceed to the next more open stages of our practice.*

Only from such a secure platform can we allow for the subtle, open-ended and *uncontrolled* practice of Direct Awareness without constantly falling back into the old habits of the thought/attention-knot with its disturbing effects on our emotions and the rest of our psychophysical being. If we are not thorough in preparing the ground through Passive Awareness and a deep level of relaxed inner quiet, such as Samatha, we will continue to struggle with the same problems which have undermined our practice all along and may never know exactly why our practice cannot deepen beyond a few intermittent states of inner quiet, bliss and beauty.

Samatha could therefore be seen, not only as a final gesture of the activities of attentive awareness in relation to its objects: it is also a *doorway through which to enter into the subtle, non-dualistic aspects of our practice.* This is what makes the practice of Samatha such a valuable part of our self-transcending process.

However, we should take great care not to become so attached to this inner state of quiet that we mistake it for the *fruit* of our practice or for true unity consciousness. Because Samatha often displays a remarkable quality of joy and pure beauty, bordering on bliss, many students of life have not looked beyond this state for the wider, inclusive possibility of wholeness and sustainable emotional equanimity. Whatever qualities the state of Samatha may exhibit, these should still be seen as part of our practice, and not the fruit of practice. As a movement on its own, it does not have the power to neutralize or eliminate the deep tendencies of fragmentary living and reactive emotional/psychological conditioning which form the basis of our dualistic vision.

We could therefore either remain fascinated, and become conditioned, by the experiences within the state of Samatha, or we could use it as a point of departure for further enquiry. If we choose to remain there, and make this state of inner quiet the focus of our practice, Samatha will become an obstruction to our further development. We have to appreciate that Samatha is still a state next to other states. In its inwardness it is exclusive and cut-off from our ordinary living reality.

We therefore need to *wake up* from Samatha, as we need to wake up from any other state of attentive absorption, if we are to enter into the delicate and subtle practice of Direct Awareness. The opportunity that Samatha affords us can only be fully realized when this exclusive state itself has been transcended as part of the process that ultimately leads to the simplicity of the non-dual.

This brings us to the next very important stage of our path where we will explore the practice of direct, non-dual experience.

Part Two: The Practice

SUMMARY OF PRACTICE

PURPOSE:

- To stabilize attention by gaining control over its random and habitual movements.
- To observe the movements of attention into the contents of thought.
- To frustrate the habitual creation of the thought/attention-knot.
- To create a secure and stable platform from where to move into all other aspects of inner work - psychological and self-transcendent.

PRACTICE:

- Find a comfortable position with minimum outside distraction.
- Feel relaxed into your own bodily position.
- Close your eyes and sense your immediate environment: bodily sensations, thoughts, sounds. Relax into the general sense of being present where you are.
- Bring attention to some inner object of focus such as the breath, inner darkness behind the eyes, your hands, your favorite mantra, such as OM etc..
- Isolate one of these to use as your object of attentive focus.
- Notice your inability to hold attention stable on its object.
- Persevere – not with force and determination, but by not giving up in your efforts to hold attention stable.
- When you notice attention has moved from its object, bring it back to the object.
- Should any emotional material arise which demand your attention, take note of this, and let it go. Come back to the object of meditation.
- Use 'minding?' randomly to bring your wandering attention back to its object.

Spirituality Without God

- Allow states of deep quiet, bliss, openness of heart, love etc to be present for as long as you feel comfortable with these and return to the stabilization of attention on its original object.
- Invite and enjoy the clarity of insights which may appear. These are natural to your state of inner quiet. Do not dwell on them for too long. Come back to the primary practice: holding attention stable on its object.
- Try to sense how attention leads awareness wherever its goes. Play around with attention and notice how it takes awareness to each new area of focus.
- When attention becomes stabilized, move it around the body, hold it stable for a while on one object and move it further along to other areas of focus.
- Notice how attention diminishes your field of awareness in its exclusive focusing on a single object.
- Open your eyes, and use external objects as points of focus. Do not interpret what you see, hear etc. Merely let the eyes come to rest on an object and allow attention to stabilize itself there.
- Bring attention back to your inner darkness and allow it to remain deeply attentive of this. Hold this for as long as possible. Develop Samatha in this way. Use very little effort. Just relax completely into the inner darkness behind your eyes. Allow states of bliss, well-being, joy and clarity to remain in your awareness if they present themselves. Come back to the inner darkness.
- Hold this position stable for as long as possible.

Chapter Fourteen

THE PRACTICE OF DIRECT AWARENESS

1) Understanding Direct Awareness

Once the practice of Passive Awareness has been well established in us, and we are able to participate in the deep quietness of Samatha, or any similar state of inner quiet, we will be well prepared for the next, most important aspect of our practice: Direct Awareness.

Direct Awareness is the first real gesture we make towards the possibility of directly experiencing beyond the separate self-sense. This is a rather subtle form of participatory practice and is evidenced by a presence of *bodily feeling-sensation* that reveals the truth of the non-dual nature of things, not dependent on our traditional view of sense-perception, or on our ability to pay attention or to think.

As we have seen with all the earlier forms of practice, as well as our general participation in this work, it is important to have a clear prior understanding of our involvement with any particular aspect of practice. Without being guided by such insight and understanding, our work will lose its focus and may easily get side-tracked by some specific experience, or experiences, within the vast potential of our delusory, dualistic vision.

The same applies to the practice of Direct Awareness. As this practice points to a radical departure from working with attention and thought as our main instruments, to working with awareness alone, it is imperative that we understand the context within which we will approach this aspect of our work.

The most fundamental consideration that informs the path of self-enquiry and self-transcendence is the notion of wholeness. Wholeness is the non-fragmentary self-revelation of the living moment. Whatever we may believe to the contrary, everything appears quite naturally and holistically by itself, and while we are awake, the total field of present arising, including our own psychophysical appearance, is nothing other than the undivided truth of the living moment. To be human, *is* to be the undivided truth of present arising. This non-dual present moment is therefore not objective to, or separate from, our own psychophysical appearance. No clear line can be drawn between us as presumed experiencers, and what we believe to be objective reality – the experienced.

If the world truly existed 'out there' for us to perceive as something objective to, or separate from, us, duality would have been the only truth available to us: wholeness would not have been possible. But as our enquiry into Direct Awareness will reveal, *it is wholeness that is real and duality that is unreal.* And because our total field of present experience is one undivided reality, it is fragmentation and duality which, in truth, is not possible. Rather, they are based on an illusory, dualistic vision which has to be recognized for what it is and gradually transcended.

Fragmentation and duality are misconceptions created and sustained by thought. They are thus only apparent as delusion. We are not the perceivers of an objectively existing reality. In wholeness there is nothing separate from where to observe any part of this living, non-dual process. Our entire path is therefore directed towards the removal of everything we have added to the simplicity of our present experience which creates the appearance of division and fragmentation. And as wholeness is the simplest form of human experience, it may be clear that any aspect of such fragmentary activity would constitute a complication, or unnecessary elaboration, that we impose or project onto this great simplicity.

Part Two: The Practice

In truth there is only wholeness. Yet, in our uninspected ways of doing things there is *only* the appearance of fragmentation and the conditionality this presumed fragmentation imposes on our lives. Human existence is therefore characterized by the paradox of nurturing and exploring an ever widening field of fragmentation through science, technology, religion, philosophy, mysticism and other ideas upon ideas, while we remain totally unaware of the wholeness which lies unmanifest, as our deep potential, at the root of human life..

Once we become sensitized to the fundamental non-dual truth of the natural and true status of things, we could enquire into ways that may deliver us from every vestige of fragmentary presumption. Wholeness, and that which presumes itself to be separate from it, are two categorically different states of experience. And as wholeness is the truth, and fragmentation a misunderstanding, and therefore untruth, it will always be our fragmentary vision that will be the factor of conflict, unrelatedness, unhappiness, alienation and separation. This fragmented vision will dominate our lives for as long as we believe in this uninspected presumption of dualistic living.

Yet, although in the ultimate sense, fragmentation is a misapprehension of reality, and thus an illusion, it nevertheless presents itself to our living experience as absolute reality and truth. We live our fragmented, dualistic vision in the same way as we live the air we breathe and feel the heat from the sun on our skins. It is as real as every loss and every gain. It is the stuff of which wars are made, and is the fertile soil from which our political and religious masters can manipulate, control and destroy us. Fragmentation or duality is not just a deep sense we have of things. It has become a total *condition of existence* where we have accepted and have become completely identified with a notion of reality that totally negates the natural and holistic order of things.

This is an important insight to keep in mind, because if we are not merely looking for superficial behavioral modifications within the relative, illusory world of fragmentation, it may be clear that the change we are looking for will have to manifest in us in the same *direct and intimately-felt* way as the presumed reality of our fragmented ways of living.

Spirituality Without God

Our path, if it is for real, cannot be something we merely add to ourselves as we would add another skill or religion to our lives. The change will have to be so absolute, so self-evident and directly felt, that it will show itself also as a condition of living reality. The only difference would be that such a life, revealed as the non-dual nature of things, will be based in the totality of present experience, and not as a fragmented aspect of it. Whereas our uninspected reality is evidenced by the sense of alienated struggle, a life lived from the disposition of the non-dual is one of great simplicity, order, Intelligence and charity.

Direct Awareness will make it experientially true that *knowledge is not the instrument through which wholeness manifests.* The non-dual requires no instrument through which to reveal itself. When all obscurations to this great simplicity have been removed and transcended, humanity remains complete as its own expression: whole and self-revelatory. It cannot be known. There is always only 'What Is'.

What makes our path a radically humanistic endeavor, is that nothing we will be working with lies beyond our human experience. As much as all un-truth has its measure within our human condition, equally should we not search for the truth of non-duality anywhere outside human life. All that is required is for us to allow for the removal of the obscurations to this truth through correct practice and right living.

This proposition will gradually become part of our lives as we engage in the non-dualistic practices of Direct Awareness. We will explore forms of practice that will allow for everything to remain as it has always been prior to us duplicating and interpreting this open field of experience within thought.

A living reality freed from these compulsive and largely unconscious impositions naturally displays its own holistic order of intelligent and compassionate living. We do not want to become holy, saintly, mystical or godly. These are all manifestations of the same confusion we have inherited from the mystical traditions and organized religions. To be holy or mystical is to be fragmented. *We merely want to be fully and completely human.*

Another crucial aspect of Direct Awareness that we shall discover, is that it could be applied as part of a process which comprehensively addresses our deeply hidden emotional and psychological disturbances. In fact, while being dominated emotionally by the disorderly components of our ego/'I'-centered psychology, no sense of wholeness is possible for any sustainable period. The sustainable equanimity associated with aligning our emotional responses with non-dual reality will always remain open for disruption unless we gain deep insight into these and transcend all our unnecessary emotional reactivities. Direct Awareness is ideally suited to many aspects of emotional work as it allows us to *feel* our way through these complications rather than relying merely on understanding them as disturbances within our being.

As we shall discover, the practice of Direct Awareness has therefore a twofold purpose: it allows us to transcend into the non-conceptual, direct experience of wholeness, while at the same time has the potential to facilitate a comprehensive enquiry into our psychological and emotional patterns of reactivity and disturbance.

Every step we take along this route, and every gesture we make toward different aspects of this practice, have to be informed and guided by our greater vision of wholeness until this vision itself falls away by non-use through the direct experience of that towards which it has been pointing. What remains when all concepts of reality have fallen away is nothing but our own direct, feeling experience of the true Advaita or non-duality.

And if we allow ourselves to be guided by such an understanding of life, we may proceed with our enquiry into the directness of experience from the secure knowing that this process will facilitate, in a practical and realistic way, the gradual unfolding of our natural condition. The practice of Direct Awareness is the single most potent instrument to bring this transition about.

2) Practicing Direct Awareness

We have seen that the practice of Samatha is characterized by a relative equilibrium between attention and awareness. This makes for a deep and profound sense of inner quiet because attentive awareness has come to rest in a conscious state of silence and non-movement.

However, having gained this subtle control over the movements of thought, attention and awareness, Samatha nevertheless requires a certain effort to be held in place. This is an important, recognizable component of all forms of inner absorption. As we have seen, Samatha should still be regarded as a state next to other possible states which remain influenced by a subtle division between the observer and the observed.

Even if it may appear to be the case, the inner darkness or silence is not all that is present during Samatha: in itself, it is not a state of wholeness. Intimately bound with these experiences is still the marginally effortful activity of attention that holds the whole thing in place. And even more integral to this process of absorbed attention is the ever-present (however subtle) activity of thought which quietly informs us that because we are paying attention to our inner darkness, we must be separate from that to which we are paying attention. So, in Samatha the separate self-sense is still alive and active, however subdued and unobtrusive.

However, as we have deliberately allowed for Samatha to be our point of departure into the experience of Direct Awareness, we need to find a way that could lead us beyond this inner quiet and which, at the same time, *is consistent with the effortless nature of non-dual arising.* We cannot force our way into effortless Being. We can only allow for the conditions which facilitate its revelation through a conscious process which transcends those functions within us that obscure it.

While we are thus finely attuned to our state of inner quiet in the presence of a deeply felt-sense of conscious attention, we may experiment with the *relaxation of attention.* As we have seen, attention is not the appropriate instrument for the

Part Two: The Practice

realization of wholeness because of its exclusive functioning. Samatha itself is the ultimate form of such exclusive operation. We need, therefore, to learn how to *relax* attention from within the experience of Samatha in order to enter fully into the practice of Direct Awareness.

We have observed that Samatha is held in place by an act of attention. This state inherently requires attention to remain focused on our inner darkness for it to prevail. Without this effortful act of attention, the state of Samatha will lose its coherency. If for instance, during Samatha, we lose concentration and allow attention to slip back into the content of thought, Samatha will be lost. However, to allow for the non-dual to become evident we have to find a way of *consciously relaxing attention from within the state of Samatha without sacrificing the conscious aspect of that state.*

This would imply that the relaxation of attention will not diminish the quality of awareness present during Samatha. We will simply relax attention and thereby remove one of the main constituents of the state of absorbed attentiveness, leaving us only with the direct, and conscious, experience of our inner, self-existing silence or darkness.

As a useful introduction to the practice of the relaxation of attention, we could just remind ourselves that attention can generally only focus on one thing at a time. It may move with great speed from one object to another, giving the *appearance* of continuity of focused awareness, but careful observation will reveal that it literally jumps from one object to another in its work of focusing, defocusing and refocusing awareness on aspects of present arising. And it is this inability of attention to hold itself stable on more than one object in any given moment that we could use to our advantage when we enter into the practice for its relaxation.

For this we could devise a simple exercise whereby we again bring attention to hold itself completely stable on the sense of inner darkness. Ideally we should bring ourselves as close as possible, or fully into, to the state of Samatha. Once the instruments of thought and attention have become stable, and we are well established in our inner quiet, we give attention the instruction to become aware of *two points of focus at the same time.*

To do this, we could use any two bodily objects or experiences, but ideally, especially during our initial attempts to feel our way into the practice, it would be easier to keep our attention focused on our inner darkness, while we *simultaneously* attempt to focus in on another bodily aspect. For the second point of focus, we could use any object or bodily sensation, such as our inner warmth, the hands touching, the air as it passes through our nostrils, the feeling of the tongue touching the palate and so on. We will then try to remain focused on *both* the inner darkness and the newly introduced bodily sensation of the hands, the feeling-sensation and so on. The point of the exercise is merely to try to focus attention on *both of these objects simultaneously,* while we remain conscious of what we are doing.

Quite naturally we will soon discover that attention cannot deliver on our demand. Attention cannot focus with equal clarity on two separate things simultaneously. Rather, we will observe how it jumps from one object of focus to another at considerable speed, without managing to maintain its focus on both the chosen objects. If we stay with this experiment for a while, and remain conscious of the attempts of attention to do as it has been instructed to do, we will notice how the impossibility of the endeavor gradually wears attention down.

Because we allow ourselves to remain conscious of what is going on during this exercise, this awareness brings its own Intelligence to the situation which informs attention to stop attempting the impossible. In the light of this insight, the demand for attention to hold awareness focused on two things simultaneously begins to fragment and wither. Soon attention feels the lack of motivation to continue and begins to relax. And as it relaxes its frantic efforts to function contrary to its natural ability, (which is to focus on one object at a time) a new and rather subtle experience presents itself: *we become aware of the direct experience of the inner darkness behind our eyes.*

Part Two: The Practice

Through conscious relaxation of the isolating function of attention, we are now left with a subtle sense of being directly 'in touch' with this inner darkenss.

We have therefore moved from focused, attentive awareness (the state of Samatha) to a more relaxed and direct awareness which is not bound by the exclusive focusing of attention. What is most interesting about this kind of awareness is that it displays a deep feeling sense of *non-divisiveness between its 'object' and itself.* There is the sense that the inner darkness of which we are aware cannot be separated from us being aware of it. The content of awareness and the awareness of the content becomes one experience of present arising. And because our practice had priorly been well established in Samatha, where the whole instrument had been sufficiently stabilized, we can quite easily remain in this open, aware state with no effort to hold it in place by a deliberate act of attention. We are just directly aware of the darkness in our head area.

Also, we now see the value of our earlier practice of securing a stable inner environment for the work we are engaging in. For although attention is no longer present, and we apply no effort to keep the Direct Awareness of our inner darkness in place, we nevertheless do not revert back to the random, habitual movements of thought and attention. The stability established during the event of Samatha has literally spilled over into the experience of Direct Awareness.

What also becomes evident is that it is not attention, but *awareness itself* that is conscious of this inner darkness. In this we make a significant discovery: when attention relaxes its hold on consciousness, it is clear that consciousness itself is the 'observing' component of this experience. No 'I', as the presumed observer, remains as central headquarters from where we believe we experience our darkness. In this diffused, but finely tuned sense of awareness, no separation can be felt, intuited, or in any way experienced between the content of awareness and awareness itself. Here these processes are shown never to have been two distinct aspects of experience. Our inner darkness and the awareness of this inner darkness are experientially revealed to be one unitary process.

Consciousness and the content of consciousness are one indivisible process of present arising..

Whereas Samatha was therefore still characterized by a subtle sense of the observer, during the state of Direct Awareness this witness is absent. This is because when attention relaxes, thought relaxes. The conscious non-movement of attention brings about the non-movement of thought. *And when thought relaxes, the 'I'-sense withers and falls away by itself,* as it is nothing but a creation of thought. This shows us that we can be *fully conscious without being self-conscious.* All that remains when the inner actor is no longer present is the Direct Awareness of our inner darkness.

When we have thus managed to feel our way into this introductory practice of Direct Awareness, we could refine our approach to allow for a more seamless transition from dualistic to non-dualistic experience. Yet, it is very important that we practice with this primary exercise until we have become well established in our ability to relax attention and to experience beyond the confines of the separate self-sense.

3) Full-Bodily Awareness

Once we have felt ourselves into the relaxation of attention and have comprehensively explored the directness of the experience of our inner darkness and silence, we could, with full confidence enter into the next phase of our work. We need to simplify the shift from Samatha to Direct Awareness. For this we again have to enter the state of Samatha or an equivalent measure of deep, inner quiet.

We have seen that to maintain the attentive state of Samatha, it is most practical to use the inner darkness as our object of meditation. When our eyes are closed, this darkness is already present. All we need to do is to allow for attentive awareness to focus on it in a subtle, unforced, yet very conscious and alert way. And it is the *feeling-sense* of this inner darkness that becomes the vehicle for our further enquiry into Direct Awareness.

So, instead of attempting to become aware of two objects simultaneously as we did during our preliminary exercise, this practice will involve a *sudden relaxation of attention* for the inner darkness to remain effortlessly in our field of awareness. Here the proficiency we gained with allowing attention to relax as explored during the previous exercise becomes pivotal to the success of this practice. There we noticed that in order to become directly aware of this inner darkness we needed to *feel* it rather than to hold it as an object of attentive awareness. The *feeling-sensation* of the darkness was crucial for the revelation of the non-dual sense of the experience.

During this more advanced phase of letting go of our dualistic vision, we simply relax attention instantly, *catching it almost by surprise.* We already have the sense of what it *feels* like to have attention completely relaxed. Here we just enter into the relaxation of attention in a sudden shift from attentive awareness to Direct Awareness of our inner silence. We do this by simply *feeling* or s*ensing* the darkness directly, without paying attention to it. We allow the darkness to be present by itself. It is *already* part of our situation and therefore integrally contained within the awareness of it. With no effort and no will to hold anything in place, the direct experience of this inner darkness becomes self-evident the moment attention relaxes its hold on consciousness.

As we have observed during the first exercise, this darkness will initially appear to be only in our head area, somewhere behind our eyes. This is still the consequence of using Samatha as our point of departure where we held attention stable on the inner darkness in our head. However, during this experiment we become aware that as soon as attention relaxes its focus on this darkness utterly and completely *the darkness immediately 'spreads' throughout the whole body.* This happens quite naturally and without any effort on our part. We are left *only* with the conscious, non-dual experience of the darkness, and here the darkness is clearly experienced as self-aware content. Darkness and the awareness of the darkness reveal themselves as one undivided process of *full-bodily presence.*

And not only do we become directly aware of this whole-bodily presence, we also experience the non-divisiveness of our inner darkness and silence, and the awareness of these.

And it is at this point where we enter the practice of 'non-doing' or 'no-effort'. There is simply no-one around who is either doing anything, such as paying attention to the darkness, or noticing it. Yet, the presence of the experience of darkness and silence is unmistakably, and *experientially*, real.

Having thus suspended attention and thought as willful activity, we are left with an inward sense of *whole-bodily presence*. It will also become clear that, as our eyes will be closed at this point, the sense we have of the 'body' will not be of any physical, bodily structure as such. It will be mere sensation. For instance, to 'feel' the presence of our hands where no hands can be detected as objects of sight, would be e already to have fallen back into the *thought-projection* of our hands, and then to mistake this thought for reality. What is present where thought might project a pair of hands is just mere non-conceptual sensation. On present evidence, while our eyes are closed, there are simply no hands to be experienced. There is just sensation with no borders to demarcate something called 'hands'.

This becomes true of our whole body. *It is present as mere sensation.* It is self-aware, and in this condition nothing about it can be separated into any sense of observer and observed. There is just the sense of one non-dual inward process completely aware of itself as *mere sensation*. This is the state of undivided, full-bodily awareness.

At this point the Zen saying: 'Sitting quietly, doing nothing; Spring comes, and the flowers bloom by themselves' begins to make sense. The Soto Zen term 'Shikantaza' (just sitting) also seems to apply. Inward stillness, untouched by thought or attention, reveals itself as a total, non-dual, 'full-bodily' and effortless presence.

During this experiment, it once again becomes clear that we can be *fully conscious without being self-conscious*. Self-consciousness is an unnecessary elaboration on the simplicity of undivided reality. Although still limited to a rather specialized field of conscious awareness (the body), we have here direct experiential proof that the 'observer' is not necessary for anything to appear. Rather, when the previously presumed 'conscious principle', the 'I' as the observer, is absent, a considerably greater feeling of awareness, naturalness, reaxation and wholeness emerges.

As will become clear when our practice moves to the final stage of Integration, this complete relaxation into the non-dual feeling sense of the body, serves as the 'vehicle' for the revelation of the living reality of the non-dual throughout our entire field of experience. However, we start our enquiry with the body simply because in the bodily context it is quite easy to feel how any experience arises by itself, requiring no mediation for it to be. As a form of practice, and to develop a strong sense for this non-dual experience, we make use of the body because of its ready availability.

This practice is repeatable and the results will always be the same. It presents us with a controllable measure against which we could discern between being caught in the activity of thought and attention (or any other state of attentive absorption), and the directness of unmediated experience. *This is an absolutely crucial shift in our eventual sustainable identification with the non-dual.* We should not underestimate the value of developing this ability of full-bodily awareness. It is the true foundation of our practice, and will prove to be at the core of transcendent living.

As part of our practice, this will reveal itself as the most critical watershed along our path of self-transcendence. It brings us not only to the direct experience of an aspect of our present field of awareness, but clearly positions us in the *effortlessness that will evidence every aspect of our final Integration into the wholeness of life.*

If our interest is the realization of this wholeness, not as concept but as a living experience, we will be well advised to experiment with these types of practices many times over, and in different forms, until attention begins to settle down by itself and to participate without resistance in relaxing beyond its habitual movements.

This practice is as far as our formal meditative enquiry could take us relative to Direct Awareness of the physical body. The path to the wholeness of life lies through the psychophysical being as a whole: mental, emotional and bodily. Once firmly established as a form of whole-bodily practice,

Direct Awareness could be integrated into our entire field of living experience. This aspect of our work will be explored in the last chapter: *'Integration'*.

However, there remains considerable work ahead of us that have not been addressed during the process of establishing the practices of Passive Awareness and Direct Awareness. This work centers on the deeply-rooted psychological/emotional reactivities so characteristic of our pre-inspected lives. *We cannot bypass our fragmented mental, emotional and psychological complexities.* These could be *temporarily* put aside during our formal meditative work while we develop the subtle instruments of Passive Awareness and Direct Awareness. But once these practices have found their measure within our conscious potential, and we can more freely allow for the non-dual experience of the body as a whole, we need to return to our emotional/psychological work.

No sustainable equanimity is possible unless we free ourselves from the deep, often debilitating disturbing tendencies of our hidden emotional material. Before we could therefore proceed with the final Integration of our practice into our lives, where alone the question of true freedom becomes relevant, we should first attend to these inner patterns of emotional resistance comprehensively and with considerable care.

This is the work of both Contemplation and Direct Awareness. In the following three chapters we will use our experience, as well as the instruments we have developed along our enquiry up to this point, to explore our deeply conditioned mental and emotional complexities in considerable detail. When we have worked through these, our psycho-physical being as a whole will be sufficiently prepared to enter the final stage of our practice: Integration. Only then could our freedom become sustainable, realistic and dependable.

One last aspect of the subtle state of direct bodily awareness is worth mentioning. This deep non-dual experience of the body often reveals itself not just as an objective, impartial and unemotional inner affair. Direct Awareness is a profoundly deep and enriching experience. While we are in the full-bodily state of non-dual awareness, we may often enter into very deep states of bliss, feelings of love, tremendous sensitivity, clarity, purity and Intelligence. These are *not* states of attentive absorption: rather they are natural expressions of our full-bodily Being and differ from all other earlier states of attentive absorption in that they take place in the context of full, non-dual awareness.

When the self is not, life is already full of its own profoundly human qualities. And if we are fortunate, we may sometimes be presented with a sense of what it means to be perfectly and completely overcome with the total presence of Being. This is a profound and deeply moving experience filled with intense passion and uncontaminated, pure emotion. It feels as though the whole of life is expressing itself through us in one single moment of living truth.

During such blessed moments we are touched so deeply that every part of our being takes on its true revelatory form. During this great simplicity our emotions are transformed into love, bliss and a tremendous sensitivity of feeling. What is physical becomes the process of awareness/Being. Thought is translated into Intelligence. And what previously presented itself as the 'I' is revealed to be the sum-total of all of these, with no one left to notice it.

This directly experienced realization is probably best described by the words: 'I am THIS, there is only THIS'.

SUMMARY OF PRACTICE:

PURPOSE:

- To allow for the direct experience of whatever arises in the present moment free from dualistic presumption.
- To develop a useful and practical instrument with which to approach and transcend sensitive and deeply embedded emotional disturbances.
- To establish the disposition from where Integration could take place.

Spirituality Without God

PRACTICE:

- Be restful, feel secure and positive. Trust your inner nature.
- Feel your way into the practice of Passive Awareness. Use all the techniques you have learnt during Passive Awareness to keep your inner state quiet and steady.
- Use the darkness behind your eyes as your object of attention.
- Keep attention stable in this darkness. Take your time and allow for a deep state of inner quiet (Samatha) to come over you.
- When Samatha is stable, try to become aware of two objects at the same time. Experience the impossibility of this. Attention can only focus on one thing at a time.
- Attention relaxes and what remains is the direct experience of the inner darkness behind your eyes.
- It becomes evident that awareness itself is conscious of the darkness.
- Experience the non-divisive truth of direct experience. The darkness exists by itself.
- Awareness and the content of awareness are directly experienced to be one undivided process of present arising.
- Practice this many times over until a considerable degree of proficiency has been attained.
- The next part of the practice is to go back to Samatha and from there to relax attention *suddenly* from its object of inner darkness.
- Relax *completely* into this darkness and experience the diffusion of the darkness throughout the whole body.
- Again the darkness is present directly and immediately without mediation by thought or attention.
- Feel the entire body-sensation, first as darkness, then as pure general alive sensation. No borders, just the direct full-bodily sensation.

Part Two: The Practice

- Experience full awareness of the body without being self-aware. At this point the observer has been transcended.
- This is Direct Awareness of the body.
- Hold this disposition for as long as is comfortable.
- Feel the truth of the words: 'I am THIS. There is only THIS', while you are present *as* the full-bodily experience.

Chapter Fifteen

WORKING WITH CONTEMPLATION

The insight and understanding of the human situation which this book communicates are based on two distinct forms of enquiry. The first has to do with arriving at a clear view of our overall situation through insight, clear comprehension and introspection. Here we look at the ways we function and how we think about things. We also investigate many aspects of our psychological and emotional responses to both inner and outer experiences. We begin to understand ourselves from a wider and more comprehensive perspective based on our own clarity and self-enquiry. This is facilitated not only through clear insight and right understanding, but is also informed by the Intelligence that becomes available to us during the practice of Passive Awareness.

As we have seen, Passive Awareness is a valuable instrument we develop to deal with many aspects of our dualistic vision. Because we learn how to look at things as they are in themselves, without the habitual interference of thought-projections, we gain considerable insight and clarity about our world, both inwardly and outwardly. Passive Awareness could thus be seen as an instrument of passive, yet critical and intelligent, observation of our *relative*, dualistic functioning. It serves our understanding of things in a very objective and comprehensive way. This is why this kind of practice is such a valuable instrument for all contemplative investigation into ourselves.

Contemplative enquiry could be seen as a natural extension of the instrument of Passive Awareness which we use during the examination of many aspects of our cognitive and emotional being. It affords us with all the tools to arrive at a realistic and vitally important understanding of both ourselves and things in general. In the process we are freed from much of the problems associated with certain aspects of our emotional/psychological disturbances. And it is this area of investigation we will pursue in the course of this chapter.

The second area of investigation concerns itself not with insight or understanding as such, but rather with the non-dual *experience* of things. As we have seen in the previous chapter, here we enter into the subtle experiences of non-doing, effortlessness, and Being. But, as we indicated before, the ability to enter into a direct sense of things also makes it possible for us to access our emotional world in a very *immediate* way. This is why it is important that we first have to develop the ability of Direct Awareness, before we use it as an instrument for investigating our deeply rooted emotional and psychological reactivities.

Working with Direct Awareness in the context of these problem areas will be explored in Chapter 17: *Working with Psychological and Emotional Reactivities.*

Much of what is proposed, and shared, in this book concerns itself with this *relative world* of presumed separate existence and the possibility of seeing into the illusory, self-created nature of that which binds us. From this understanding it may be clear that we will have to explore the many *relative* issues that surround, influence and condition our lives from the point of view of a kind of enquiry which facilitates such work. Passive Awareness, in the form of contemplative enquiry, will more than adequately assist us in this.

During contemplative work we will discover many aspects of ourselves. Often we may have to confront issues we have previously denied or suppressed, simply because of our often unfortunate conviction that we are not capable of dealing with deep emotional issues within ourselves. But if we are patient, and approach things with an open mind and an open heart, we will soon discover that there is nothing to be afraid of and nothing which lies beyond our potential to investigate, understand and transcend.

So let us start by looking at how the practice of Contemplation might elucidate aspects of our inner complexities and assists us in freeing ourselves from the binding effects these have on our being.

We have seen that contemplative enquiry is an extension of the practice of Passive Awareness and is thus a very useful instrument for enquiring into matters such as the relationship between thought and emotions. This type of enquiry is of critical importance because of the *deeply conditioned interaction between thought and emotional responses.* Thought plays a crucial and determining role in many kinds of emotional and psychological reactivities. It may not always be immediately evident, but behind many reactive forms of emotional response we find a thought (or thoughts) that triggers, informs and often sustains it.

We do not only *feel* our emotional and psychological reactivities, we also *think* them. We may have the sense of simply feeling hurt, done in, rejected, inferior, inadequate, unloved and so on. But if we observe ourselves closely, we will notice how many of these feelings are preceded and informed by *thoughts* of inferiority, rejectedness, inadequacy or hurt.

In many of these emotionally reactive responses, thought is often the initiating component. *We often first think a disturbance before we feel it reflected in our emotions.* And because of the overwhelming effect of such emotions on our being, we are generally unaware that an integral part of what we believe we feel, is intimately tied to the thought that precedes, accompanies and sustains it.

This brings us to the most important aspect of contemplative enquiry: it does not concern itself with embedded memories of past hurts and other forms of residual, memory-based emotional disturbances. Rather, contemplative exploration could be seen as an attempt to get to grips with the *mechanisms* which facilitate the appearance and sustenance of any present emotional response. Reactive emotions are the *symptoms* of the inappropriate functioning of inner processes. If we therefore want to deal with our emotional disturbances comprehensively and adequately, we have to investigate the *inner functions* which produce them. We cannot merely use the disturbed state as it gets presented to us and try to overcome it through some kind of resistive, or mere analytical approach to it. By the time we actually experience a disturbed emotion, it is already well established in the conditioned functioning of the *instruments which produced it*.

No doubt, the content of past emotional experiences cannot be ignored. They clearly form part of our reactive impulses. However, it is exactly because of the important role these play in our relationships with both others and our world in general that we need to enquire into the possibility of dealing with these in a new and creative manner. And the way of Contemplation suggests that we put aside the *historical content* of our emotional reactivities and rather approach each incident as it arises as a *process* of inner functioning.

In this way we may discover a different kind of resolution based on observing both the processes which facilitate the manifestation and the binding nature of these types of emotional disturbances. Contemplative enquiry allows us to stay with what is happening *in the present moment* and thereby affords us with the opportunity to come to a clear understanding of how we participate in the creation and maintenance of our disturbed emotional states. Such clarity, based on our own observation of how we function, provides the disposition from where our deeper Intelligence could bring its own insight and freeing lucidity into the situation. All we need to do is to observe ourselves with an open and receptive attitude.

During contemplative work our interest is therefore to observe and transcend the manner by which thought elicits emotional and psychological reactive feeling-responses as a general process active within us, without us becoming involved in the *emotional content* or storyline of the disturbance as such. For this we will make full use of the ability we gained during the practice of Passive Awareness, which is to hold an object relatively stable for a period of time to gain access to it, thereby allowing it to teach us about itself

To start this enquiry we could bring attention to focus consciously on our inner darkness. As we have seen, when our eyes are closed, this darkness is present by itself and is thus an easy object for attention to focus on. This will stabilize attention and allow us the inner space to explore an aspect of ourselves of which we are generally quite unaware. When things begin to settle down, and we experience the relative quiet of stabilized attention, we could remain with this conscious process for a while and get deeply, yet consciously, into the feeling-sense of our inner quiet. The deeper the experience of this inner quiet, the better. *Contemplation requires a stable and relaxed atmosphere to do its work.* We should therefore not underestimate the importance of establishing ourselves firmly in the conscious feeling-sense of deep silence before we start our contemplative investigations.

The reason for this is threefold: first, it is impossible to look at a specific aspect of ourselves when we are in a state of unsettled attention where it moves in a random, unconscious and habitual way from thought to thought, or object to object. The second important reason for starting our contemplative enquiry from a disposition of inner stability and tranquility is that we will often be working with rather volatile thought/emotions. Inner silence needs to be well in place for us not to become so overwhelmed and disturbed by the material we work with that the whole process becomes counterproductive. The third, and perhaps most crucial aspect of establishing this inner quiet, is that only in this state of conscious awareness is our deeper Intelligence afforded the opportunity to do its insightful and liberating work.

Once this has been allowed for, we could start by consciously projecting a mild, emotionally disturbing situation into our field of awareness. For instance, we all know what it feels like to experience the sense of inferiority. For the purpose of our present exercise we could imagine finding ourselves in a somewhat insecure situation where normally we would feel slightly inferior – such as when we are in the presence of a person of authority, or faced with something we have to do but about which we feel a little insecure. This should be quite easy as we all have areas of relative insecurity about our ability to perform in relation to others which might trigger feelings of inferiority and insecurity. Of course, for the purpose of this exercise any other mildly disturbing emotion may be used.

Part Two: The Practice

As we begin to sense this conscious, self-induced feeling of inferiority, we allow ourselves to stay with the feeling-sense of it for a while and try not to move away from it. We just allow attention to remain focused on it in quite a gentle and non-aggressive way. This may be somewhat uncomfortable at first, but we will soon discover that the practice we are engaging in as a form of *conscious* exercise, is in no way different to what we generally allow to happen to us unconsciously: we experience all kinds of emotional disturbances throughout our lives while we generally remain totally unaware of the processes which at any moment are responsible for these states. We simply suffer our feelings of inferiority, inadequacy, lack of self-worth and so on without being in touch with how these develop within us.

What we will attempt to do from here is to hold onto this mild feeling of inner disturbance and to use the skills we have gained through the practice of Passive Awareness to make this sense of un-ease available to both our conscious awareness and to our deeper Intelligence. In this way we will gain a clearer understanding of what this state is all about.

Careful observation will soon show us that what we presumed to have been a mere *feeling* of inferiority is in fact priorly informed by the *thought* of inferiority. It is the thought of inferiority which creates and sustains the feeling of inferiority. For us to feel inferior requires the intimation from thought that we are inferior. This of course would imply that if the thought of inferiority is absent or marginalized, our feeling of inferiority will also be absent or greatly diminished. So, in order for us to allow for the relaxation of the offensive thought-projection, we could devise a simple exercise which may help us to do this.

We could start by identifying and isolating the *thought* of inferiority and then to focus our attention on this thought aspect of the disturbed feeling. *The reason for doing this is to frustrate the unconscious association between the negative thought and its negative emotional counterpart.* By separating these, and focusing our attention consciously and exclusively on the thought that triggered the emotional response, we fragment the thought/emotion 'reality' by bringing conscious awareness into the situation.

We have seen that attention and awareness have a close working relationship. Where attention goes, awareness goes. And by using attention consciously in this manner, we literally make the unconscious, conscious. We become clearly aware of how thought evokes an emotional response by bringing our conscious attention to this process. In other words, for the sake of this experiment, we make the *thought-aspect* of the disturbing experience our object of meditation.

Here we again observe the critical importance of the work we engaged in during our practice of Passive Awareness where we acquired the skill of holding attention stable on any chosen object. We may recall how we allowed attention to remain stable by keeping its focus on our inner darkness. Contemplative practice makes use of exactly the same skill. We identify the area of focus (in this case the *thought* of inferiority) and allow attention to remain stably focused on it *without any intention on our part to effect any change to either thought or feeling of inferiority..*

We may also remember how insight developed from the inner stability of thought and attention. Conscious awareness led to insight and clear understanding. So, by holding attention consciously stable on the thought of inferiority, we try not to judge, evaluate, understand or get rid of the disturbed emotion. We merely stay with the thought that is responsible for this feeling. In this we establish an entirely different relationship with our emotional disturbance: we allow our deeper Intelligence space to enter the process. And this naturally leads to insight into the thought-created emotion. We obtain clarity with regard to the unnecessary functioning of thought as it projects the image of inferiority. We clearly begin to see the false for the false.

We observe with great clarity what we are doing. And what we are doing in that moment is *thinking* our own inferiority. In the light of our deeper Intelligence the whole inferiority-project begins to lose its coherency, as well as its acutely disturbing potential. From this deeper perspective the notion of inferiority as such suddenly seems rather absurd. It is something we create within ourselves and then proceed to believe in the apparent reality of our own projection. Inferiority has no existence separate from the mind that projects it, yet, we experience it as though it has a kind of inner objective status – as though we are really inferior. Here we again observe how easily it is for us to mistake thought-projections for reality.

Another insight which may present itself during this enquiry into inferiority is its close link to the functioning of the ego in its endless comparative struggle. In Chapter 4: *Components of the Separate Self-sense,* it became evident how the ego is most fundamentally based in comparison. It is always active *as* comparison. Here we again see this ego-tendency at work. To imagine ourselves in the company of someone we believe we should feel inferior toward our ego measures its own standing in this relationship and decides that in comparison to the other person, it somehow does not meet the mark.

The thought of inferiority is founded in comparison. And comparison, as a function of the self-image, is itself revealed as part of the inappropriateness of the feeling of inferiority. In its widest sense, we clearly observe how the emotional disturbance is created and sustained by thought, and how this unnecessary elaboration within our psyche binds our emotions into the feeling of inferiority. At this point, we simply stop *doing* inferiority.

We have therefore done nothing *to* the feeling of inferiority as such. We have merely allowed ourselves to view it from a more intelligent and therefore more comprehensive perspective. *Our natural Intelligence does the healing for us.* The error is corrected without us trying to correct it from within the measure of the error itself.

At the same time we notice how the disturbed emotional residue begins to fade and simply wither in the light of clear comprehension and insight. We find ourselves established in a sense of freedom from the implications of the thought/emotion which a few moments earlier appeared very solid and real. And this is a direct result of allowing, through silent observation, for the introduction of an Intelligence that has no concern for the dreams we mistake for reality. Through insight into the functioning of disorder, a new way of intelligent, participatory relationship to things gets established. A new order comes into being, based on Intelligence and insight.

Intelligence transcends the dream together with its accompanying emotional reactivities. And this we discover as a natural consequence of contemplative enquiry. What was previously experienced as a deeply *personal*, feeling-sense of inferiority now becomes an observable, *impersonal process* which we allow ourselves to notice and leave behind from within the silence and Intelligence of our contemplative disposition.

Once we have found our way into this process of passively 'interfering' with our projected thought/emotion, we could naturally extend this practical experiment to many other similar situations. Both the thought and emotional content may vary, but the principle of how to approach these remains the same. Having been sensitized to this way of inner functioning, and having gained experience through further experimentation, we may develop sufficient confidence in this approach to introduce it into many real-life situations.

We simply continue to separate the thought from the emotion whenever we sense a reactive disturbance gathering momentum in us. Gradually we will notice how the apparent reality of the entire thought/emotion syndrome begins to fade and lose its hold over us. Not only will we gain confidence in the possibility that we may relieve ourselves from the distressing symptoms of such reactive thought/emotions, we will also steadily lose faith in all mental/emotional reactive responses, regardless of the apparent seriousness, and genuineness, of their content. In this way contemplative practice greatly enhances the possibility of freedom from these forms of unnecessary emotional reactivities.

If we now compare this type of contemplative work with more traditional forms of psychoanalysis where we are advised to enquire deeply into the *content* of our past hurts and repressed emotional material, we could draw some useful comparisons between these two forms of self-enquiry.

Part Two: The Practice

One of the most important distinctions between psychoanalysis and contemplative enquiry is the lack of formal preparatory work in the former. No doubt, attempts are made to allow the client to relax and feel their way into the psychoanalytic session. But whereas contemplative enquiry is grounded in a well developed ability for conscious, inner attentiveness and calm, psychoanalysis shows little interest in such thorough preliminary work.

In the latter, the history of past hurts and repressed shadow material is investigated and considered in the context of our ordinary thinking. The past gets reflected in terms of present understanding, and analyzed to gain greater insight into how the whole emotional disorder was originally constructed. Contemplation, on the other hand, does not concern itself primarily with the content of any hurtful past incident. Rather, it endeavors to bring into play an Intelligence which is of a different order and quality to that of the problem.

Self-analysis takes on a certain sequential and causal logic. This logic rests on the assumption that knowledge about the past will correct an emotional disturbance in the present. Yet, however true the historical connection between our present, emotionally reactive states and such past hurts might be, the knowledge of this connection seems to make little difference to the way we continue to feel about these past incidents. Neither does it address the powerful tendencies to experience the same distressing feelings in the future.

By analyzing myself I may gain an understanding of the reactivities I experience about many aspects of my relation to others and myself. For instance, I may discover that I was not given enough love by my mother, or that I was dominated by my father, or not respected and appreciated for who I believe I was; but such knowledge of past emotional hurts has no inherent insight to cut through its own logic of justified present disturbance.

Knowledge about knowledge has no inherent healing power. It attempts to *explain* the emotional disturbance in terms of its historical background, but such explanation often tends to be mere justification for the way we feel. The reason for this failure is that no new energy has been brought into the process of self-analysis. Self-analysis works with the known and knowable. It is essentially memory-based and works with the same instruments in the same fragmentary way that brought about our problems in the first place. We may end up having considerable knowledge *about* our problems, but such knowledge can never transcend the problems created by memory-based knowledge itself.

The whole process of self-analysis is suspect, because it depends on our disorderly and conditioned, memory-based thinking to inspect aspects of itself objectively and with clarity. It is like expecting a corrupt police department to inspect and report back on its own corruption: it generally only leads to a further falsification and suppression of evidence. Until an honest person, with a fresh mind and an open heart, is given full authority to lead the investigations, nothing of real consequence could happen. Only when the quality of investigation comes from a different source than that of the problem, is there any possibility for clearing up the confusion.

And, as we have seen, this is where contemplative enquiry differs markedly from other forms of introspection. It allows for the introduction of our deeper Intelligence in the context of inner silence and mental stability to bring new clarity and vision to the problems created by the unconscious projections of thought.

Thought inspecting thought only results in further justification, greater confusion and inner conflict. As an instrument for self-enquiry and self-understanding, thought, in itself, is inherently flawed. We need to allow for a new energy of insight and Intelligence that is founded in observation and inner stillness to re-cognize the entire interaction of emotional and mental reactivities. Contemplation affords us with such a radically different approach to our complexities. It is also very empowering, because we have the sense of being able to observe and participate consciously in our inner world the very moment it is happening. We are no longer tethered to our hurtful past. We fully acknowledge the presence of what we think/feel about the past, but approach it in a way that enables us to see directly into the *mechanisms* that facilitate our emotional distress in the present.

Part Two: The Practice

In this way we not only objectify our emotional reactivities (and thereby rendering them accessible for true investigation and clear insight), we also allow ourselves to look directly at what is happening within us when such states are present. Here we begin to observe the functional sequence and logic of our emotional disturbances as *processes,* rather than investigating their historical, memory-based justifications.

In conclusion we may just reiterate that there is nothing that determines the continuation of our uninspected living other than our disinclination to look at ourselves with clarity and a fresh, open attitude. When we become inwardly alive to all the things that limit and condition our being, it will be evident how we have allowed ourselves to be dominated by aspects of our functioning which should never have been given the freedom to control our emotional life the way they do.

When thought/emotion is not active, we begin to sense a subtle relaxation and a feeling of quiet equanimity and this we naturally intuit as our home-ground. It is a state of simplicity and gentleness. The natural order of human life exhibits a relaxed state of participatory emotional equanimity that cannot be *destroyed* by the inappropriate use of our inner faculties. These can, and do, however, *obscure* the subtle movement of our inner equanimity. When we become conscious of how we function as disordered, fragmented and emotionally challenged human beings, we do not *add* anything to what we already do in the form of counter-strategies or defense-mechanisms. The awareness and Intelligence we bring to our situation are sufficient to effect all the necessary changes effortlessly.

In this regard it is also interesting to note that Intelligence works most subtly as an act of non-doing. When it discovers any inappropriate or unnecessary activity, it simply allows this to fall away through non-use. *It has no compulsion to correct the error by effortful means.* Our responsibility is merely to allow this to happen. In the context of correct inner work, our problems will *self-correct,* without us having to do anything about them.

SUMMARY OF PRACTICE:

PURPOSE:

- To work effectively with emotional disturbances which have a strong thought component as their motivation and foundation.

PRACTICE OF CONTEMPLATIVE ENQUIRY INTO EMOTIONAL DISTURBANCES:

- Allow yourself to become restful and be willing to work intimately with your emotions.
- Find a quiet place where you could feel secure and happy to be on your own.
- Sit down, take a few deep breaths and feel the relaxation of your body-mind. Calm down as far as possible. Get out of head and into your senses.
- Appreciate that you will be working only with the instruments you have acquired during Passive Awareness.
- Slowly allow your attention to settle onto the darkness behind your eyes.
- Hold attention stable on the darkness for a while until you feel completely relaxed into the situation.
- Again feel the deep inner quiet of Samatha.
- Project a slightly disturbing emotion into your field of awareness and allow yourself to come to rest in the feeling-sense of this emotion.
- Do not become distracted or anxious to be in such close proximity to a slight feeling of disturbed emotion.
- Notice how the disturbed feeling is motivated by the *thought* which informs and sustains the feeling.
- Do not attempt to analyze or dissect the emotion. Merely allow attention come to rest in it and remain with it completely.

Part Two: The Practice

- Make no effort to get rid of the disturbing thought/emotion.
- At this point, shift attention deliberately to the thought-aspect of the feeling, making the thought behind the feeling your object of attentive awareness.
- Become aware of how you are *thinking* your emotion and not primarily *feeling* it. The feeling only follows the thought of disturbance.
- Become sensitive to how the *content* of the thought elicits the specific content of the emotional response to it.
- Notice how a new insight arises which simply refuses to continue with the projection of the offensive thought. This is a sign of your unfolding inner Intelligence.
- You notice how you stop *doing* your emotional disturbance.
- When the thought of the disturbance disappears, you notice how the emotional reaction begins to fade and finally fall away.
- Once you have experimented with this type of exercise sufficiently to give you faith in your own ability to relax out of disturbing thoughts, you may experiment with real-life situations.

Chapter Sixteen

CONTEMPLATION AND REALITY- CONSIDERATION.

*I*n Chapter 5: *Intellectualism and Reality-consideration*, we noticed how the intellect cannot enquire beyond its own measure. The relative vision of the intellect gets informed by the limited intelligence that functions in the context of past experiences, and the projection of these through the present into the future. We intimated that a new and different kind of Intelligence would have to be uncovered for us to arrive at a radically new and fresh insight into the way we and our world function. To seek clarity from within the limitations of knowledge-based thinking, is to keep treading water while we believe we are moving forward to greater insight and understanding.

Having worked with contemplative insight as we did with our thought/emotions, we gained valuable experience of how to *feel* our way into contemplative enquiry. Here we allowed for an awakened Intelligence to do its work and to assist us to investigate and break free from many of the binding activities of our deeply conditioned thought/emotions. We also noticed that the insights associated with this process are only possible in the context of a stable and quiet inner environment.

This is why any realistic consideration of other aspects of our lives could also greatly benefit from a similar stable and quiet disposition of conscious awareness. Many of the considerations presented to us in *Part One* are material we could work with contemplatively so that we engage these not merely from an intellectual point of view, but could allow them to be pondered in a conscious and contemplative circumstance. This is how we make these reality considerations part of our lives and therefore *aspects of ourselves*, rather than for them to remain merely on the level of knowledge and thought.

During reality-consideration we do not investigate intellectual and philosophical questions merely for the satisfaction of mental curiosity. Philosophy generally only adds words upon words, logic upon logic, idea upon idea. Often these tend to be completely unrelated to the real circumstance of our lives. And as we have seen, such speculation only results in further confusion.

Contemplative reality-consideration leads us to a direct understanding of many aspects of how we think and feel about things from the perspective of our deeper Intelligence. Prior to such penetrative investigation we relate to things in a confused, conflicting and limited way. Reality-consideration is therefore of paramount importance in our quest for freedom from dysfunctional relationships with others, and our world in general. It allows us to see things as they are, and construct our worldview on lucidity of perception and insight, rather than mere thought-constructs.

Contemplative reality-consideration is one of the most effective methods through which to restore our true and realistic connection to our world. It helps us to look at things from beyond the confines of the dream, and to bring new clarity and an open-ended spirit of enquiry to our situation. And because this kind of enquiry is founded in our deeper Intelligence, the process by which we become *realists* takes place in a creative and participatory environment.

At this point we have had sufficient exposure to many forms of contemplative enquiry to appreciate that when our inner Intelligence is brought into the equation, we can afford to look at things factually and realistically without fear or resistance. We begin to sense that to live with facts is indeed considerably more valuable and practical than to try to make sense of our lives through our thought-projected world. We have nothing to fear from reality: we only have to learn to resonate with it as far as possible.

Another important aspect of reality-consideration is that it literally considers reality before it concerns itself with the security-seeking tendencies of the separate self-sense. This is why reality consideration could be applied to so many aspects of our deluded vision. It seeks truth rather than the fulfillment of the demands of the ego/I. It by-passes these demands and this allows us to re-orientate our functioning in line with reality.

One of the most important consequences of this kind of inner work is that there are hardly any limits to the depth in which anything could be explored. We may often start our enquiry with just one area of investigation in mind, such as what would constitute honesty, compassion, ethical behavior, or we may look for the meaning and value of honesty, or enquire about god, faith, the need for security, justice, 'I'-consciousness, duality; the value of formal meditation etc. Yet, when we deeply enquire into these we observe how our investigation leads us to related, more fundamental aspects of these considerations, where we begin to see the matter in a considerably wider context. It becomes evident how the investigation of one concept leads to another related and more comprehensive one. Soon we begin to experience a pattern of *interlinking insights* which affords us with a considerably more comprehensive picture than the one with which we started our enquiry. This leads to a natural broadening of our outlook and affords us with a new, wider, and often liberating, view of things.

We may recall that during the practice of Samatha we naturally and spontaneously developed insights as a result of our practice. However, during Samatha these insights tend to appear rather randomly. Contemplative reality-consideration works in a methodical way, and don't rely merely on occasional insights which might bring us intermittent moments of inner clarity. Here we make systematic use of this very valuable and revelatory ability of insight. Because we work with a silent mind and stable attention, our inner environment is properly attuned to being receptive for the intimations of our deeper Intelligence. Here we deliberately use inner silence and our awakened Intelligence to contemplate aspects of our world and our relation to it.

So, to start this kind of enquiry, we could enter the state of inner calm in exactly the same way as we did when we worked with our thought/emotions. We just allow ourselves to become restful and quietly predisposed so that our psychophysical being could become receptive to new insights which might occur. As we have done before, we could use our inner darkness as our object of focus, and once we have stabilized attention in this way, our inner environment will be well prepared for contemplative enquiry.

For this we could bring any problem or aspect of our understanding of things gently into the field of awareness. For instance, we may want to look into the notion of 'effort' in the context of meditation. This is an important consideration, not only because it is a rather unresolved issue for many practitioners and teachers alike, but that once we have discerned for ourselves exactly what this word implies in its functional reality, we could move from there into true effortlessness. Few of us know exactly what this word implies in the context of meditative enquiry. Investigating this aspect of our path could prove to be rather interesting, if not of vital importance.

For the sake of this experiment, we will approach the matter as we would normally approach all kinds of contemplative enquiry. This will afford us with the sound basis from where to proceed with our work.

When we therefore bring the notion of 'effort' to our inner quiet, we make no effort to understand the word. We do not immediately direct all our energy to come to a clear conceptual grasp of the exact meaning and nature of what it means to make 'effort'. Although this may be our normal approach to solving problems, the contemplative way suggests that we enter into this kind of enquiry *passively, not actively*. We completely abandon any willful activity, other than just very subtly holding our attention onto the word 'effort?'. There is no demand from thought to reach a quick answer: rather we just come to rest in a general attitude of inner questioning.

By doing this, we allow ourselves the inner space to remain intimately with the object towards which our enquiry will be directed. We simply allow attention to come to rest on this word and to stay with it in a conscious and alert way. The question has already been asked. We are already in a spirit of enquiry. We have already established that we would like to gain insight into this matter. *Having asked the question, our mental work is finished.* We neither wait for an answer, nor do we think about the question. To wait for an answer is to create an inner tension which inhibits the flow of intuitive understanding. Perhaps our approach to this could best be described as an attitude of free-floating enquiry, where the spirit of enquiry is more evident than the demand for an answer.

For the sake of this particular exercise, however, we now need to create a somewhat artificial situation whereby we deliberately loosen our grip on our inner stability, thereby consciously allowing thought to start to enquire into this thing called 'effort' in a kind of mental, effortful manner. In other words, we introduce into our background state of inner quiet the movement of thought as it begins to search for answers to this question. *We try to do this without losing too much of our inner stability and clarity.* By becoming attentive to how thought tries to solve the problem it now works on, we learn, from a relative disposition of quiet, how effort really operates and what it actually looks like. In this way we become both the experiment and the experimenter. We consciously partake in and observe an inner process which normally may not be within our ability to investigate clearly.

The moment we allow thought to begin its search for answers to the question of effort, we notice how it endeavors to find these answers within its own categories. *Thought knows nothing but itself*, and cannot operate beyond itself. So, when it looks for an answer to any challenge, it always searches its own database for clarity and definitive answers. It becomes evident to our quietly observing disposition how this search of thought is in fact rather effortful. It becomes clear that the effort of thought to come to an answer is an attempt to move from here to there. From not knowing to knowing. From what is, to what should be.

And it is this inner tension between what is and what should be that is the basis of all effort in the context of meditative enquiry: we do not understand, and we want to understand; we are not enlightened, and we want to be enlightened; we notice that our concentration is poor and we want it to be better; we think we are not spiritual enough, and we want to be more spiritual and so on. It becomes clear that all effort is motivated by the demand for the change from this to that. And this we observe directly happening within us as thought attempts to find answers to the question of effort. All effort is goal directed, and the establishment of any goal is a projection of thought into some thought-projected future. We further notice that any presumed movement within thought is no movement at all. For thought to seek and to find is to do so within its own paradigm. It seeks and finds nothing but aspects of itself. Thought dances around in circles while believing it is going somewhere.

At this stage we need not place any value-judgments over what we observe. In other words, the point of our exercise is not to teach us *how to work* with what we observe, but rather just to make us aware of how we could look at something through contemplative investigation. The movement of effort is observed against the background of silence and non-movement.

Contemplative reality-consideration has the potential to open an enquiry into every aspect of our lives so that we may gain fresh and more comprehensive understanding and insight into the way we experience things in general. And integral to this enquiry is also to discover how projection and transference distort our vision. Again we have to see these processes in operation. Reality-consideration is ideally suited to discern between projected and transferred reality on the one hand and experience which is not tainted with interpretation on the other. So, perhaps we could just briefly also look at these processes from a contemplative perspective to discover how this may allow us to come to greater clarity about these.

When we find ourselves well established in our inner silence, it will be perfectly sufficient for us just to touch very lightly on the question and not to attempt to force any answers 'from the beyond'. We simply place a question mark over these two concepts while we remain consciously aware of our situation. We again make no effort to come to an answer, or to gain any insight into or clarity about the question. We also put aside what we might know about these concepts or what we have read or previously intuited about them. All we do is to keep our spirit of enquiry wide open and allow these concepts to remain at the center of our focus. The only function of attention in this exercise is to hold these words as *objects of attention* stably within our field of conscious awareness. Nothing more is required. We simply enter into a state of attentive awareness, holding our attention loosely focused on these two concepts of projection and transference.

Perhaps we could just remind ourselves that Passive Awareness is *alive* awareness. It is passive only insofar as it accommodates a stable inner environment. And it is this stability which gives the process the freedom to be fully alive and alert. No energy is wasted on unnecessary movements of thought and attention. In this situation the instrument becomes a conscious pool of receptivity which quietly reflects the insights and clarity our deeper Intelligence provides. And it is to this subtle, but highly aware state that we present our question regarding 'projection' and 'transference'.

Being alive to our inner processes, we will soon observe that projection happens when we project a name, or image onto someone, something or some aspect of life. We name things for practical purposes. And when we relate to such names, it is understood that no name or description is identical to the person or thing itself. The word tree, is not the tree. The name of the person, is not the person. Projection is merely to facilitate communication, recognition, description and functional relationship. The ability to project is here clearly seen to be a useful and necessary instrument of the body/mind.

From within the silence of our contemplative disposition, we could look at any object, give it a name and notice that the naming as such does not interfere with our relationship with the object. Whether I call a towel a towel or a computer a computer or a plant green, white or yellow makes little difference to how I relate to the object. This aspect of projection has a certain neutral functionality to it. It merely serves to duplicate experience in thought which in turn allows for verbal communication. The relative separation between naming and that which has been named remains intact. Generally we do not mistake the name we give to something or someone for the thing or person themselves. In its broadest sense we could say that the appropriate use of projection establishes an appropriate link between the suchness of things (that things are) and the world of the known (what things are).

Part Two: The Practice

However, if we now extend our experiment with projection to include subjective, value-judgments, things take on a rather different nuance. Once we include in our projections issues such as like and dislike, good and bad, moral and immoral, ethical or unethical, beautiful and ugly, right and wrong, etc., things are not so clear any longer. When we project one of these qualities onto a person or object, it becomes more difficult to discern between the projected thought and the object itself. It is no longer clear whether the projection stands totally free from the object onto which it has been projected. Here we observe how our projection loses its *neutrality* and mere mental duplicating ability. In other words we do not only give something a name and know that the name is a mere duplication in thought with regard to the object we have named.

During this kind of subjective projection, our projection tends to take on its own form. We can no longer discern clearly between the image we have projected onto the object and the object itself. That is, we mistake thought for the thing, and this subjectively-projected reality, which we mistake for objective reality, may be called transference. We have literally transferred our own subjective value judgments onto things out there and *then believe that these qualities are inherent to the object of our projection.* And, as we have seen, we do this with people as much as with objects.

During transference we therefore establish a self-enclosed pocket of unconscious relationship with an *aspect of ourselves*, mistaking this for objective reality. Once this error has been committed, we are no longer capable of discerning between thought projections and transferred reality. The one has become the other. Thought has *become* form.

And, interestingly, the sensitivity of our contemplative state will reveal that the moment projection is translated into transference, we are again firmly established in the thought/attention-knot. The pocket of unconsciousness in which we mistake our thought-projections for reality, is nothing other than the living dream-state of the thought/attention-knot. At this point of transference we leave behind all sense of reality, and enter the world of illusion or Maya. Transference creates 'reality' where there is only thought.

Spirituality Without God

We clearly observe that the act of transference is a movement in illusion. And while caught in this illusion, we are totally out of touch with reality. We could also say that here we observe a clear situation where we cannot distinguish between that which is created and sustained by thought, and that which is not.

Once this insight into the distinction between projection and transference has been well established, and we are able to utilize the projective ability of thought in a useful and practical way, (without allowing it to become transference), we would feel more comfortable to explore other similar concepts from our contemplative disposition. We will gain confidence in our own ability to observe our functioning clearly and to arrive at our own insight of things.

Again we need to emphasize that contemplative enquiry always investigates the *larger* picture. During this kind of investigation, we do not concern ourselves with the specific content of the projection or the transferred state as such, that is, trying to see how distorted, stupid, unintelligent, true, false, valuable, disconnected or unrelated the content of the projection might be. Rather, we simply observe with clarity and insight the *inner processes* which are responsible for the act of both projection and transference. This is true reality-consideration. We arrive at the truth of things not merely through thinking about it as objectively as possible, but by using the clarity of our inner *perceptive Intelligence* to re-cognize a world which so often exists for us merely as unconscious transferred reality. This is how we make the unconscious conscious, leaving its content available for intelligent self-correction.

Once contemplative enquiry becomes aware of these mechanical defaults in the way we operate, we begin to develop a sense for recognizing them the moment they appear. Consequently we begin to see and experience things as they are prior to transference. We see things in their 'suchness'. Over time, we gradually develop the ability to become aware of these illusory processes as they arise, and by allowing our awareness to be sensitive and alive to our inclination to fall back into some aspect of thought-created reality, we gently pre-empt such thoughts from taking on the appearance of reality. We begin to live with things as they *are*, rather than what we project and transfer them to be.

Reality-consideration, in the context of the Intelligence of contemplation, should therefore be regarded as of equal importance to working with our inner emotional and psychological material. What we project inwardly as psychological and emotional complications, 'I'-consciousness and ego-consciousness, are of the same illusory nature as that which we project and transfer outwardly onto our world of experience. All these are created, informed and sustained by thought.

Implied in this kind of contemplative work is that we begin to develop a healthy skepticism with regard to many aspects of our lives which previously we have taken for granted as irreducible fact. From personal, direct observation of how we allow ourselves to be deluded by secondary processes (such as thought-transference) the realization begins to dawn that we are not our thinking. Thought is merely one of our very valuable instruments. It need not, and in fact *cannot*, define us.

Reality-consideration could effectively be used in many different kinds of enquiry. We could literally take any subject we wish to explore, and by allowing it to be pondered by our inner silence, we may gain valuable insights into many aspects of our lives. There is no limit to the depth and range of such enquiries. It is a truly remarkable instrument for obtaining clarity about ourselves. In its purest form, such reality-consideration could be seen as the most subtle and detailed approach to mental investigation. It is as close as we will ever get to complete unconditioned thinking.

SUMMARY OF PRACTICE:

PURPOSE:

- To gain deep insight into the way things appear to us.
- To get our general thinking in line with reality.

Spirituality Without God

PRACTICE:

- Gain access to your own inner quiet through the practice of Passive Awareness.
- Hold your silence by sensing the stability of thought and attention.
- Trust your inner Intelligence to provide answers to any serious question you may bring into your field of open awareness.
- From within your inner silence project the question or word which is the basis of your enquiry.
- Do not think about the matter. Merely allow the question to remain as asked, allowing your inner Intelligence to do its work. Do not demand or await a reply.
- Rest merely in a free-floating *attitude* of enquiry.
- Become aware of your resistances to seeing things clearly and factually.

Chapter Seventeen

WORKING WITH PSYCHOLOGICAL AND EMOTIONAL REACTIVITIES

General Introduction

In Chapter 9 we established that a clear relationship exists between self-transcendence and the need to effectively neutralize all mental, emotional and psychological reactivities which fragment and distort our lives. Through self-enquiry we developed sensitivity to how these emotional disturbances offer a continuous flow of resistance to the living moment. From this it became clear that we generally do not approach our interaction with life with an open and emotionally responsive attitude. On the contrary, our responses are mostly conditioned and fragmented, which generally bind our emotional energy in a narrow range of pre-determined reactivity. This reactivity contracts around itself and thereby supports the illusion of the separate self-sense.

It may be useful again to remind ourselves that to transcend any aspect of our inner confusion, whether reactive emotional material or patterns of conditioned thinking, it is important for us first get to know these intimately through self-observation and intelligent participation in the processes which create and sustain them. Nothing that creates resistance, conflict, fragmentation or division can be by-passed or left out from our enquiry. To do so would leave us vulnerable to the continued effects of these mostly unconscious modes of dysfunction on our being.

Once we understand that the path of self-transcendence concerns itself essentially with the recognition and transcendence of everything which places a limitation on our sane, happy and integral relation to life, we may appreciate how important it is to come to terms with our emotional and psychological shadow material. If our interest is to free ourselves from the symptoms of every manifestation of fragmentary living, it will be evident that these require our dedicated and most intimate consideration.

Any residual resistances, whether physical, mental or emotional/psychological which have not been brought into the light of our own awareness, and transcended, will remain as unconscious potential within us, and will continue to exert their control over us. The process by which we free ourselves from these reactivities has to be active and effective within us for our self-transcendent work to be truly sustainable. For this we need to remain vigilant that our inner work does not in itself become a block to further investigation.

For instance, during meditation, we may often have rather intense and very beautiful experiences which may inspire us to believe that we have touched upon the deepest levels of Being or have come upon the essence of life itself. Often these are indeed early signs of true non-dualistic unfolding. But because the instrument as a whole has not been thoroughly prepared, these become mere fleeting experiences with little or no sustainable, long-term effects. And because these are so special and intense, we tend to *keep these experiences in memory* and recall them over and over to remind and convince ourselves that we have indeed reached beyond the confines of the separate self-sense. But for as long as we remain absorbed in the *memory* of any inner experience, however profound and moving, such a memory itself will become a barrier to our further development.

Of themselves, these states are to be enjoyed and welcomed as part of our unfolding. They will inevitably present themselves from time to time, but they should not be mistaken for the fruit of our practice. As we have seen, these are mostly exclusive, inward states, and become apparent only in a certain limited field of conscious awareness or attentive absorption. This is why we should not be motivated to meditate on these in the faith that they will be sufficient to relieve us from the plight of the total self-sense with its necessary emotional and psychological disturbances.

Part Two: The Practice

For our current work, it is important that we appreciate and understand the profoundly debilitating effects of our negative emotions on our lives. Nothing disturbs us more intimately than the manner in which we react emotionally to situations in a habitual and uncontrolled way. The power with which our emotional patterns control almost every aspect of our being should make this perfectly clear. Psychological and emotional reactivities are inner functions which we should approach with care and a genuine desire to understand and transcend. Together with other forms of mental conditioning, these form the most formidable barrier to the realization of our natural, non-dual reality. We need, therefore, to attend to these with *at least the same attention to detail as they bring to their own fragmentary functioning.* We should never underestimate the destiny-creating power of our uninspected emotional and psychological shadow material.

These reactivities have to be addressed as processes of disturbance when they are active within us, and cannot be bypassed by entering into what we believe to be some form of 'spiritual' practice which provides us with all sorts of mystical states of absorption. Working on these deeply-rooted disturbances is as integral to our self-transcending process as any other form of meditative or contemplative practice.

As we have seen, we *are* the path we will have to walk. Distinct from our resistant patterns of emotional and mental life, there is no path. When these have been transcended, the path itself has been transcended, and when our living reality is no more active *as* dilemma and contracted being, the simplicity of life itself becomes its own natural revelation.

Self-transcendence and Emotions

Most spiritual, religious and mystical paths share one rather unfortunate tendency: they often project human emotions as something inimical to what they propose as a truly spiritual way of life. According to this misconception only unenlightened mortals enjoy their senses and the full expression of their emotional potential, while the spiritual sages have been described as having gone beyond such human 'weaknesses'.

Spirituality Without God

This misunderstanding has led many sincere students to believe that they should detach themselves emotionally from the world if they are really serious about self-transcendence or spiritual life. In many cases this has led to the practice of inhibiting and debilitating disciplines where considerable restriction has been placed on the free and open-hearted unfolding of their emotions in the context of both their spiritual practice and everyday lives.

The humanistic approach to self-transcendence does not set itself on such a collision course with our human condition, especially our emotions. It is only when we pursue some presumed Other-worldly or metaphysical ideal that we will be vulnerable to being convinced that every aspect of this world, including our emotions, are necessarily of a lesser order than the world of our Gods or the Great Beyond towards which we are suppose to aspire. Such misconceptions positioned spiritual life in direct opposition to the rich soil of human experience from within which alone free and intelligent living could flower.

The spiritual path is nothing other than the gradual unfolding of our own human potential. To transcend the separate self-state is not to arrive somewhere 'Else'. And when the spiritualization of our being is complete, so will be our *humanization* which will include the free and joyful participation of our natural emotional potential in every aspect of our lives.

To transcend self-limitation is therefore not to reject or marginalize our emotions. Rather, when the self with all its self-centered desires, motivations and inhibitions have been transcended, we become founded in the emotions of compassion, equanimity and charity. And because the self-transcended condition has no need for the kind of desperate search for objects and states with which to identify itself, as we observe in the 'I'-conscious state, all our sensations and emotions can function freely and joyfully, while our lives remain informed by our deeper Intelligence and holistic disposition.

Having said this, we may nevertheless appreciate why the traditions have mistakenly taken such a strong position against our emotional life. We have seen that the 'I' regards itself as the center of our being and, while feeling separate from its entire field of experience, cannot but search for things with which to identify itself (See: *Part 1: The Destiny of 'I'-consciousness*). By this, the self-sense has created for itself a destiny of seeking. Through its self-imposed feelings of separateness, loneliness, isolation and alienation from life, it is constantly seeking for ways to relieve itself from the consequences of its own presumed reality.

During these early enquiries, it also became evident that one of the main strategies of the 'I' is to attach itself to things in a rather indiscriminate way. In the process it binds itself to objects, people and circumstances, as well as philosophical, political and religious ideas. Through this, we, as bundles of 'I'-conscious activity, assume a defensive, often violent, position against all that threatens these sources of identified security. We respond to things in a strategic way, always protective of everything we have attached ourselves to in our vain attempt to eliminate the anxiety inherent in the self-conscious state.

So, perhaps this is what some of the traditions observed which led them to the conclusion that we should detach ourselves from our emotions so as not to suffer this ego-based reaction to our indiscriminate urge to attach ourselves to things. Through detachment from the world, they argued, we would be more amenable to attach ourselves to God.

However, what escaped the attention of these traditions is that emotions, whether conditioned or natural cannot be repressed in this manner. Here they have clearly missed the mark. Uninspected emotional detachment addresses only the symptoms associated with uninspected emotional attachment. Detachment does not relieve us from the underlying dilemmas of alienation and loneliness *inherent in the 'I'-conscious state* which, as we have seen, necessitates attachment and identification.

Forceful detachment is nothing but suppression. Through such counter-strategies we may attempt to put a lid on our ability to feel freely over the entire spectrum of our emotional potential, but such an uninspected, emotionally restrictive measure will only lead to other forms of psychophysical disorder. Our emotions are deeply rooted in our being and require a much softer and more intelligent approach if we were to work with them constructively to allow for their natural expression.

Ours is a path of *transcendence*, not willful elimination or detachment. Every aspect of limitation needs to be observed, understood and transcended. Our natural emotional responsiveness is an integral component of human existence and as such do not need our interference. Being totally identified with the separate self-sense, we have already interfered with the natural function of our emotions. This is why we find ourselves in the state we are in. The point of self-transcendence is for us to enjoy life fully without the impositions and complications which the separate-self necessitates. This we can only do when we have brought our emotional potential into the very center of our spiritual, self-transcending quest. From here a harmonious relationship could be established between our emotions, the rest of our spiritual unfolding and our ordinary living experience.

Our emotions are one of our most precious gifts. We need to nurture them and allow them to become an integral part of the function of our non-dual human condition. Only then can they serve the broader destiny of our humanity as a whole, and inform every activity with a true and free emotional Intelligence. To be fully 'spiritual', is to fully human. And to be fully human, is to have the full potential of our emotions available to us at every instance of free and participatory relationship.

The path of self-transcendence is the path of gradually allowing our humanity to shine through the ignorance of the ego/I-process with its debilitating effects on our emotional lives. Ours is not a path of becoming so 'spiritual' that we lose our humanity and become emotionally-neutral 'saints'. For a 'spiritual' path to frown upon any sane and coherent development of our emotions is for it to frown upon a very real and important aspect of life itself.

From this it may be evident that if we regard the functionally sane and necessary aspects of our emotions as an integral part, not only of our lives in general, but also of the process of awakening to the non-dual nature of things, we cannot avoid addressing those *reactive* emotional disturbances which are part of our present fragmentary, life-constricting relationships with our world..

Freedom in the human context is an open-ended way of life where real choices can be made relative to us engaging in long-term, emotionally responsive and trustworthy relationships, not only with ourselves, but with others and the world in general.

Our path is not to be associated with a chronic and debilitating non-involvement with, or forced detachment from, our work, talents, interests, loved ones and other aspects of daily living. *Our natural condition is not at odds with true participatory human activity.* Rather, it allows us the freedom to express ourselves fully and without fear and to enjoy our natural emotional responses as part of the fulfillment of our non-dual condition.

The only difference between natural living, and the emotional responses associated with it, and the reactive, fearful emotional mode generally experienced in the self-conscious state, is that when we act from the former, we allow the psycho-physical being complete freedom to explore itself in an open-hearted and open-minded way. This is not possible from within the contracted state of the ego/I. The 'I' simply has too much to protect, and therefore to fear, to show any interest in the true freedom of human expression.

Looking at the problem

Each disturbance in our body-mind calls for a specific kind of healing-response. For instance, it could be considered inappropriate medical intervention to treat a symptom without thoroughly investigating its possible causes. One would not interfere with a higher than normal bodily temperature unless the exact cause of it has been established. For this a thorough diagnosis is required, and only then could intervention be contemplated as a possible appropriate option. The same is true for our emotional responses to life. We cannot expect to be healed emotionally by merely reacting to our inner disturbances in a repressive or defensive way. Rather, to be healed emotionally requires our most subtle co-operation with, and careful investigation into, every aspect our emotionally disturbed experiences.

Our ordinary functioning tends to address only the moment to moment demands of the psychophysical being to the best of its ability, but it is generally not capable of going deeper into the more subtle aspects of ourselves. In fact, the way we ordinarily function, displays a remarkable lack of insight and awareness to many of the processes and motivations which support and sustain our ongoing emotional and psychological disabilities. We need therefore to find very specific ways to allow these disturbances to reveal themselves in a conscious and coherent manner. Only when we render them consciously available to our investigative, deeper Intelligence and learn to appreciate and respect them as part of our present state, can we begin to work with them, and not against them.

From such a realistic and participatory perspective, which is based in a feeling of self-acceptance and willingness to learn about ourselves, we will notice that our perceived difficulty, or inability, to deal with our emotions is not because nature has not provided us with the necessary instruments with which to approach this aspect of ourselves in an effective and coherent way. Rather, we have just never allowed ourselves *sufficient intimacy* with our emotional reactivities to discover ways of relieving ourselves from their negative effects. *We have tended to resist, suppress or avoid these.* In this way we have remained vulnerable to their debilitating influences over us because we never allowed ourselves to get to know and understand them intimately from a disposition of clarity and empathy.

We have seen that every aspect of our enquiry needs to be approached in a way, or ways, appropriate to its specific needs and dysfunctional demands. We simply cannot address our emotional disturbances from the disposition of our ordinary, rather mechanical and conditioned way of doing things. And whereas many aspects of our ordinary living may require only this level of mechanical participation, resolving the subtle dynamics within ourselves which produce our psychological and emotional dysfunctions demands a deeper level of participatory Intelligence.

Part Two: The Practice

No doubt, such Intelligence is always available to us and ready to become part of our functioning. Our responsibility is to discover ways for allowing it to do its work. This is why we first developed our abilities through Passive Awareness and Direct Awareness before we could start working with our volatile, emotional tendencies as we will be doing here. Unless these have become an integral part of our 'skillful means', we will not have sufficient space and inner quiet from where to resolve any emotional disturbance in a sustainable way.

If, while we are still in the process of developing our observational skills and other inner abilities, we feel that our emotional problems are really too difficult for us to deal with or endure, it may indeed be useful and practical to consult the professional advice of a considerate and insightful therapist. However, once we begin to undertake any aspect of this work by ourselves, we should ensure that we have found a calm and secure disposition of quiet within ourselves from where we could proceed with our work If our work has ripened sufficiently through these practices, we are ready to engage our emotional and psychological complexities in the context of Direct Awareness.

The broader context of emotional disturbance

When we approach our emotional disturbances we enter into a complexity of emotional interference-patterns, profound human potential, ignorance, conditioning, a life's history stored in memory, hopes, fears, needs and expectations - all trying to make sense of things through our ongoing interaction with life.

We are not something separate and functionally different to any or all of these qualities. This often results in us feeling that our problems are rather unique and specific only to ourselves, which, in turn, creates the deep feeling-sense that our problems are too private and personal to have them explained or even approached in any general terms. And of course such an assessment would have considerable merit. No general approach can ever fully and comprehensively attain the depth and subtlety of enquiry necessary to come to an understanding of our personal inner world.

Spirituality Without God

Yet, paradoxically, it is exactly for the reason that we feel ourselves so individual and unique, that it may be useful to start our enquiry from a somewhat wider perspective and to work our way from there to our own, more personal situation. It is often easier to place something in its personal perspective *after* we have developed an understanding of the broader context within which our problems arise. This creates valuable space for our enquiry to discover its own order within a more objective approach. Such an approach removes us from the immediacy and immersed acuteness of our specific problems so that we may gain insight into aspects of ourselves as they manifest also in the lives of millions of others like us.

Should we, therefore, approach our emotional reactivities in this rather impersonal manner, we will discover that there are indeed critical areas of common dysfunction which point to how we tend to deal with the challenges of life in rather similar ways. Through this we develop a sense of *objectivity* towards those aspects of ourselves we often believe to be unique to our own situation. But once we observe how others around us behave, think and feel, it will soon become apparent that most of us suffer the same general problems of feelings of lack of love and appreciation; an unstable, circumstantially based self-image; fear of failure; a relative inability to extend ourselves to others for fear of rejection; a problematic social persona; an acute, and rather painful sense of self-centeredness; alienation; embedded post traumatic reactive emotions and a wide range of other emotional insecurities, inconsistencies and reactivities founded upon the separate self-sense..

Of course, seeing these qualities of emotional disability in others has no power to relieve us from the plight of our own specific areas of confusion and emotional sensitivities. Where such observations may become meaningful and healing, though, is when we start to appreciate that we are not alone, or unique in our struggles, and that our problems may have a more universal quality than being purely the result of our own subjective, inner assessment of ourselves. Realizing that we are not the only ones who may be somewhat, or even greatly, disturbed, could serve as a healthy reminder that to be human is to have the ability to develop inappropriate and dysfunctional ways of relating to ourselves and our world.

In this there is nothing new or even personal. We have been doing this for as long as we have been human. Working therefore with ourselves in any specific way, is always to work with aspects we have in common with millions of others like ourselves. What appears to be specific to us, is also specific to others, often perhaps just in a slightly modified expression. We are all confronted with fundamentally the same emotional challenges and by the mere fact that we *share a common humanity*, we tend to deal with these in surprisingly similar ways. This is why it is important to sensitize ourselves to this impersonal component of our inner work. This may help us to look at things in a more objective, less self-absorbed way.

Discovering the right instruments

Given that through the practice of contemplative investigation we came to a clear understanding of the processes which are mainly responsible for our *mentally-based* emotional reactivities, and how to work with these in a freeing manner, we could now enquire whether there may be an equally effective way of neutralizing and transcending our deep, emotionally disturbing tendencies which are not so clearly based in thought.

During contemplative work we approached matters from an observable, *objective* point of view. We used the sensitivity of Passive Awareness to see how thought creates certain reactive emotional disturbances. By separating the thought/emotion unity, and allowing our attentive awareness to remain focused on the thought of disturbance as its object in a fully conscious environment, we frustrate and fragment the processes that generally result in these kinds of thought-created emotional responses.

The question we now ask is whether there is an equally appropriate way of working with our emotions whereby we may transcend those deep tendencies of emotional reactivity which cannot clearly be connected to thought? We have seen that it is important to make a distinction between those emotional reactive states which could be dealt with in a contemplative manner, and those which will respond better to Direct Awareness. Not all emotional disturbances can clearly be traced back as having their origin in a particular identifiable thought. Many just seem to appear as mere emotion, and it will be these we will be working with here. We will use the ability we gained through the practice of Direct Awareness in an effort to relieve ourselves from the effects of such debilitating emotions.

This naturally implies that we will be working in a completely different way than we did during our contemplative investigations. In our present enquiry we leave all objectivity behind and instead enter into the subtle *feeling-experience* of our emotional disturbances as such. Only Direct Awareness can facilitate this without leaving any emotional residue.

When we enquire into these emotional complexities, using Direct Awareness as our mode of operation, it is useful to remind ourselves that we will be working with these disturbances in a most direct, non-intellectual manner. Here we are not so much concerned with gaining insight and a clearer understanding of any specific problem, or even seeing into the nature of its development: rather, we will remain with the *feeling-sense* of the disturbance as a form of direct experience. During this direct involvement with such emotional disturbances these get transformed or translated into pure feeling.

In all work that involves Direct Awareness there is always a sense of translation. By this we understand that we allow the object of our enquiry to become *so completely part of our total field of experience* that no division remains between the emotional state we work with and ourselves as the presumed separate one having the experience. This is why we use the instrument of Direct Awareness for this emotional work: it translates separation into wholeness; disturbing emotional content, into pure feeling/emotion.

Beginning the process

In order to enter directly into our emotional world, it is again important that we start our enquiry from the conscious, inner quiet of Passive Awareness. We have seen how Passive

Part Two: The Practice

Awareness affords us not only with the inner stability necessary to work with many aspects of ourselves, but how it is also accompanied by an Intelligence which is not of the order of our conditioned thinking. By establishing ourselves in the inner quiet and focused attention of the state of Samatha, we allow ourselves to come *into very close proximity* to our feeling-world before we continue to the next phase of working with Direct Awareness.

The experiments we will enter into require that we fully understand and appreciate the nature of the work we will undertake. As it is very difficult, and (due to the sensitive nature of all emotional work) also not advisable, to use real-life emotional disturbances to work with at this early stage, we will follow the same route we have taken with contemplative enquiry. We may recall that we started our contemplative enquiry by first creating a mild emotional disturbance to give ourselves the opportunity to *have something concrete to work with*, without the danger of being overwhelmed by the content of some deep, reactive, emotional shadow material.

We could therefore usefully start our present experiment in the same way. Our first task will be to establish the general principle and basic technique through which we plan to approach this aspect of inner exploration. Later, when our practice is stable and secure, we could widen our emotional experience to include real-life situations and allow even deeply disturbing states to present themselves to our inner awareness and Intelligence without any fear of being taken over by such states. Once the *principle* has been established, we will realize that all these types of reactive emotions are of the same nature and could be addressed in much the same way. They all arise and dominate our lives to a greater or lesser extent because they have been allowed to do so as *uninspected and unconscious inner processes*.

So, when everything has settled down, and we feel ourselves becoming absorbed in our inner darkness and silence, we again consciously project any mildly disturbing emotional incident from memory. This could be any insignificant incident that happened to us. For instance, it may be something someone said to us that upset us, or something we have said to another over which we feel a little guilty or sad, or a mildly embarrassing incident that took place at work, on the tennis court, at a party, and so on. We are merely trying to recall some incident of mild emotional disturbance to elicit an emotional response to work with.

It is important to appreciate that we are not entering into a state of war with ourselves. Neither are we out to prove how much emotional pain we can endure. The point of this exercise is to create a *mild emotional disturbance* within us so that we could establish an intelligent working relationship with it in order to discover, *in principle*, how to approach, and work with, all such emotional reactivities.

Again it may be worth reminding ourselves that what we are doing here is not different to what we often, unconsciously, do to ourselves: we allow negative emotions to arise and take control of our being. During our present exercise we enter into a similar process, but this time with *conscious awareness* where we select the degree of emotional disturbance we feel comfortable with for the purpose of the experiment. We do it volitionally and from a position of confidence, inner silence and Intelligence. In fact, we merely bring into conscious awareness a function that has been ruling our lives for many years, and which have never been challenged, or enquired into, in such a conscious and direct way.

This exercise allows us to take full control of the situation and thereby gives us the confidence that we are indeed capable of investigating these matters for ourselves. Nothing forces us to engage in this work but a deep interest in our own emotional disharmony and the potential to free ourselves from such unbalanced states. These disturbances are integrally part of our uninspected being, and requires our most empathetic cooperation if we are to free ourselves from them.

A little perseverance will soon show us that we have nothing to fear from imagining simple scenarios of emotionally charged incidents in order to learn how we function as emotionally challenged individuals. We cannot free ourselves from anything unless we first make it fully conscious by allowing it to remain with us for careful inspection. This is how we make the unconscious, conscious, and thereby rendering every aspect of it available for intelligent recognition and transcendence.

If we are thus successful in imagining this emotionally charged incident or situation, the next step is to focus our attention on the actual *feeling* of the emotion. From our disposition of inner quiet, we allow attention to hold itself stable on this feeling-sensation until we become perfectly comfortable with being in such close proximity to a mildly disturbing emotion. We bring no value judgments or interpretation to this process. Thought is quietly tucked away in our inner calm and all that is present is the *attentive awareness* of the mildly disturbing *feeling sense* of the emotion.

This is a subtle and participatory process that requires sensitivity and care. We are not used to remain volitionally in such close proximity to our negative emotions. We usually just become aware of the negative content of our disturbances and immediately attempt to escape from these by diverting attention to something else more exiting or positive. We seldom allow our negative emotions to remain with us consciously and deliberately. As this is a new experience for us, we need to tread gently, but with confidence and quiet determination.

So, once we have managed to hold the *emotion in stable focus*, we will notice that whatever thought-aspect it may still contain, becomes marginalized. Here we have the opposite to what happened during contemplative enquiry where the emotional aspect was diminished while we were focusing exclusively on the thought behind the emotion. In both these exercises we may now appreciate the tremendous value of having established early in our practice the ability to *isolate, and stabilize*, any aspect of our functioning so that we may work with it as may be necessary. By holding attention stable on the emotion as such, we can now proceed with our work of Direct Awareness.

Direct Awareness and Emotional reactivities

Up to this point we have been working with the feeling-content of the emotion as an *object* of Passive Awareness. We have remained passively aware of the feeling-aspect of the emotion. However, this passive-aware relationship does not have the ability to enter into the actual *feeling-sensation* of the emotional disturbance as such. This is why we need to allow for the more subtle practice of Direct Awareness to facilitate this process.

Having thus allowed our attention to settle gently on the feeling aspect of the disturbing emotion, the next step is to *relax attention itself* so that all that remains is the mere feeling-sensation of it.

We may recall that during our practice of Direct Awareness we learnt how to relax attention away from its object to allow for the Direct Awareness of the 'object' to remain present by itself with no effort on our part whatsoever. During this present exercise we do exactly the same. We *suddenly and spontaneously relax attention* away from the emotional feeling which leaves the emotion present as an integral part of our conscious awareness. The feeling simply remains present when all effort to keep it in place is abandoned. We could say here we have *become* the feeling, as there is no sense of 'me' as the observer noticing the feeling as object. All that is present is the feeling-sensation as such. Here we have entered into a true state of effortless Direct Awareness of the mere feeling-sensation of the disturbed emotion.

At this point it may again be interesting to notice that we have no 'sense-organ' with which we 'perceive' this emotional state. It is just directly present in our field of awareness with no-one 'sensing' it. It becomes perfectly self-evident that the emotion as pure feeling-sense is present with no separation between the emotion and the awareness of it. The awareness of the emotion, and the emotion itself, become one single process of emotion/awareness. The feeling cannot be separated from the awareness of it.

The most startling discovery that presents itself at this point is that the moment Direct Awareness allows for the simple, direct feeling-presence of the emotion, the emotion loses its *specific quality of disturbance* and is translated into a very sane and simple sense of *pure emotion.* And this natural feeling-sense is not just a gray, emotionally neutral experience. Rather, we feel a deep human warmth that is not held in place by any effort on our part whatsoever. This direct experience of pure emotion is further accompanied by a profound sense of relief and body-mind relaxation. Here we allow ourselves to experience the deep emotional and mental equanimity associated with our natural condition.

We are left with just a free feeling-sensation of clarity, sanity, and an openness of heart. This proves beyond doubt that when we remove the obscurations to our natural, effortless condition, what remains is a purity of experience that has been there all along, but that was never allowed to reveal itself.

Normally we only know our emotions as *content-dominated and content-controlled*. In other words, we only know our emotions as positive or negative experiences. We never experience our emotions as *pure feeling*, without any specific content. At this level of participating in our own processes, we are not concerned with transforming the negative emotion into a positive one. Rather it is merely to allow the disturbing emotion to remain fully present *as it is*, negative or positive. From within the very same experience that presented itself as dilemma, flowers the simplicity of pure, present feeling-emotion that is inherent to our non-dual human condition. The emotion of disturbance has been *translated* into the pure emotion of equanimity.

When the disturbed emotional content is translated into pure emotion, we also begin to sense the continuous presence and functioning of our deeper Intelligence, *which is also contentless, unconditioned and pure. A*nd because this brings to our situation nothing but uncontaminated pure Intelligence, it can serve our humanity and humaneness unconditionally. Soon we begin to appreciate the validity and beauty of this different quality of life, and this motivates us to become alive to our ability to *feel beyond emotional contraction* into the simplicity of our present situation.

Evidently this new quality is nothing but an unfolding of our true humanity. Life, simplified to its natural order, *is* spiritual life. And here it becomes apparent that no distinction can be drawn between the spiritualization and the full *humanization* of our being. These are not vested in God, Brahman, the Self, Atman, or some ultimate unifying Principle. Merely to be human is to have this potential available to us. It only needs to be uncovered for it to become self-revelatory.

Again it is important to remind ourselves that this is a delicate and gentle process where we cannot rush into our deeply-rooted emotional disturbances in the hope of pushing them aside or eliminating them by force. We need to approach these with great humility and reverence. We have to respect and appreciate that which has controlled us for so many ages. The pain of our disturbed emotions informs us that we are doing something wrong. Like a true Guru, it points us directly to the problem itself. Yet, we have to be rather judicious in our approach when we work so intimately with such subtle processes as our emotionally disturbed conditions. Through the practice of Direct Awareness we meet these inner disturbances with such deep intimacy. They are allowed to unfold and be translated into pure emotion – leaving no trace of disturbed emotional residue. Translation is possible only when the disturbance is recognized to be of the same fundamental quality as the healthy condition into which it is translated. Both emotional disturbance and purity of emotion are of the nature of emotion.

A significant insight we receive along the way is that we need not suffer our emotions the way we do. Our body-mind is fully equipped to *break the habits* of emotional reactivity. We just need to call upon the instruments already present within us, and allow them to function intelligently and coherently. Every emotional reactivity can be approached in the manner we explored above. In truth there are no greater or smaller emotional disturbances. Some may be deeper ingrained into our psyche, but they are all created, and given validity, in an unconscious environment. Once we have learnt the *principle* of how to approach them in such a non-confrontational, yet direct, manner, we will be in a position to extend our new ability to include a more comprehensive working relationship with our emotional disturbances in general.

And this, finally, brings us to the consideration of Integration and the wholeness of Being.

Part Two: The Practice

SUMMARY OF THE PRACICE:

PURPOSE:

- To free our being from unnecessary emotional and psychological reactivities.
- To prepare the ground for sustainable self-transcendent, holistic living.

PRACTICE:

- Find a quiet and secure place where you will be free from too many outside disturbances and distractions.
- Feel yourself into the inner silence of Samatha.
- Hold attention stable on your inner darkness.
- Project a mild emotional disturbance into your field of experience. Do not use a real-life situation as this may be too sensitive to handle at this early stage.
- Allow the feeling-sense of the emotion to settle while you remain in close proximity to it through the kind of 'witness' position of Samatha.
- Always feel you are in full control of this exercise. Do not allow yourself to become overwhelmed by any material you work with.
- When you feel completely comfortable with being so close to this negative emotion, allow attention *suddenly* to drop away from the emotion, as you did during the second practice of Direct Awareness.
- Notice how the specific negative content of the emotion gets translated into the simple *feeling-sense* of pure emotion.
- Experience the profound inner psychophysical relaxation that comes over you.
- Experience the directness of the purity of emotion, the sense of well-being, the softness of heart, the availability of unconditioned Intelligence to shine through into your life.

- This practice could be extended to many aspects of your disturbed emotional reactivities. Once it has been allowed to stabilize itself as part of your functional living reality, you will be able to draw on it whenever old patterns of reactivity attempt to control your being.

Chapter Eighteen

INTEGRATION
Toward the Wholeness of Being.

Once we have mastered the practices which allow for sustainable emotional equanimity and the non-dual truth of the living moment, we have prepared the entire psychophysical being for living unstrategically and effortlessly *as* the wholeness of life.

From here a subtle process of gradual *re-adjustment of all our faculties* takes place by itself. Each of these faculties gradually begins to re-align itself with the wholeness from which it has always been an integral part. This is not an active process of willful activity. Rather, as the sense of separation withers in the light of our growing non-dual awareness, every aspect of our being and functioning is simply experienced as already integrated into the non-dual nature of things. Wholeness replaces the presumption of fragmentation and begins to shine through as the true foundation for human living.

Whereas the inner state of Samatha served as a platform from where to launch into direct, full-bodily awareness, the latter now serves as a gateway into the sustainable realization of the non-dual. Once we have become skillful in allowing for this deep state of non-dual bodily awareness to establish itself firmly within us, the instruments will be in place for the Integration of our entire being into every aspect of our living experience.

As we have seen, when, during the practice of Direct Awareness, this deep psychophysical relaxation is complete, and our full-bodily sensation exists *entirely by itself* as mere presence or sensation, it also becomes self-evident that for this to be the case, no effort is necessary, or even possible. There is absolutely nothing we can positively do for this simplicity of bodily wholeness to be the case. Direct Awareness requires no mediator such as thought, attention, the witness, effort of will or any other inward activity for it to reveal itself as an ongoing movement of non-dual experience. This is why it is called 'Direct Awareness' as opposed to any notion that some mediation is necessary between us and any aspect of our field of experience.

An interesting and fundamental challenge we now seem to face is how to allow for the integration of this non-dual bodily-sense into our entire field of experience. *Non-duality has to become functional in every aspect of our lives* and has to be able to retain its conscious equanimity in the face of the challenges of life. That is, Direct Awareness has to find its measure and living reality in each and every moment of present arising. Only then will our freedom be complete and sustainable. But how do we move from the non-dual experience of the body, to the wholeness of our total field of living reality? And is there to be such a movement at all?

These are vital and rather subtle questions which point us beyond any sense of dualistic vision. We have sensed the truth of our full-bodily awareness. While our eyes were closed this non-dual bodily experience presented itself as undivided reality. Yet, however beautiful and true the living reality of the non-dual bodily state is, this too has to be incorporated into our quest for ultimate freedom from our dualistic vision. As we have seen, what was true as non-dual reality in the context of the direct experience of the body now needs to become the *functional reality* of our total field of present experience.

But before we proceed with this aspect of our enquiry, we again have to remind ourselves of the nature of true human-centered self-transcendent work. We need to be very clear that our enquiry does not depend for its final resolution on the presumed existence of some Primordial Essence or Ground of Being with which we finally have to merge or with which we have to realize our already-existent identification. *Human life, explored to its deepest and most subtle levels of manifestation, knows only itself,* and our enquiry into the non-dual is relevant to successful living only insofar as it establishes the appropriate relationship between ourselves and our total field of experience.

If this world is founded in dualistic vision, where fragmentation forms the basis of all experience, (including the fragmented state of God and humankind) the fulfillment of human life as non-dual reality would not be possible. Non-dualism has to be discovered as an expression of our total human situation in any living moment. It has to be seen and experienced directly as one undivided process of present arising, and should in no way be equated with the unification of some presumed inner principle (the soul) with its God.

Once we have perfect clarity with regard to the notion of wholeness or non-duality as an expression of *human* life, and nothing else, we could enter into the next very important consideration relative to the question of self-transcendence and the nature of undivided experience.

To orientate ourselves for this final gesture towards the wholeness of life, we need to consider a very fundamental truth with regard to the experience of the non-dual state: *diversity of appearance is not a sign of fragmentation.*

As is the case with all other aspects of our enquiry, this is not a mere philosophical, intellectual statement. To understand this truth of the non-dual state is crucial to the final flowering of our work. Such an understanding will orientate us to the simple truth of the undivided nature of human experience.

So, what do we mean by the statement: 'the diversity of appearance is not a sign of fragmentation'? By this we understand that although there appear many diverse objects, states of mind, feeling-sensations, emotions and so on in our field of present experience (diversity of experience), these do not constitute a world of *self-existing* things where everything exists as something categorically separate from everything else. The diversity of objects, etc., no doubt exists, but these cannot be separated from our *human experience of them.* In its most fundamental expression, human experience cannot be divided into clearly defined entities such as subject and object. *Diversity is therefore not in conflict with the notion of wholeness* or undivided reality. In any moment of living reality, there is just the total, undivided truth of present human experience.

This is an important insight and will experientially be confirmed by our work with Integration. Although our uninspected intuition may lead us to believe the contrary, diversity of appearances does not necessitate fragmentation with its implied notion of duality. Quite the contrary is true: all diversity exists as the wholeness of the living moment.

Perhaps we could use the atom in relation to its sub-atomic particles as a metaphor to gain more clarity on this matter. The atom and its subatomic particles cannot be separated. Without the diversity of particles, the coherency of the atom makes no sense. So, although the particles are different from one another, they nevertheless form an integral part of the atom as a whole. From this perspective there exists not only a mutually dependent relationship between the subatomic particles as diverse forms within the whole process of the atom-appearance, it also becomes clear that no single component of the atom exists categorically separate from it or from one another. This diversity within the atom is therefore not a form of fragmentation of the atom. Rather, the sub-atomic particles are integrally part of the whole, and thus also part of the non-dual nature of the atom. From the point of view of the atom as a whole, its parts are inherently an integrated aspect of itself.

When, during the practice of Direct Awareness, this metaphor is translated into the reality of experience, and serves no longer merely as an argument to confirm our mental understanding of the non-dual nature of present experience, it becomes evident that no aspect of diversity has any inherent self-existence. Or to put it differently: there is no wholeness without content, and no content without wholeness. Slightly amended we see this reflected in the Mahayana Heart Sutra which also makes the point that 'Emptiness is Form and Form is Emptiness'.

There may be many ways of adequately explaining this non-dual truth of life, but there is only one way of *experiencing* it. It has to be our own, presently-experienced and directly-felt truth. The living reality of it has nothing whatsoever to do with its description. And this is the question implied in our *apparent* dilemma of moving from our non-dual bodily experience to true integral living: is there any direct link between this bodily experience and the rest of our field of diverse experience?

In truth there is no link. As we have seen, there is nothing truly separate 'out there' which exists categorically separate from anything 'in here'. Direct Awareness reveals that nothing has been discovered 'inside' the body that is not already true of our *total* field of experience. In the full-bodily experience there is the sense of undivided inner presence. *From here we do not attempt to integrate this 'inner' truth with the rest of our world.*

Rather, as we open our eyes, and become aware of a wider field of experience, we *immediately* sense the same quality of undividedness which is present in the full-bodily experience to be the case with the things we now hear, see, feel, smell, and so on. None of these have a quality of being truly separate from us. We need not, and cannot, *forcefully integrate* our inner wholeness into an experience which is already whole. What becomes perfectly evident is that every one of our senses reveals their *non-separation* from the things they 'perceive'. In this way, the entire field of diverse experience assumes a subtle non-dualistic character.

Integration is therefore not a willful activity attempting to establish a relationship between 'inner wholeness' and 'outer fragmentation'. It is also not to bring some *inner unitive principle* out into the world of fragmentation through which to unify the diversity of experience. Rather, Integration is the awakening of all our faculties from the *disposition of full-bodily wholeness* into every aspect of our functional interaction with life. And this is the key to Integration. *All we need to remain aware of is our non-dual bodily experience.* This direct bodily experience of the non-dual not only underlies our own sense of wholeness, it underlies, and is already perfectly identified with, every aspect of present experience.

Perhaps this needs a little further exploration. For this we could just step back to the practice of Direct Awareness. Here we remain in the feeling-sense of non-dual bodily experience with our eyes closed, and we are simply conscious in the context of the body. This naturally reduces our field of present experience and therefore does not allow for *all* our sense-faculties to function as would normally be the case had we been busy with our everyday activities. As wholeness is firmly established in the body, all we need to do is to remain aware of this non-dual bodily sense when we become active in the world beyond our formal practice. When we move from the closed-eye bodily disposition to the open-eye state of normal functional awareness, nothing 'outside' will any longer appear as categorically separate from our awareness of it.

This is a very important realization. *Once we have removed the principle of fragmentation and separation from within ourselves* (such as we have allowed for during the practice of Direct Awareness), what remains reveals itself to be whole over the entire spectrum of our present field of experience. When we allow all our faculties to become operative beyond the full, non-dual bodily sense, all human experiences take on the form of non-dual reality.

Wherever attention may then direct awareness, wholeness will be the case, because the *factor of division*, which exists only *within* our psychophysical being, and which has presented us with the *illusion* of the observer and the observed, has been transcended. This leaves the necessary functioning of attentive awareness free to do its work without us having the burdensome sense of inner separation from that to which we attend and become aware of.

The truth of non-dual bodily awareness now becomes true of our total living reality. By not falling back into our deluded state of self-contraction, and by remaining consciously open and vulnerable to the non-dual truth of our entire psycho-physical being, *every other experience of manifest existence reveals itself to have been of the same non-dual quality all along*. The simplicity of this has just been obscured by unconscious inner activities.

Our path of humanistic self-transcendence therefore never leaves the human condition. Its point of departure is the same as its point of arrival: human life. The only difference between the two is that in the case of the latter we have relinquished all the illusions we have brought to our living reality which created the illusion of duality.

Part Two: The Practice

We are born non-dual, with the *potential* to have this revealed in our ordinary living. However, having acquired a false sense of separateness through the uninspected use of certain of our faculties, this revelation never established itself as the functional reality of our lives. When, through recognition and correct forms of practice we awake to this inherent non-dual truth of present experience, it becomes self-evident that fragmentation was a mere illusion, and that wholeness has been the true basis of our living reality all along. Only in the reality of this truth are we alive to the deep joy of what it means to be truly, non-dualistically, human.

Everything *is* because we *are*. Without us, there is nothing. Yet, humankind is not only the measure of all things. *The total field of present arising is equally the measure of humankind.* We *are* the world, and the world *is* us. And this is true, not as a mere idea, but in a practical, experiential and very real sense. This is the self-revelatory truth of life as it unfolds from moment to moment while we remain open and alert to the non-dual bodily experience as we function in the world.

Integration is therefore the art of *conscious recognition and instant relaxation*. We recognize any state of *inner contraction* and relax beyond it into the wholeness of the body, and therefore into the non-dual nature life. And as we establish ourselves more clearly in the relaxed felt-sense of things, we will gradually lose faith in all our programs of separation and fragmentation which manifest as the 'I'-consciousness state. We will learn how to recognize these resistances to the living moment as they arise. This immediate recognition of the habits of self-contraction allows us to relax out of the conditional states of limitation they create, and simply to feel our way back into the wholeness of the body and thereby into the wholeness of life itself. *This is not a function of willful self-manipulation: it is a perfectly natural expression of our inner Intelligence and awareness.*

Through this practice of instant recognition and relaxation we learn that we need not dwell in any state that is more complex than the simplicity of the whole-bodily experience. Gradually our ability to relax becomes complete, because we learn the art of how to relax directly from any state of unconscious attentive awareness, or emotional contraction, right back into the wholeness of present experience. In the process we do not correct any aspect of the lesser states. They no longer concern us. They are allowed to be as they are. They just gradually fall away by non-use.

Progressively we become identified with the wholeness of the living moment that has only Intelligence, compassion and humaneness as its inspiration and motivation. From here, life as wholeness takes care of itself. The more we allow this process of recognition and relaxation to become our ability, the deeper we will become established in the non-dual nature of existence which naturally reveals itself also as our true human identity.

Wholeness manifests not only as a feeling of inner joy, sanity and equanimity, but also most profoundly as an alive sense of intelligent participation in everything we do. In this way human life becomes the fulfillment of its own non-dual potential. We have no purpose other than to allow for the realization of our inherent wholeness and to live both *in* and *as* this disposition of the non-dual or true Advaita.

In time, we will become so well established in this that even the process of recognition and relaxation becomes unnecessary. We begin to live *as* the non-dual truth and our identification with it becomes complete.

And this great simplicity of the wholeness of Being always unfolds as nothing other than a natural expression of our total human condition, where alone resides love, compassion, Intelligence and humaneness.

About The Author

Möller sees himself as a student of life. He has studied and practiced most of the traditional mystical teachings, and after a lifelong, passionate engagement with these, he finally realized that the true Advaita (non-duality) is an expression of the fulfillment of human life alone, and is therefore not founded in any supra-human entity of any description.

This realization is evident in everything Möller communicates. He has a passion for going beyond mere description, intellectual understanding and knowledge, directing his enquiry instead to the heart of the human spirit and the possibility of sustainable self-transcendent living. For Möller a single question has to be answered: how to translate ideas into living reality?

It is this question that has motivated him to remain resolute in his own self-enquiry and self-transcendent work, the expression of which is shared in his first book: *Spirituality Without God*.

Möller lives a quiet life with his wife, Lize, in a rather remote part of South Africa called the Little Karoo – an arid, mountainous, sun-drenched place of peace and quiet.

Möller welcomes creative and well-considered interaction with those who have read, studied and experimented with his work. Anyone is welcome to contact him at: mollerdlr@telkomsa.net

Printed in the United States
64744LVS00010B/49